THE RECEPTION OF BACH'S ORGAN WORKS
FROM MENDELSSOHN TO BRAHMS

THE RECEPTION OF BACH'S ORGAN WORKS

FROM MENDELSSOHN TO BRAHMS

Russell Stinson

OXFORD
UNIVERSITY PRESS

2006

OXFORD
UNIVERSITY PRESS

Oxford University Press, Inc., publishes works that further
Oxford University's objective of excellence
in research, scholarship, and education.

Oxford   New York

Auckland   Cape Town   Dar es Salaam   Hong Kong   Karachi
Kuala Lumpur   Madrid   Melbourne   Mexico City   Nairobi
New Delhi   Shanghai   Taipei   Toronto

With offices in

Argentina   Austria   Brazil   Chile   Czech Republic   France   Greece
Guatemala   Hungary   Italy   Japan   Poland   Portugal   Singapore
South Korea   Switzerland   Thailand   Turkey   Ukraine   Vietnam

Published by Oxford University Press, Inc.
198 Madison Avenue, New York, New York 10016

www.oup.com

Oxford is a registered trademark of Oxford University Press

Library of Congress Cataloging-in-Publication Data
Stinson, Russell.
The reception of Bach's organ works from Mendelssohn to Brahms / Russell Stinson.
p. cm.
Includes bibliographical references (p.).
ISBN-13 978-0-19-517109-9
ISBN 0-19-517109-8
1. Bach, Johann Sebastian, 1685–1750. Organ music.   2. Performance practice (Music)—
19th century.   3. Organ music—Interpretation (Phrasing, dynamics, etc.).   I. Title.
ML410.B1S856 2006
786.5'092—dc22   2005011111

1   3   5   7   9   8   6   4   2

Printed in the United States of America
on acid-free paper

But it is only at his organ that he appears to be at his most sublime, most audacious, in his own element. Here he knows neither limits nor goal and works for centuries to come.

—Robert Schumann

Contents

viii   Contents

THE RECEPTION OF BACH'S ORGAN WORKS
FROM MENDELSSOHN TO BRAHMS

Introduction

THE RECEPTION OF BACH'S ORGAN WORKS during the nineteenth century—the era of the so-called Bach revival—was a phenomenon that involved not only church musicians from St. Petersburg to New York but also several of the most prominent composers in all of music history. To judge from the surviving evidence, four members of the latter group were particularly influential in how they championed this repertory. Their activities within this realm form the subject matter of the present book.

To study the ways in which this quadrumvirate reacted to Bach's organ music is a fascinating line of inquiry. Of fundamental importance, of course, is the fact that they borrowed from Bach's organ compositions in creating their own masterpieces. But their "compositional responses" to the repertory were exceedingly diverse, including, in addition to keyboard works, chamber, orchestral, and vocal compositions. Luckily, they also responded to the music in ways other than compositional. They performed it, edited it for publication, transcribed it for other media, taught it to their pupils, analyzed it, and reacted to it aesthetically as well as emotionally. They ensured its "afterlife."

No comprehensive discussion of this topic exists. Put another way, no one has ever attempted to consider with any degree of inclusiveness how any of these four individuals responded to the model of Bach's organ music. Nor has anyone ever explored how the four influenced one another in this regard, even though this is an absolutely critical aspect of the topic. Just consider that Mendelssohn introduced Schumann to many of Bach's organ works and that the young Brahms was probably introduced to several of these same pieces by virtue of his membership in the Schumann circle. Although he never really belonged to this circle, Liszt was personally acquainted with both Schumann and Brahms. He also shared with each of them mutual acquaintances, such as the organist J. G. Schneider, the pianist Carl Tausig, and the organist-painter J. J. B. Laurens, who made an impact in their own right as "receptors" of Bach's organ works.

In more general terms, experiencing Bach's organ works through the eyes and ears of these four titans immeasurably increases one's appreciation of the music. Take, for example, the "Great" Fugue in A Minor, BWV 543/2, which Mendelssohn played at the organ as a pedal showpiece; which Mendelssohn and Brahms used as a compositional model; which Schumann taught to his wife, Clara; which Liszt and Brahms (and Clara Schumann) regularly played at the piano; and which Liszt published as a piano transcription and taught to his legions of piano students. What is more, Schumann attended and reviewed Mendelssohn's only public performance of the movement, Liszt heard Clara play her piano transcription of it, and Clara eventually played Liszt's transcription.

Naturally, I have presented my own thoughts and findings throughout. At the same time, I have gathered and synthesized a great deal of preexistent information, much of which has never before appeared in English. (I have also furnished my own translations of numerous items, in each instance giving the original text in an endnote.) For their help in locating secondary sources, thanks are due to my librarian-colleagues at Lyon College (especially Kathy Whittenton), the University of Chicago, Duke University, the University of Illinois, Rice University, Ohio State University, the University of Houston, and the University of Memphis. In addition, I would like to thank the Bach-Archiv Leipzig, the Houghton Library (Harvard University), and the Johann-Sebastian-Bach-Institut (Göttingen) for providing me with photocopies of their holdings.

In researching primary sources, I was fortunate enough to do on-site work in several European archives. I would like to express my sincere gratitude to the archive of the Gesellschaft der Musikfreunde (Vienna), the Music Section of the Bodleian Library (Oxford), the Robert-Schumann-Haus (Zwickau), and the Goethe- und Schiller-Archiv (Weimar) for allowing me to examine editions of Bach's organ music owned by the four composers under investigation here. I am particularly indebted to the directors of the first three of these archives (Otto Biba, Peter Ward Jones, and Gerd Nauhaus, respectively) for answering my many questions and for being such gracious hosts. I am thankful as well to the Staatsbibliothek zu Berlin for granting me access to certain Mendelssohn autographs in its possession and to the parish of St. Peter-upon-Cornhill (London) for permitting me to peruse the Mendelssohn autograph on display in the church's organ gallery. My travel was funded by grants from Lyon College and the American Bach Society.

For assistance of various kinds, I would like to thank Styra Avins, Catherine Bordeau, James Brokaw, John Michael Cooper, James Deaville, Reinmar Emans, Walter Frisch, Virginia Hancock, Hans-Günter Klein, William Parsons, Paul Ranzini, Nicholas Temperly, Larry Todd, Peter Wollny, and Rudolf Zuiderveld. A special word of appreciation goes also to Peter Ward Jones and Wm. A. Little, for reading and commenting on my discussion of Mendelssohn's "grand tour." I must thank Professor Little a second time for allowing me to see, prior to its publication, his article on Mendelssohn and the Prelude and Fugue in E Minor, BWV 533, and a third time for his extraordinary generosity to me as I was beginning my work. Finally, I would be remiss not to thank Kim Robinson of Oxford University Press for her patience and understanding throughout the different phases of the project.

ONE

Felix Mendelssohn Bartholdy

As far as the subject of this book is concerned, Mendelssohn represents an embarrassment of riches. In composing his approximately thirty organ works,[1] he routinely took the organ music of Bach as his model. Numerous eyewitness accounts evince that he performed Bach's organ compositions his whole life, both as an organist and as a pianist. And he edited for publication over seventy of these pieces, most of which had never before appeared in print. Mendelssohn's reception of Bach's organ works is also attested to by a multitude of letters written by and to him, many of which record his aesthetic and emotional response to the music. The picture that emerges from this documentation is that Mendelssohn promoted Bach's organ music as a performer, scholar, and ambassador-at-large. In so doing, he helped to bring this historical repertory into the mainstream of musical life in the early nineteenth century.

Youth

Mendelssohn spent his formative years in Berlin, at that time a bastion of musical conservatism.[2] Three of Bach's most important pupils—his sons Wilhelm Friedemann and Carl Philipp Emanuel and the theorist J. P. Kirnberger—had lived there, and by the turn of the nineteenth century the city boasted the strongest Bach tradition in all of Europe. The Mendelssohn family was an integral part of this legacy. Felix's great-aunt Sara Levy, a student of Wilhelm Friedemann Bach and patroness of Carl Philipp Emanuel, was recognized throughout Berlin as a harpsichordist who specialized in the music of the Bach family, and her extensive collection of music manuscripts included several keyboard works by J. S. Bach.[3] Felix's mother, Lea, had, like her mother, studied under Kirnberger.[4] She gave the child his first piano lessons.

By June 1819, at the age of ten, Mendelssohn had begun to study composition under Carl Friedrich Zelter, another pupil of Kirnberger's and director of the Berlin Singakademie. This group concentrated on the music of J. S. Bach, and Felix joined its chorus in 1820. Nine years later, he would conduct the Singakademie himself in Bach's St. Matthew Passion, a pivotal event in the early Bach revival.

It stands to reason that Zelter served as a catalyst for his student's initial exposure to Bach's organ music. For one thing, Zelter saw to it that the instrumental ensemble (*Ripienschule*) of the Singakademie featured organ works by Bach on its programs. There are documented performances of the first two Trio Sonatas, BWV 525–26; the Concerto in G Major after Prince Johann Ernst, BWV 592; and especially the Fantasy and Fugue in G Minor, BWV 542, which seems to have been a staple of the repertory.[5] The vast library of the Singakademie also contained numerous organ compositions by Bach.[6] Mendelssohn, then, presumably had ample opportunity to hear and study the music in this milieu. His compositional studies with Zelter, which clearly reflect the theoretical tradition of the Bach school, probably introduced him to various organ works as well. At any rate, one of the fugue subjects penned by the old man into the boy's counterpoint workbook is virtually identical to that of the "Little" Fugue in G Minor, BWV 578.[7]

In 1820, while his studies with Zelter continued, Mendelssohn began organ lessons with August Wilhelm Bach, the most prominent organist in the city. August Wilhelm was a leading proponent of the organ music of J. S. Bach (no relation), both as a performer and as a teacher.[8] As organist of St. Mary's Church, he presided over a sumptuous, three-manual instrument considered Joachim Wagner's masterpiece.

August Wilhelm, however, seems only to have resented his star pupil—because of his superior musicianship and otherwise. Another of his students, one Karl Gottlieb Freudenberg, recalled that

> the prominence of little Felix made him [A. W. Bach] suspicious and envious. Mendelssohn wanted to have an unpublished Bach fugue from him, but he wouldn't give it to him, and to me, who had copied it out, he said, "Why does the Jew-boy have to have everything; he has enough as it is. Don't give him the fugue." I did, however, straightaway give this Bach-relic to dear Felix, who showed such youthful charm in his manner, whereupon he was delighted and shook my hand, "Freudenberg, I'll never forget you for this gift," and he has kept his word.[9]

Freudenberg's tale is well documented, for there exists in Mendelssohn's hand a copy of Bach's Prelude in E Minor, BWV 533/1, titled *Praeludium für*

Orgel von Seb. Bach, that ends with the inscription "received from Freudenberg at the Akademie and copied on 9 December 1822" (see figure 1–1).[10] This
source represents one of only two surviving copies of Bach organ works in
Mendelssohn's hand. A manuscript copy of the prelude, along with its fugue,
owned by A. W. Bach has also survived.[11] Perhaps, then, Freudenberg remembered incorrectly that Mendelssohn had copied only the fugue, since
the only logical conclusion is that he copied both prelude and fugue working from a lost manuscript in Freudenberg's hand that contained both movements. Another possibility is that Freudenberg, like many other nineteenth-
century organists, used the term "fugue" to refer to any prelude-fugue pair
by Bach. One can also infer, of course, that this prelude and fugue was one of
the first Bach organ works played by Mendelssohn, something that can be
said of many organists since. It is the easiest organ prelude and fugue Bach
ever wrote.

Freudenberg's report—which eerily recalls a famous episode from
J. S. Bach's youth in which the composer's older brother refused to let *him*
copy a manuscript of keyboard works—reminds us that by this date over
two-thirds of Bach's organ compositions still awaited publication.[12] Not
until about ten years later was the E-minor prelude and fugue published. If
an organist wished to add a Bach work to his library, he often had to copy it
by hand, just as generations of his forebears had done.

A. W. Bach was also jealous of the Bach collection owned by the Mendelssohn family, a goodly portion of which was catalogued between 1823 and
1833 by Felix's sister Fanny.[13] According to her inventory, the family owned in
1823 various unspecified organ preludes, an organ toccata, and "6 Praeludien
u. Fugen f. die Orgel," a listing that must refer to the print, *Sechs Praeludien
und SECHS FUGEN für Orgel oder Pianoforte mit Pedal von Johann Sebastian Bach.* Issued originally in 1812, this edition of the six preludes and fugues,
BWV 543–48, was by 1823 the most popular print of Bach's organ works available.[14] Over the next three years, the family acquired nine additional organ
works by Bach: an unspecified fantasy; a fugue in G minor (presumably BWV
535/2, 542/2, or 578); the Passacaglia in C Minor, BWV 582; the Pastorale in F
Major, BWV 590; the four "duets" from Part 3 of the *Clavierübung,* BWV
802–5; a prelude and fugue in G major (presumably BWV 541 or 550); and a
fugue in C minor (presumably BWV 537/2, 546/2, 549/2, 574, or 575).

The same year that Mendelssohn began his organ lessons, he started to
compose for the instrument. Nine organ works from the period 1820–23 have
survived, and they amount to nothing so much as a tribute to J. S. Bach. Three
of them are transcriptions, undoubtedly for two manuals and pedal, of three-
voice fugal exercises from Mendelssohn's counterpoint workbook for Zelter.
As such, they may be modeled after Bach's Trio Sonatas for organ, works admired by Zelter and included in Sara Levy's collection of Bach manuscripts.[15]

Figure 1–1 Manuscript copy of the Prelude in E Minor, BWV 533/1, mm. 1–25, in the hand of Felix Mendelssohn Bartholdy, dated 9 December 1822 (Staatsbibliothek zu Berlin—Preussischer Kulturbesitz, Musikabteilung mit Mendelssohn-Archiv, Mus. ms. autogr. Mendelssohn 2, p. 166)

Figure 1–1 ctd. Manuscript copy of the Prelude in E Minor, BWV 533/1, mm. 26–32, in the hand of Felix Mendelssohn Bartholdy, dated 9 December 1822 (Staatsbibliothek zu Berlin—Preussischer Kulturbesitz, Musikabteilung mit Mendelssohn-Archiv, Mus. ms. autogr. Mendelssohn 2, p. 167)

Three other works from this period are the Fantasy in G Minor, the Chorale Variations on "Wie gross ist des Allmächtigen Güte," and the Passacaglia in C Minor. A probable exemplar for the fantasy is Bach's similarly rhapsodic Fantasy in G Minor, which may have been Zelter's favorite organ work of all. Variation 2 of "Wie gross ist" presents the chorale tune in a series of canons at different intervals, not unlike the final movement of Bach's Canonic Variations on "Vom Himmel hoch da komm ich her," BWV 769.[16]

Composed in May 1823, the passacaglia is without question an imitation of Bach's Passacaglia in C Minor. Mendelssohn, too, chooses a pedal theme of eight bars, followed by approximately twenty variations, and, like Bach, he often employs the same figuration for two consecutive variations. Also like Bach, Mendelssohn transfers the theme to the right hand midway through, accompanied only by fast scalar figures in the left hand (see examples 1–1 and 1–2), then arpeggiates the theme between the hands (see examples 1–3 and 1–4), and ends with the theme once again played on the pedals. In no other organ work does he so closely follow a Bachian model.

We do not know when Mendelssohn got acquainted with Bach's passacaglia (which, according to Fanny's catalogue, was not acquired by the family until 1825). Another question is whether he could have, at this stage in his development as an organist, played the piece in its entirety. For as late as 1831

Example 1–1 Passacaglia in C Minor, BWV 582

Example 1–2 Felix Mendelssohn Bartholdy, Passacaglia in C Minor

(in a letter to be discussed later), he confessed that he could not perform Bach's "major" organ works because of their demanding pedal parts. The fugal section of Bach's passacaglia, which contains more than its fair share of pedal sixteenth notes, might have proved impossible.

Mendelssohn would not compose another organ work until 1829,[17] but he seems to have regularly played the instrument during this interim, especially outside Berlin. His travels afforded him many opportunities to try new organs, and he took full advantage. The exact nature of these performances surely differed from place to place, but for the most part they appear to have been private, informal affairs at which he either improvised or played Bach (usually from memory, it seems). This pattern would become his habit whenever playing the organ.

As early as 1821, Mendelssohn is known to have to sought out organs to play while traveling with his family,[18] and during a vacation to Switzerland in the summer of 1822, he wrote to Zelter about an instrument by Aloys Mooser whose pedalboard was decidedly inadequate for the music of his favorite organ composer: "In Bulle, a small town in the canton of Fribourg, I found an excellent organ in very good condition. . . . [But] the pedals reach only to high A; B and C are missing, so that nothing of Bach's can be played on it."[19] Nine years later, he would register the same complaint about an organ in Munich.

Example 1–3 Passacaglia in C Minor, BWV 582

A rather different opportunity presented itself in Paris in the spring of 1825. Felix and his father, Abraham, himself a Bach devotee, had traveled there in order to accompany Abraham's sister Henriette back to Berlin. They stayed for about two months, which gave the youth ample time to perform his own compositions and meet the city's musicians. Felix, however, had nothing but disdain for the latter. Just read what he wrote to Fanny:

> You say I should try and convert the people here, and teach Onslow and Reicha to love Beethoven and Sebastian Bach. That is just what I am endeavoring to do. But remember, my dear child, that these people do not know a single note of "Fidelio" and believe Bach to be a mere old-fashioned wig stuffed with learning. The other day, at the request of Kalkbrenner, I played the organ preludes in E minor and A minor. My audience pronounced them both "wonderfully pretty," and one of them remarked that the beginning of the prelude in A minor was very much like a favorite duet in an opera by Monsigny. Anybody might have knocked me down with a feather.[20]

The most noteworthy fact here is that Mendelssohn, all of sixteen years old, was openly proselytizing for Bach's music, with particular reference to the organ works. And the favorable response of his "converts" suggests that he enjoyed some measure of success. This audience at least appreciated Bach as more than a stuffy academic. Nonetheless, Felix was appalled by their ignorance.

Example 1–4 Felix Mendelssohn Bartholdy, Passacaglia in C Minor

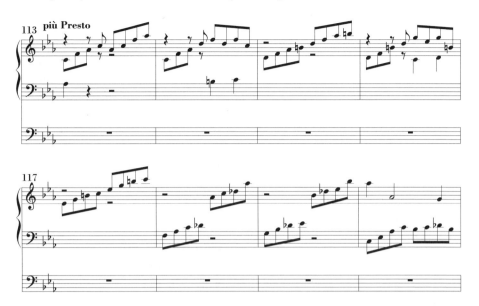

He did not act entirely on his own. He had been encouraged in the first place by his older sister Fanny, a fellow Bach aficionado who advised her brother on musical matters his whole life. Fanny herself was a wunderkind who at the age of thirteen had surprised her father by playing from memory twenty-four preludes from Bach's *Well-Tempered Clavier,* an almost unbelievable feat. She also seems to have shared her brother's particular passion for Bach's organ works, considering how often he refers to these pieces in his letters to her.

"Kalkbrenner" was the piano virtuoso Frédéric Kalkbrenner, a leading Parisian musician.[21] In addition to asking Felix to play Bach, he may have assembled whatever audience was present. Kalkbrenner had been a guest of the Mendelssohns in Berlin two years earlier, at which time he heard both Felix and Fanny perform. He, too, played Bach, which for a French musician then was hardly the norm. Indeed, Felix would report several years later that Kalkbrenner played *organ* works by Bach.[22] There can be little question that he (and Fanny) influenced the Frenchman in this regard. Since Kalkbrenner is not known to have played the organ, he probably rendered these works at the piano. Felix may have done likewise, for he mentions nothing in his letter about an organ, just organ music—all of which suggests that the setting was a salon rather than a church.

What were these "wonderfully pretty" pieces? The "prelude in E minor" was probably the same prelude in E minor that Mendelssohn had copied from Freudenberg. As for the other selection, the famous Prelude in A Minor,

BWV 543/1, is a likely candidate. This is the only organ prelude in A minor by Bach that Mendelssohn is known to have played, and it of course opens the aforementioned print of the six preludes and fugues, BWV 543–48.

A few months after the Parisian sojourn, the Mendelssohns were visited at their home by Sir George Smart, an English conductor and organist. Smart wrote in his journal that "young Mendelssohn played a clever fugue, pastorale, and fantasia of Sebastian Bach, all on the organ with a very difficult part for the pedals which his sister played upon the pianoforte."[23] Smart's mention of an "organ" in a domestic setting comes as a surprise, and he may be referring not to the instrument per se but to organ *works* that Felix and Fanny played exclusively on the piano (or on two pianos, since Smart also heard that evening an "overture" by Felix performed by the two siblings "on two pianofortes"). Still, Smart describes the performances he witnessed in such detail that one is inclined to take him literally.

It seems very unlikely that the Mendelssohns, despite their wealth, owned a fully equipped pipe organ, complete with pedals. Had they owned such a large instrument, would there not be some record of it? Therefore we may rule out the possibility that Felix had a pedalboard at his disposal but still required his sister's help because of his limited pedaling ability. A more plausible scenario is that the instrument was a chamber organ or reed organ sans pedals. Might it have been an orgue expressif (a predecessor of the harmonium) similar to the one the youth had encountered in Paris a few months earlier?[24] Smart reports that the Broadwood piano on which Felix played had been purchased by his father in Paris, suggesting that an orgue expressif might have been procured there as well.

The music performed that night surely included the Pastorale in F Major, BWV 590, Bach's only composition by this name. According to Fanny's catalogue of the family's music library, the Mendelssohns acquired this piece in 1825, the same year that a print of the first movement was issued in Berlin by Schlesinger.[25] Felix could also have been introduced to the Pastorale by his organ teacher A. W. Bach, whose handwritten copy of the first movement survives,[26] or by his friend, the music critic and theorist Adolph Bernhard Marx, in whose journal (the *Berliner allgemeine musikalische Zeitung*) the first movement of the Pastorale had appeared a few months earlier. Only the first movement—which was probably the only movement played—has a pedal part, and it consists of little more than pedal points. Accordingly, the "very difficult" pedal part played by Fanny must have belonged to one of the other two pieces, whatever they were.

Evidence surrounding Fanny's wedding in 1829 to the painter Wilhelm Hensel implies that the Pastorale was also a favorite work of Fanny and her father. On the day of her wedding, the two of them met with the organist Eduard August Grell to discuss what he might play. As Fanny wrote to Felix (who had been detained in England): "Father had suggested the *Pastorella* for the recessional, but I couldn't find it and Grell didn't know it."[27] The familiarity of the reference ("*the* Pastorella") suggests a known quantity, and no work comes to mind besides the most popular organ pastorale ever written, that by Bach.[28] Since just the first movement seems to have circulated widely, Abraham was probably requesting that movement only.

To return to Sir George Smart, his report verifies that music making in the Mendelssohn household included the organ works of Bach and that persons other than the immediate family attended. These gatherings—especially the famous Sunday "musicales"—drew not only the cultural elite of Berlin but also any number of visiting artists. Hence the important realization that Mendelssohn introduced Bach's organ music to foreign musicians in the comfort of his own living room as well as on his travels abroad.

His letters to his family document two later examples of his teenage performances of Bach organ works. The first took place in 1828 in the town of Brandenburg, on a "very good" organ by Joachim Wagner.[29] Here, for about two hours, he played from memory "preludes" by Bach, as well as the Prelude in E Minor and the Pastorale. A year later he was in Hamburg (ready to embark on his first trip to England), "tickling" the magnificent J. G. Hildebrandt organ at the church of St. Michael with works by Bach.[30] It was Holy Week, though, and the church's organist insisted on quiet registrations.

The Grand Tour

Mendelssohn's "great trip" (as he called it) of 1830–32 represents the longest *Bildungsreise* undertaken by a musician in modern times.[31] He visited Austria, Italy, Switzerland, France, and England, as well as many different cities in his native Germany. Quite literally, his reputation spread across Europe. As he broadened his cultural horizons, he played all manner of concerts, kept busy as a composer, and met as many different musicians as possible. His already strong interest in Bach's organ works only intensified as he learned new compositions and improved his organ technique.

Mendelssohn left Berlin in mid-May 1830. His journey began in effect as a Bach pilgrimage, with stops in Leipzig and Weimar. In Leipzig, he sold one of his string quartets to the publisher Breitkopf & Härtel, which, as a salute to his zeal for all things Bach, presented him with manuscripts of a Bach cantata and organ work, neither of which he knew.[32] He stayed in Weimar a full two weeks, often in the company of the octogenarian Johann Wolfgang von Goethe. Mendelssohn had met the poet in 1821 on a trip to Weimar with his teacher Zelter and had visited him there three times since. During these visits the two discussed music, and the young man performed at the keyboard.

Not surprisingly, he played a good deal of Bach. Goethe had admired Bach's music for decades, and he and Zelter corresponded extensively with each other on the subject.

Both of these elder statesmen appear to have revered Bach's organ works in particular. In Zelter's case this is certain, for here was someone who regarded the organ as Bach's "essential" instrument. He had written to Goethe in 1827 that the organ represented for Bach a kind of inner sanctum wherein the composer forged his own, transcendent style: "The organ is Bach's own peculiar soul, into which he breathes immediately the living breath. His theme is the feeling just born, which, like the spark from the stone, invariably springs forth, from the first chance pressure of the foot upon the pedals. Thus by degrees he warms to his subject, till he has isolated himself, and feels alone, and then an inexhaustible stream passes out into the infinite ocean."[33]

In a subsequent missive, Zelter again portrayed the organ pedals as the foundation of Bach's genius: "I could support . . . your conviction of the effect of organism upon the intellectual nature. . . . One might say of old Bach, that the pedals were the ground-element of the development of his unfathomable intellect, and that without feet, he could never have attained his intellectual *height*."[34] However fanciful, these same ideas had probably been preached by Zelter to his protégé.

As far as Goethe is concerned, surely he knew that his adopted hometown of Weimar was where Bach had composed most of his organ works. And through his friendship with the organist J. H. F. Schütz, a student of Bach's pupil J. C. Kittel, he probably heard these works on a regular basis. Of the six Bach manuscripts known to have been owned by Goethe, two contain organ compositions.[35]

Mendelssohn performed on the organ just once during his visit with Goethe in 1830, in the church where Bach's cousin Johann Gottfried Walther had served as organist and where both Wilhelm Friedemann and Carl Philipp Emanuel Bach had been baptized. As he later explained to Zelter:

> One day [Goethe] asked me if I would not care to pay a compliment to craftsmanship and call on the organist, who might let me see and hear the organ in the town church. I did so, and the instrument gave me great pleasure. . . . The organist offered me the choice of hearing something learned, or something for the people (because he said that for the people one had to compose only easy and bad music), so I asked for something learned. But it was not much to be proud of. He modulated around enough to make one giddy, but nothing unusual came of it; he made a number of entries, but no fugue was forthcoming. When my turn came to play to him, I let loose with the D-minor toccata of Sebastian [Bach] and remarked that this was at the same time learned and something for the people too, at least some of them. But see, I had hardly

started to play when the superintendent dispatched his valet downstairs with the message that this playing had to be stopped right away because it was a weekday and he could not study with that much noise going on. Goethe was very much amused by this story.[36]

Scholars have generally assumed the work in question to be the famous Toccata in D Minor, BWV 565.[37] Nonetheless, no argument has ever been made either pro or con this supposition despite the fact that Bach composed another toccata in D minor for organ, BWV 538/1, known as the "Dorian" (because it is notated in D minor without any flats in the key signature, along the lines of the dorian mode). Of course, BWV 565 is now regarded in certain quarters as inauthentic, but this theory originated only about twenty-five years ago.[38] Throughout the nineteenth century and for most of the twentieth, musicians not only accepted the work as genuine but hailed it as one of Bach's boldest. Which is to say that whoever the composer is, the piece deserves to be discussed within the context of Bach reception.

The evidence points unambiguously to BWV 565, mainly because Mendelssohn knew the Dorian not as a toccata but as a prelude. We may conclude this from a letter (soon to be discussed in its own right) written to his family in 1831 in which he requests to be sent copies of six different Bach organ works, including a "Prelude and Fugue in D Minor," which he identifies by notating the first two beats of the Dorian toccata. Moreover, Felix at some point acquired a manuscript of the Dorian in the hand of the violinist Eduard Rietz, titled *Preludio e Fuga di Giov: Seb: Bach.*[39] Rietz, who died in 1832, was a Bach enthusiast and close friend of the Mendelssohns; he was also a professional music copyist. According to Fanny's catalogue, three of the Bach-organ manuscripts that had been acquired by the Mendelssohns between 1823 and 1825 were copies by Rietz that he had donated to the family. It seems likely, then, that Rietz had also donated to the Mendelssohns his copy of the Dorian and that Felix adopted the title of the work found in this manuscript.

In terms of aesthetics, there is really no reason to doubt that on some level Mendelssohn deemed BWV 565 especially appropriate for popular consumption. By calling the piece "something for the people," he was no doubt mocking the local organist,[40] but its style is simple and direct: the hands frequently play in unison; the diminished-seventh chord is shamelessly exploited; and dramatic, "rhetorical" pauses are tossed in for good measure. By calling it "learned," Mendelssohn may have meant merely that the composer was exceptionally erudite.

Bidding farewell to Goethe for the last time, Mendelssohn next headed to Munich for a stay of about two months and then to Vienna, where he would remain from mid-August to October. There he visited the baritone and Bach expert Franz Hauser. The two had met in 1825 while Hauser was visiting

Berlin (and at which time he sang for Zelter the "Quoniam" from Bach's B
Minor Mass).[41] The year prior to Mendelssohn's arrival in Vienna, Hauser
and his scribes had prepared a manuscript containing numerous organ works
by Bach.[42] Hauser no doubt showed this source to his young colleague. Mendelssohn is also known to have continued his organ playing on this visit, which
almost certainly means that he continued playing organ works by Bach.[43]

When Mendelssohn departed Vienna in October for a nine-month tour
of Italy, he took with him a volume of Luther's chorales given to him by
Hauser.[44] Over the next few months, this present would inspire him to compose a whole series of cantatas on these hymns, including one on the Christmas chorale "Vom Himmel hoch da komm ich her."[45] This cantata seems to
be modeled after Bach's Canonic Variations for organ on the same chorale,
for both pieces open with the same descending-scale figure set as a canon
(see examples 1–5 and 1–6).[46] They are also in the same key. It may or may
not be significant that Hauser edited the Canonic Variations for publication
the following year.[47]

Very late in 1830, while Mendelssohn was in Rome, Hauser mailed him
what was essentially a Christmas present, a manuscript copy of Bach's organ
partita on "Christ, der du bist der helle Tag," BWV 766. Hauser himself
penned the source, which is dated 22 December 1830.[48] A month later, the recipient expressed his heartfelt appreciation: "Dear Hauser! As I write to you,

Example 1–5 Canonic Variations on "Vom Himmel hoch, da komm ich her," BWV 769,
Variation 1

Example 1–6 Felix Mendelssohn Bartholdy, chorale cantata "Vom Himmel hoch, da komm ich her," first movement

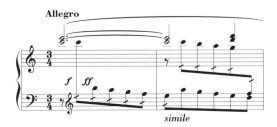

I must begin with a word of thanks. Once again you have sent me a heavenly chorale by Bach, in your own hand, and the whole thing looks so elegant and tidy, and yet scholarly too, just like my room in the Bärenmühle. You know indeed what joy this must bring me."[49]

Thus Mendelssohn thanked Hauser both for the manuscript itself and for its handsome appearance. He may also have referred to the Bärenmühle out of gratitude, since Hauser, who was already living in this building when Mendelssohn arrived in Vienna,[50] had presumably helped him secure lodgings there. In any case, this gift provided Felix with a further unpublished Bach organ work, as this partita would not appear in print until 1846, when editions were issued by C. F. Peters and by Mendelssohn himself.[51] Evidently, this was not the first chorale by Bach that Mendelssohn had received from Hauser.

Mendelssohn seems to have played the organ rarely during his nine months in Italy, probably because he "did not find a single one in good order,"[52] and by the time he arrived in Switzerland in late July 1831, his technique must have deteriorated. To compensate, he began to practice the instrument with a vengeance, naturally with a focus on Bach. In late August and early September he did little else. He wrote to Goethe about the monks at the monastery in Engelberg, who, even though they "had never even heard the name of Sebastian Bach," enjoyed his performance of "a couple of Bach fugues" on their organ.[53] But the letter he penned to his family a week later, while stranded (because of flooding) in the village of Sargans, reveals infinitely more:

Today I played [the organ] the entire morning, and I have begun to study the instrument seriously, because it is actually a shame that I cannot play Sebastian Bach's major works. In Munich, if I can manage it, I intend to practice an hour every day, because today, after a couple hours' work, I have already made progress with my feet (*nota bene:* sitting). Rietz once told me that Schneider,

in Dresden, played him the D-major fugue from the *Well-Tempered Clavier* [at
this point, Mendelssohn notates the first ten notes of the subject of the D-
major fugue from Book 1 of this collection] on the organ, and played the bass
line on the pedals. This had hitherto appeared so fantastic to me that I could
hardly comprehend it. It occurred to me again at the organ this morning, so I
instantly attempted it, and I at least see that it is far from impossible, and that
I will learn how to do it. I succeeded pretty well with the theme, so I practiced
as many passages as I knew by heart from the D-major fugue for organ, the F-
major toccata, and the G-minor fugue. If I can find a decent, unbroken organ
in Munich, I will learn this method, and I look forward like a child to playing
such pieces down on the pedal. The F-major toccata, with the modulation at
the end, sounds as if the church were about to tumble down. That cantor was
awesome.

After an intense practice session at the organ that afternoon, he resumed:

I practiced on the organ until dusk and was trampling furiously on the pedals,
when we suddenly noticed that the low C sharp on the Subbass was humming
away, softly but continuously. All of our pushing, shaking, and stomping on
the pedals was of no avail, so we had to climb inside the organ, among the
thick pipes. The C sharp continued to hum—the fault lay in the windchest—
and the organist was greatly disconcerted because tomorrow was a feast day.
Finally, I stuck my handkerchief into the pipe, and there was no more humming but no C sharp either. All the same, I played continuously [he notates
here the first five beats of the subject of Bach's Fugue in D Major for organ,
BWV 532/2] and it is already going rather well.[54]

Just what does this letter reveal? Most important, it tells us that Mendelssohn still lacked—at least, according to his standards—the pedal technique necessary to perform Bach's "big" organ works. Furthermore, his comment about Johann Gottlob Schneider's performance of the D-major fugue
from the *Well-Tempered Clavier* bespeaks a limited understanding of pedal
technique in general. Mendelssohn was amazed that anyone could pedal this
fugue subject, which begins with a barrage of thirty-second notes.

Pedaling this subject reminded him of Bach's only *organ* fugue in D major,
BWV 532/2, and his Toccata in F Major, BWV 540/1, both of which make
extraordinary demands on the feet. Seen in this light, the "G-minor fugue"
was presumably the Fugue in G Minor, BWV 542/2, Bach's only organ fugue
in that key with a virtuosic pedal part. Mendelssohn may have gotten acquainted with this fugue through Zelter, as suggested earlier, or through his
organ teacher A. W. Bach, who printed the movement in his anthology,
Orgel-Stücke für das Concert (Berlin, 1829).[55] He may have learned the D-major
organ fugue through Rietz, for at some point he acquired a manuscript copy
of the movement in Rietz's hand.[56] That Felix played these works "by heart"

suggests that he had known them for some time. Still, considering his prodigious memory,[57] one should not make too much of this.

The letter raises other issues as well. To judge from the second musical example inscribed by Mendelssohn, he used the head motive of the D-major organ fugue as a kind of pedal exercise starting on low C sharp (even though he notated it starting on D). There is also his anticipation about playing other harpsichord pieces by Bach on the organ, *pedaliter*. Playing Bach's harpsichord works on the organ was nothing new to him,[58] but rendering them as pedal showpieces apparently was. Most interesting of all, at least from an aesthetic perspective, Mendelssohn enthused over the startling move to G-flat major in measures 424–32 of the F-major toccata.

He arrived in Munich two weeks later. There he wrote to Zelter: "Now I am going to the organ at St. Peter's to study some Bach fugues with my feet. The bearer of this [letter] can tell you all about it."[59] Perhaps, then, he continued to focus on the pedal parts of Bach's D-major and G-minor organ fugues. The courier was presumably a member of the Mendelssohn family, any of whom would already have read Felix's letter about his organ playing in Sargans.

Still in Munich a fortnight later, he again wrote to his family about his organ playing:

> I also play the organ every day for an hour. But unfortunately I cannot practice as I wish because the pedalboard lacks the five uppermost notes. Thus I cannot play any of Sebastian Bach's passage work on it. But the stops are wonderfully beautiful, especially for chorales. The heavenly, liquid tone of the instrument is edifying. In particular, Fanny, I have discovered the stops that ought to be used in playing Sebastian Bach's "Schmücke dich, o liebe Seele." They seem actually made for this piece and sound so touching that I am invariably awestruck when I begin to play it. For the moving parts I have an eight-foot flute, and also a very soft four-foot flute, which continuously floats above the chorale tune. You know this effect from Berlin. But here there is a manual with reed stops on which I can play the chorale tune, so I use a mellow oboe, a very soft four-foot clarion, and a viola. This renders the chorale tune so subdued and glowing, it is as if distant human voices are singing from the depths of their heart.[60]

Mendelssohn begins this excerpt by assuring his family that he has kept the vow he made in Sargans to practice the organ an hour a day. He then complains that the pedalboard of the organ on which he was practicing (still that of St. Peter's?) evidently extended no higher than g or a, which precluded playing on it any of Bach's "passage work," a term that in this context should be interpreted as fast, wide-ranging figuration. But this organ was, he seems to suggest, perfect for relatively slow chorale arrangements featuring a solo reed melody and flute accompaniment. The work he refers to as an ideal candidate for this classic registration is the famous arrangement of "Schmücke dich, o liebe Seele," BWV 654, from the so-called Great Eighteen chorales, Bach's only setting of this hymn for the organ.

This was not the first time Felix had cited this piece in one of his letters. A month earlier in Lindau he had written to his family: "Yesterday I rode here from [St. Gall] . . . and found in the evening a wonderful organ, where I could play 'Schmücke dich, o liebe Seele' to my heart's content."[61] Clearly, the work had become one of his favorites, and it would remain so until his death. We do not know when or how he got to know it, but his remark to Fanny that she had heard "this effect" in Berlin may refer less to flute stops in general than to this organ chorale in particular. Perhaps, then, he had studied "Schmücke dich" with A. W. Bach. Fanny, who accompanied her brother to his organ lessons,[62] may even have been present when Felix played this work for his teacher.

He would remain in Germany for another two months. By mid-November he had arrived in Frankfurt, where he was a guest of Johann Nepomuk Schelble, the director of that city's St. Cecilia Society. Like Zelter's Singakademie, this ensemble concentrated on early music, especially Bach.[63] Mendelssohn had met Schelble in Frankfurt in 1822, at which time he heard the group perform a Bach motet. More specific to our concerns, Schelble is known to have prepared for this ensemble an orchestral transcription of one of Bach's organ works, the Prelude in C Minor, BWV 546/1.[64] He also owned numerous manuscript copies of organ chorales by Bach.[65]

During his visit to Frankfurt in 1831, Mendelssohn received the best and worst of news from his family. They had first written that his younger sister, Rebecka ("Beckchen"), was engaged to the mathematician Lejeune Dirichlet, then that his aunt Henriette ("Jette") had died. In a letter addressed to Fanny, begun on 14 November, he responded:

> Oh my dear little sister and musician, today is your birthday, and I wanted to congratulate you and wish you good cheer, and then came your letter about Aunt Jette, and now any real joy is certainly over with. Yesterday the engagement announcement came, today this one—things are strangely back and forth. I want to give you one of the new unbelievably moving Seb. Bach organ pieces that I just got to know here—they are fitting today in their pure gentle solemnity. It is as if one were listening to the angels in heaven singing.
>
> *The 17th.* I wanted to write out the piece when I was starting the letter, then in the evening set aside the paper, and in the morning when I arose it had already been finished—Schelble had arisen earlier, having heard me speak of it, and got there before I did. From this small tidbit, you can fill in the rest of the details of my life with him for yourself; every moment he puts me to shame with his generosity. . . .

Now play this chorale with Beckchen, as long as you are together, and think of me while doing so. At the end, when the chorale melody begins to flutter and dies out way up in the air, and everything dissolves into sound—there it is surely heavenly. There are many others as well, just as powerful, but they are more remorseful. This one fits today exactly, and so I am sending it, and my regards to you and Hensel [Fanny's husband], and I wish that you will remain mine, as I am yours.

N. B. The chorale is with double pedal, eight feet. Schelble arranged it thus, not a note is missing.[66]

Mendelssohn's emotional reaction here to what was presumably an entire collection of Bach organ chorales owned by Schelble is of special interest. On the face of it, he does not respond so differently than he did to "Schmücke dich." He even employs the same "singing" metaphor, only with angels rather than humans. (The imagery of angels also agrees with the use of "flutter" and "air" toward the end of the letter.) But whereas his response to "Schmücke dich" had primarily to do with how that piece sounded on a particular organ, he now reacts to the music itself. He was also touched, no doubt, by the chorale texts involved. Whatever these pieces were, they moved him profoundly and gave rise to a whole range of feelings.

We can better understand his remarks only by identifying the work he mailed to Fanny. Our best clue, of course, is his description of how the work concludes: the voice that states the chorale tune begins to accelerate ("flutter") and eventually cadences on a very high pitch ("way up in the air"). To judge from the pitch reference, the voice range must be soprano. Of the hundreds of organ chorales either composed by or attributed to Bach, only one really fits this description: the popular setting of "Wir glauben all an einen Gott, Vater," BWV 740. Four versions of this work survive, and they differ with respect to the placement of the chorale tune (whether in the soprano or tenor) and the number of pedal voices (whether one or two).[67] But the most familiar version of this piece, known as BWV 740, presents the hymn tune in the soprano and contains a double pedal part, as mentioned in Mendelssohn's postscript.

Example 1–7 shows that the final bars of this version of "Wir glauben" closely match Mendelssohn's words. On beat 3 of measure 27 the right hand plays the last note of the hymn, which it has presented mostly in quarter and half notes. Four beats later, thirty-second notes begin to take over and continue for six beats; by means of rising sequences, the passage winds up an octave higher than it started. These sequences become almost unbearable to the listener, supported as they are by a dissonant combination of a dominant-seventh chord and tonic pedal point. When the resolution finally comes—and it is prolonged further by a very long quarter-note appoggiatura—the

Example 1–7 "Wir glauben all an einen Gott, Vater," BWV 740

sense of relief is overwhelming. All the voices ("everything") at last "dissolve" into a tonic triad ("sound"). There is no sweeter or "heavenly" moment in the composition.

"Wir glauben" is a sweet-sounding work in general, due not only to the use of the major mode but also to frequent parallel thirds and sixths and an overabundance of tonic harmonies.[68] (This quality might explain why Mendelssohn found this chorale less "remorseful" than the others in Schelble's collection, although the chorale text was probably a factor too.) Such traits, of course, characterize the music not of Bach but of the post-Bach generation, a claim that can also be made for certain *galant* mannerisms found in the work (see especially the first two beats of measure 7 of BWV 740). It is hardly surprising, then, that two of the four versions of this piece are attributed in a mid-nineteenth-century edition to Bach's pupil Johann Ludwig Krebs. Indeed, the general consensus today is that Bach had absolutely nothing to do with any of the four versions.[69]

A good deal of external evidence also supports our hypothesis. For one thing, both Mendelssohn and Schelble published editions of BWV 740 under Bach's name, which suggests that it was one of their favorite Bach compositions. Mendelssohn printed the work in 1846 as one of Bach's *Grand Preludes on Corales* [*sic*], while Schelble included it in volume 1 of his lost collection, *Var.[iirte] Choraele fürs P. f. zu 4 Haenden eingerichtet.*[70] Mendelssohn's edition, furthermore, prescribes that "no 16 feet Stop whatever" should be used for the double-pedal part, which is more or less consistent with his comment in the postscript about an eight-foot pedal registration (sixteen-foot stops can easily obscure the thick bass texture). He also mentions there that Schelble had "arranged" the work for double pedal. Surely it cannot be happenstance that the only extant manuscript of any version of the work is a copy of BWV 740 in the hand of Franz Xaver Gleichauf, one of Schelble's pupils and heirs.[71] All of this leads to the conclusion that Schelble prepared the version known as BWV 740. He appears to have worked directly from the other double-pedal version, which he improved upon at every turn.

Since neither Fanny nor Rebecka is known to have played the organ, Felix undoubtedly envisioned the two of them seated together at one of the family's pianos. He also knew his sisters were fond of playing Bach organ works as keyboard duets, then a very common practice. Fanny had written him two years earlier apropos of Bach's organ preludes that "Beckchen is virtuosically pounding out the pedal parts . . . and at times it does my heart good. Old Bach would laugh himself to death if he could see it."[72] (To judge from a letter Felix wrote several years later to Rebecka, the two of them performed Bach organ works together at the piano too, with Rebecka taking the pedal line.)[73] Her remarks smack of sarcasm as well as sincerity, for Rebecka, a gifted soprano, was certainly no keyboard "virtuoso." Her inadequacies as a duet partner may not always have amused her older sister, but Fanny genuinely appreciated her efforts.

Rebecka, then, would have appreciated the relatively slow rhythms of this pedal part, even if it does comprise two voices. Her brother's note about eight-foot pedal registration would have told her to play the part at the pitch written, rather than down an octave to simulate sixteen-foot stops and to avoid interfering with the performer of the manual voices. Transposing the pedal part in this way was a customary practice in playing Bach organ works at the piano, as the preface to volume 1 of the Peters edition evinces.[74] In this work, however, the pedal part may be performed at the pitch notated with only minimal encroachment upon the other player.

One can imagine that as soon as Fanny and Rebecka learned this chorale, it became a sentimental favorite. Each time they played it they would have thought not only of Felix, as he had requested, but also of the contrasting and poignant circumstances within their family at the time they had received the piece. Their brother had selected a work solemn enough to honor their deceased aunt yet pleasing enough to serve as a birthday present. The title of the chorale ("We all believe in one God") offers reassurance under any circumstance.

Meanwhile the tour continued. Mendelssohn reached Paris on 9 December and had scarcely unpacked his bags before he set about repaying Schelble for his hospitality. Five days after arriving, he wrote to Fanny:

> In the meantime, dear Fanny, please see to it that *two* copies are made of the following pieces from our Sebastian Bach file, and if possible, entirely accurate copies: Toccata in D Minor, Toccata in F Major, Prelude and Fugue in E Minor, Fantasy in G Minor, Prelude and Fugue in G Major, Prelude and Fugue in D Minor [at this point, Felix inscribes the first two beats of the Dorian toccata, BWV 538/1]. Then have one copy sent to Schelble in Frankfurt and a second one (for Hiller) to me here, unless they are too bulky to mail. . . . Hiller wants to have them at all costs. On occasion, he and Kalkbrenner play the printed organ pieces here.[75]

This excerpt introduces a second (in addition to Kalkbrenner) Parisian pianist with an affinity for Bach, Ferdinand Hiller. Mendelssohn had met Hiller in Frankfurt at the same time he made Schelble's acquaintance in 1822, and they would eventually become the closest of friends. We know nothing about the context of Hiller's or Kalkbrenner's performances, but their repertory must have included the six preludes and fugues, BWV 543–48, which by this date had been reprinted three different times.

There can be no question that Mendelssohn is talking here about organ compositions. The only instrumentation mentioned is the organ, the only musical incipit provided is that of an organ work, and the first four titles agree with those of organ works composed by or attributed to Bach that we have already discussed: BWV 565, 540/1, 533, and 542/1, respectively. It follows that the fifth title refers to the same "prelude and fugue in G major" for organ listed by Fanny in her catalogue of the family's music library. Felix appears to have chosen for his two friends not only six of his favorite Bach organ works but also six he believed to be unpublished.[76] This would explain why he bothered to designate Hiller's and Kalkbrenner's repertoire as "printed."

The task of procuring the copies fell to Fanny, who presumably either did the actual copying herself or enlisted a professional scribe to do the work. Whoever the scribe was, he or she would have worked from master copies kept in a special Bach "file." That the scribe was Fanny is suggested by four extant Bach-organ manuscripts in her hand that Felix is known to have owned late in his life.[77] That Fanny was accustomed to helping her brother along these lines is suggested by a letter she wrote him two years earlier in which she reports on forwarding "Bach organ preludes" to their friend, the writer Hermann Franck.[78] She may have sent Felix a similar parcel in late 1830 during his visit to Rome. In that instance, he had asked his family to mail him Bach cantatas or organ works for the bibliophile Fortunato Santini, who had allowed Mendelssohn to peruse his collection of Italian sacred polyphony.[79]

Even though he socialized extensively, the four months that Mendelssohn spent in Paris during the winter of 1831–32 were every bit as disappointing artistically as his trip in 1825. This was a dark time for him personally as well, as news came first of the death of his friend Rietz and then of Goethe. To make matters worse, he contracted Asiatic cholera. No doubt, then, he was relieved when on 22 April 1832 he set foot in London, where several of his closest friends had settled and where he was already quite a celebrity. He had first visited there in 1829 and during that sojourn seems to have regularly played the postlude at the Sunday morning service at St. Paul's Cathedral.[80] The cathedral's three-manual organ, by Bernard Smith, was one of the few instruments in the city at this time with a full, two-octave pedalboard (C–c′).[81] This made it an obvious choice for the music of Bach. These performances, like Mendelssohn's organ playing in general, probably consisted for the most part of improvisations and works by Bach, and they were to become a standard feature of Mendelssohn's visits to London over the next several years. To judge from one such occasion in 1837, he could play upwards of half an hour (!) with enthusiastic onlookers crowded around the console.[82] These performances were the primary means by which he advanced Bach's music in England.[83]

Mendelssohn's organ playing at St. Paul's in 1832 is well documented. As in 1829, he stayed with Thomas Attwood, the elderly organist of St. Paul's and a former pupil of Mozart. At eight o'clock on the morning of Sunday, 27 May, Attwood dashed off the following note to be hand-delivered to his friend and fellow organist Vincent Novello, then one of England's most ardent Bach champions: "Dear Novello, —Mendelssohn has just rec^d. some manuscripts of Sebastian Bach, which he purposes trying this Morn^g.: hope you will meet him —11 o'c."[84] Thus Mendelssohn was to perform again presumably in the form of a postlude, as the service began at 9:45.[85] Unfortunately, nothing at all is known about these manuscripts, neither their contents nor who sent them.

Exactly two weeks later, on 10 June, Mendelssohn is reported to have played "fugue music . . . to the amazement of all the listeners" on the organ at St. Paul's and to have "excited so much attention by his treatment of the pedal-board that a complete revolution in the style of English organ-playing may be dated from that memorable performance."[86] These references undoubtedly pertain to fugues by Bach with virtuosic pedal lines. They also provide a context for a letter written by Mendelssohn later that summer in which he remembered with great joy his performance of a "Bach fugue in A minor" on the organ at St. Paul's.[87] By this he must have meant Bach's only organ fugue in that key, the famous Fugue in A Minor, BWV 543/2, and he may well have played this very movement on 10 June. Those who witnessed his performance of this fugue were no doubt awed by its demanding pedal line, which few English organists then could have negotiated. That Mendelssohn was able to do so implies a substantial improvement in his pedal technique since his stay in Switzerland the previous year. He was now thoroughly proficient.

Another Bach organ work performed by Mendelssohn in London at this time was the Prelude and Fugue in E Minor, BWV 533. According to the organist Edward Holmes, writing in 1835, this composition "was first made known to English amateurs by the performance of Mr. Mendelssohn Bartholdy, at St. Paul's cathedral."[88] Novello claimed that Felix played this piece "frequently" and "from memory."[89]

Mendelssohn's stay in London would last two months. At the end of June, and after an absence of over two years, he was back in Berlin. The "great trip" was finally over.

Young Adulthood

Now, at the age of twenty-three, Mendelssohn realized his need for a professional position. He was the obvious choice to succeed Zelter (who had died in May) as director of the Singakademie, but his application came to naught. Instead, starting in 1833, he became music director in Düsseldorf. After about a year on the job, though, he was entertaining offers from elsewhere, and he ultimately agreed to serve as municipal music director and conductor of the Gewandhaus orchestra in Leipzig, an appointment that began in 1835. By the end of the 1830s he had amassed one of the largest collections of Bach's organ works to be found anywhere[90] and had become known, particularly in England, as an organ recitalist who specialized in Bach. Last but not least, his organ compositions from this decade betray the influence of Bach's organ music in a variety of compelling ways.

In the summer of 1832, as Mendelssohn debated whether or not to apply to the Singakademie, he attempted to publish his own edition of Bach's organ works. The earliest mention of this project is found in a letter he wrote (from Attwood's home in Surrey) to Novello during his stay in London the previous spring:

> As soon as I have a free moment, I will try to write for you the Fugue in E [Minor]; but I cannot promise whether I shall succeed, as I fear I do not recollect exactly the distribution of parts in some passages. However, I will try it, and if I do not recollect it, get you a copy from Germany, where it must now be published in a collection of organ pieces.[91]

It is impossible to tell whether Mendelssohn means just the fugue or the work as a whole. Whatever the case, after receiving the promised manuscript the following year, Novello published the prelude and fugue in his series *Select Organ Pieces.*

More tellingly, in a letter of 28 July 1832 to his Parisian acquaintance Madame C. Kiené, Mendelssohn wrote that "a friend of mine and I are now planning to publish a complete collection of his [J. S. Bach's] major organ works; as soon as it appears, I shall take the liberty of sending you a copy."[92] Two weeks later, he mentioned the edition in a letter to the pianist Ignaz Moscheles: "I think at the same time of the Bach pieces that we played together and must tell you that I have found here an entire volume of unknown works of the same type by him. I expect that all of them will now be published by Breitkopf and Härtel. There are heavenly things among them. I think they will please you."[93]

Moscheles, who had briefly taught both Felix and Fanny in 1824, was by this date one of Mendelssohn's best friends and a Bach champion in his own right. Having moved to London, he had regularly seen Felix on his sojourns there in 1829 and 1832. During each of these visits, moreover, the two had publicly performed concertos for two pianos. Did they offer the public two-piano renditions of Bach's organ works too?

Last of all, on 3 September Mendelssohn began a missive (written in English) to Attwood with the following lines:

My dear Sir, I avail myself of Mr. Moore's leaving Berlin to send you the long promised Prelude of Bach's with your favourite fugue, and with that other wonderfull piece, which I played every Sunday on your organ, & which produced so good effect with your Diapasons. I should ask you to excuse my negligence in delaying a thing which I could hope would give you pleasure, but I always waited for the publication of the whole set, which I intended to send to you. But the publisher, Mr. Simrock, being dead since that time, we have been obliged to give it to another publisher, and this will delay the term of their appearance. As soon as they are to be had, I shall send you a complete set of them, at present I hope you will play sometimes the fugue as a last voluntary and think of the time when you allowed me to do so, a time which I shall always think of, and which was a very happy one for me.[94]

From this excerpt, we learn that the collection was supposed to have been issued by the house of Simrock but that the death of Nikolaus Simrock (on 12 June 1832) had forced the editors to look for a new publisher. According to Mendelssohn's letter to Moscheles, the new publisher was Breitkopf & Härtel. He is probably referring, once again, to the E-minor prelude and fugue. This fugue, at any rate, can hardly have been the A-minor, for Attwood could not have essayed such a difficult movement.[95] Nothing is known about the other "wonderfull" work.

Recent research indicates, quite unexpectedly, that the edition cited by Mendelssohn in these four letters must be the one eventually published by Breitkopf & Härtel in the fall of 1833 under the title *Johann Sebastian Bach's noch wenig bekannte Orgelcompositionen (auch am Pianoforte von einem oder zwei Spielern ausführbar) gesammelt und herausgegeben von Adolph Bernhard Marx*.[96] We should not really be surprised by the absence of Mendelssohn's name here, since he refused for it to appear anywhere on his editions of Bach's organ chorales published by this press in 1845–46, reasoning that "only one composer's name" (i.e., Bach) should be given. The 1833 print contains the E-minor prelude and fugue, as well as three other works or movements (BWV 532, 542/2, and 565) that Felix is known to have played. As far as A. B. Marx is concerned, he was perhaps Felix's closest "friend" altogether at this time (see Mendelssohn's letter to Madame Kiené).

A total of nine free organ works by Bach are included, in the following order: Prelude in A Minor, BWV 569; Toccata in E Major (first two movements only), BWV 566; Prelude and Fugue in D Minor, BWV 539; Fantasy in G Minor, BWV 542/1; Prelude and Fugue in G Major, BWV 550; Prelude and Fugue in D Major, BWV 532; Prelude and Fugue in E Minor, BWV 533; Fugue in G Minor, BWV 542/2; and Toccata in D Minor, BWV 565. With the exception of the E-minor prelude and fugue and the G-minor fugue, none of the music had ever appeared in print. No introduction or commentary of any kind is provided, and the scores are mostly devoid of performance instructions, along the lines of an *Urtext* edition. Since Marx is not known to have even played the organ, one must assume that Mendelssohn had been the driving force all along.

The day after writing Attwood, Felix sent a second letter to Madame Kiené in which he notated in its entirety the *Orgelbüchlein* setting of "Ich ruf zu dir, Herr Jesu Christ," BWV 639. He explained that

> as I am still unable today to send you, by way of atonement, something I am working on myself, old Bach will have to be my shield and refuge; and so, on the next page, I'm writing down a little piece that I got to know here by accident a fortnight ago. . . . The upper voice is an ornamented chorale and should be played on the organ with somewhat strong registers; on the piano it must be played in octaves; or it would be best, I believe, if Mr. Baillot would "sing" the upper voice on his violins, in which case the piano would properly proceed beneath.[97]

The page containing "Ich ruf zu dir" is reproduced in figure 1–2.

Mendelssohn's comments on performance practice here are particularly telling. Not only does he suggest three different instrumentations, but he also refers or alludes to such diverse matters as organ registration, piano technique, and a *cantabile* style of string playing. His casual attitude toward in-

Figure 1–2 Manuscript copy of "Ich ruf zu dir, Herr Jesu Christ," BWV 639, in the hand of Felix Mendelssohn Bartholdy, contained in a letter from Mendelssohn to Madame C. Kiené, dated 4 September 1832 (Universitätsbibliothek Basel, Autogr.-Slg. Geigy-Hagenbach Nr. 1727)

strumentation may strike us as almost cavalier, but it typifies an era in which musicians were eager to play and hear Bach's music for the first time, using whatever resources were available. In effect, this letter is the earliest known transcription of "Ich ruf zu dir," a work also transcribed by Ferruccio Busoni, Max Reger, Leopold Stokowski, and many lesser talents.[98]

Mendelssohn's choice of violin and piano as the "best" instrumentation for this piece should be understood not as his own absolute preference but rather what he felt would be most appropriate in Madame Kiené's salon, where he had often performed. He was also well acquainted with the violinist mentioned, Pierre Baillot, evidently another regular player there. Baillot had given Mendelssohn violin lessons in Paris about fifteen years earlier, and the two performed together whenever he was in town. No doubt, then, Mendelssohn knew that Bach was one of Baillot's favorite composers.[99] He probably knew as well that Baillot's piano accompanist for his earliest Bach performances in Paris had been none other than Marie Bigot, the daughter of Madame Kiené. Bigot, moreover, had taught both Felix and Fanny. By penning "Ich ruf zu dir" into this letter, Mendelssohn was acknowledging Bach's lofty position within the Kiené-Baillot circle. These Parisians, unlike those he had encountered in 1825, were already converted.

But the instrumentation first suggested is solo organ, for which Mendelssohn recommended "strong" registers for the chorale melody. His rationale for a big sound is far from clear—the practice nowadays is a soft reed stop—especially when the thin texture and subjective text imply intimacy and introspection. Also noteworthy is his categorical description of this part as an "ornamented" chorale, since only the first five bars contain any embellishment. Did he add his own ornamentation from measure 6 on?

As a pianist, Mendelssohn knew that an idiomatic alteration at the piano was to duplicate the chorale tune at the octave. In addition, a duplication at the *upper* octave would have approximated his suggested organ registration, which would have included at least one four-foot stop (he had registered "Schmücke dich" this way in Munich). Octave doublings of this sort are commonly found in nineteenth- and twentieth-century piano transcriptions of Bach's organ works, including Busoni's of "Ich ruf zu dir."

Finally, as a chamber musician, Mendelssohn realized the effectiveness of a violin melody with piano accompaniment. His metaphorical use of the verb "sing" in conjunction with a string instrument may point to nothing more specific than a lyrical style of playing, but it suggests the use of vibrato, in imitation of the human voice. The metaphor might also have been inspired by the word "ruf" or "call" in the opening line of the text ("I call to You, Lord Jesus Christ"). Another possibility is that Baillot's playing was known for its "singing" style and that Mendelssohn is making a somewhat frivolous reference to this quality.

Meanwhile, back in Berlin, Mendelssohn pondered his chances at the Sing-akademie (and, as always, kept very busy composing and performing). When the negative verdict was finally handed down in January 1833, he was ready to leave his hometown for good. Having accepted a handsome commission from London's Philharmonic Society, he planned to premiere three works there in the spring, including the *Italian Symphony*. He also fully expected once again to play the music of Bach on the organ at St. Paul's Cathedral.

We know this from a letter he wrote to Hauser. In the first of a series of letters between the two in early 1833, Hauser informed Mendelssohn that he was preparing a thematic catalogue of Bach's oeuvre and wondered if his friend might inform him about any works he had not yet included.[100] Mendelssohn wrote back that he possibly owned no fewer than sixty such organ chorales: forty-four chorales from the *Orgelbüchlein;* fourteen of the Great Eighteen organ chorales; the double-pedal arrangement of "Wir glauben all an einen Gott, Vater," BWV 740; and the partita on "Sei gegrüsset, Jesu gütig," BWV 768.[101] (Virtually all of these works were still unpublished at the time.) In a subsequent communication, he promised to send Hauser a copy of an "E-minor prelude and fugue" by Bach, apparently another reference to BWV 533.[102]

After receiving a copy of Hauser's catalogue, Mendelssohn responded in late March with a request of his own:

> Certain pieces in your catalogue have caught my attention. Their themes are so beautiful that I would very much like to have them. And because they are mostly for the organ and because (as you know) I often play at St. Paul's, I would very much like to take them with me to London. Thus I want to ask whether you could possibly have them (especially the organ pieces) copied for me immediately and sent here, because, God willing, I depart a fortnight from tomorrow (the 14th). The pieces are the following: Fantasy for Organ in C Minor [at this point, Mendelssohn copied from Hauser's catalogue the first two measures of the Fantasy in C Minor, BWV 562/1]; chorale preludes on "Ach Herr, mich armen Sünder," "Ach Gott, erhöh mein Seufzen," "Christ lag in Todesbanden," "Herr Jesu Christ, dich zu uns wend," "Zeuch ein zu deinen Toren."[103]

In addition to the C-minor fantasy, the first, second, and last chorale settings cited here by Mendelssohn may be identified with certainty, as Hauser's catalogue lists only one work for each of these titles.[104] Both men, however, would have been dismayed to learn that most sources ascribe these three pieces (again) to J. L. Krebs, who today is regarded as their rightful composer.[105] Mendelssohn may have been drawn to this music, all of which was then still unpublished, for reasons other than its lyricism. "Ach Herr, mich armen Sünder," for example, is based on the same tune as "O Haupt voll Blut und

Wunden," a hymn that must have held special significance because of its frequent appearance in Bach's St. Matthew Passion. Mendelssohn himself composed a cantata as well as an organ chorale on this melody. As for "Ach Gott, erhöh mein Seufzen," the incipit given by Hauser suggests (correctly) a work of intense chromaticism and indicates performance on two claviers (2 Cl. Ped.). As we have already seen in the case of "Wir glauben," "Schmücke dich," and "Ich ruf zu dir," Mendelssohn seems to have had a special fondness for relatively slow organ chorales in which the hymn tune is played on its own manual.[106] Turning at last to "Zeuch ein zu deinen Toren," perhaps it was the *Affekt* marking of "Cantabile" that caught his eye.

Mendelssohn's stay in London lasted four months. It was interrupted in late May by a brief trip to Düsseldorf, where he conducted Handel's *Israel in Egypt* and was formally invited to become the city's municipal music director. Upon returning to London, with his father, Abraham, in tow, he turned his attention once again to the organ. For five consecutive weeks he supplied the postlude for the Sunday morning service at St. Paul's.[107] In a letter to his family of Sunday, 23 June, Abraham described one of these performances:

> Early today Felix played the organ at St. Paul's, and, as the bellow-blowers were already gone, Klingemann and two other gentlemen took their places. Felix played an introduction and fugue, and then improvised. Then he played with Attwood a coronation anthem by him, four hands, and afterwards three *Sebastiane*. It sounded very good. The church was empty except for two female patrons of the Philharmonic who had stolen in and listened unseen.[108]

The dramatis personae of this vignette include not only Thomas Attwood but also Karl Klingemann, a lifelong friend of Mendelssohn, who from 1827 until his death in 1862 was an official at the Hanover legation in London. Another source identifies the two eavesdroppers as the sisters Elizabeth and Ann Mounsey.[109] They were mere teenagers at the time, but both would go on to long careers as church organists in the city. Curiously, the congregation seems to have dispersed before Felix began to play.

In terms of repertory, the Attwood anthem that was rendered as an organ duet must have been either "I was Glad" or "O Lord, Grant the King a Long Life."[110] The identity of the three *Sebastiane*—a colloquialism used by Abraham for works by Bach—is unknown. Whether they were among the pieces sent by Hauser to Mendelssohn some months earlier is a moot point, since we do not know that Hauser ever responded to his friend's request. It is important to realize that the Bach works were saved for last, as a sort of climax, since several of Mendelssohn's subsequent organ performances in London were programmed according to this same strategy.

For his postlude two weeks later (7 July) Mendelssohn extemporized a fugue in C minor that he would eventually publish in his *Three Preludes and*

Fugues for the Organ, op. 37. There can be little question that this fugue was inspired by the same Bach fugue in A minor he had played at St. Paul's the previous year. Not only are both subjects conceived along the lines of a minor-key gigue, but they adopt the same syntax and contour as well (see examples 1–8 and 1–9). Both begin with a stepwise, on-the-beat ascent from the first to the third degree of the scale that clearly implies the harmonic progression of i–V–i. Both then continue with a contrasting phrase that descends sequentially, via arpeggiated seventh chords, from the sixth to the fourth scale degree. In both subjects, moreover, the second phrase is preceded by an eighth-note anacrusis on the dominant pitch. But perhaps the most important point to be made about Mendelssohn's fugue is that the technical difficulty of its pedal part far exceeds that of any of his organ works written prior to 1833. He had finally begun to assimilate Bach's virtuoso pedal style into his own compositions.[111]

Exactly a fortnight later, father and son hosted a musical soirée for their London friends in the rooms they had rented at the home of the ironmonger Friedrich Heinke.[112] Their guest list included not only Moscheles but also the pianist Johann Baptist Cramer, whom Felix had met on his first trip to England in 1829. A Bach enthusiast himself, Cramer is reported to have transcribed for string quintet the *gravement* section of the Fantasy in G Major, BWV 572.[113] At Heinke's, he performed several of his own compositions and then joined Felix at the piano for two organ works by Bach.[114] Felix played the manual voices, while Cramer, who had never seen either piece before, took the pedal part.

To conclude this discussion of Mendelssohn's visit to London in 1833, let us remember that later that year Vincent Novello published Bach's Prelude and Fugue in E Minor, BWV 533, in his series *Select Organ Pieces.* Novello's edition includes the following statement, in which he thanked Mendelssohn for supplying his manuscript source and acknowledged that Felix had often performed the work in his presence:

> For this extremely rare specimen of *SEBASTIAN BACH's* extraordinary musical genius, the Editor is indebted to the obliging politeness of his kind friend *MENDELSSOHN BARTHOLDY,* who frequently played it to him, *from memory,* at the time when there was no Copy of the Manuscript to be obtained in England. During his visit to Germany this year (1833) Mr Mendelssohn was so kind as to procure a Copy, and very obligingly allowed a transcript of it to be made for the Editor of this Work, who had so often expressed his admiration of the Composition. The writer of the present note gladly avails himself of this opportunity of expressing his best acknowledgments to a gentleman whom he considers one of the greatest ornaments of the musical art in the present age, for this as well as for other highly gratifying proofs of his liberal and friendly sentiments towards him.

Example 1–8 Fugue in A Minor, BWV 543/2

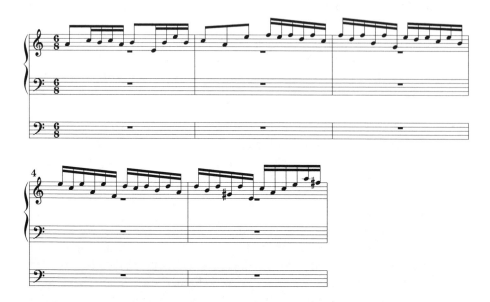

Elsewhere in this publication the Englishman saw fit to print that "For originality of Subject, masterly treatment of it, refined taste and pathetic expression,
this exquisite Fugue has probably never been exceeded, even by *SEBASTIAN
BACH* himself." That he also (incorrectly) believed his edition to have been
the very first is attested to by the note: "From a M.S. never before published."

To what extent does Novello's commentary reflect Mendelssohn's thoughts
on this composition? Surely, he could not have shared his friend's view that
such a relatively drab fugue could in any way represent the ne plus ultra of
Bach's compositional output (an assessment that bespeaks Novello's woeful

Example 1–9 Felix Mendelssohn Bartholdy, Fugue in C Minor, from *Three Preludes
and Fugues for the Organ*, op. 37

ignorance of Bach's music). And yet there can be no doubt that Mendelssohn felt a special fondness for this little piece. It was among the first Bach organ works he ever played, and it appears to be the one he had most often performed up to this point. He also thought highly enough of the piece to have it copied for his friends. Still, there is no hard evidence that he played it after 1833. As he turned increasingly to those unequivocal masterpieces on which Bach's immortality rests, this obviously youthful and somewhat clumsy opus may have lost its appeal.[115]

Mendelssohn began his duties in Düsseldorf on 1 October. His hectic schedule there allowed him precious little time to play or compose for the organ, although he continued to perform Bach's organ music on the piano at social gatherings. In at least one instance, these performances also served as parlor games, for on Sunday, 4 May 1834, at a musicale hosted by Mendelssohn in his quarters at the home of the painter Wilhelm von Schadow, he played organ fugues by Bach, with lots being drawn to see which of his comrades would negotiate the pedal part.[116] His only documented organ performance from these two years took place in the village of Werden, where, among friends and true to form, he improvised and played Bach.[117]

Leipzig beckoned. When Mendelssohn moved there in August 1835, he found himself once again in the midst of a vital Bach tradition, in the very city where the master had spent most of his career. One might even say that in certain respects Leipzig had by this date surpassed Berlin as the leading Bach center in all of Europe. The two most prolific publishers of Bach's oeuvre (Breitkopf & Härtel and C. F. Peters) were based there, and the city was home to two music periodicals (the *Allgemeine musikalische Zeitung* and *Neue Zeitschrift für Musik*) with a decidedly pro-Bach bias. The "Sebastianstadt," as Mendelssohn and Hauser called it,[118] also boasted a large assortment of Bach performers and devotees.

Except for a one-year stint in Berlin during 1841–42, Mendelssohn remained in Leipzig until his untimely death in 1847. Throughout these eleven years, his impact on the city's Bach revival was enormous. As conductor of the Gewandhaus orchestra, he led a series of "historical" concerts devoted to works by Bach, Handel, and others. Moreover, he often appeared as a piano soloist at these events. In the realm of organ music, he gave an all-Bach organ recital in Leipzig whose proceeds were used for a monument to the composer, and the Leipzig firm of Breitkopf & Härtel issued his editions of Bach's organ chorales.

He was on friendly terms with the two leading church organists in the city. One of them was August Pohlenz, organist of the church of St. Thomas, who is known to have greatly admired Mendelssohn's abilities as an organist.[119] On these premises, where Bach had lived and worked as cantor, Mendelssohn appears to have done most of his organ playing. The other organist was

Carl Ferdinand Becker, who from 1837 served the church of St. Nicholas. Becker regularly featured works by Bach on his many organ recitals in the city, and his personal library contained numerous manuscripts of Bach's organ music.[120] Mendelssohn thought highly enough of Becker's playing to appoint him, in 1843, as the organ instructor of the newly founded Leipzig Conservatory. No doubt the two spent many hours together performing and studying Bach's organ works. Late in his Leipzig tenure, Mendelssohn presented Becker with copies of his editions of Bach's organ chorales, all four of which are inscribed "in fond remembrance."[121]

Another recipient of these four volumes, courtesy of the editor, was Robert Schumann.[122] As a resident of Leipzig when Mendelssohn located there in 1835, Schumann immediately inducted him into his imaginary *Davidsbund* (League of David) under the sobriquet "Felix Meritis." Mendelssohn evidently introduced Schumann to numerous organ works by Bach, including, from the Great Eighteen chorales, "Schmücke dich, o liebe Seele." He must have played this work for Schumann early on in their friendship, for in the 24 June 1836 issue of the *Neue Zeitschrift für Musik,* apropos of his unsuccessful attempt four years earlier to find Bach's grave, Schumann wrote:

> I prefer to picture [Bach] seated upright at his Silbermann organ in the prime of his life, the music swelling out from under his feet and fingers, the congregation looking up at him raptly, and possibly a few angels among them.
>
> You, Felix Meritis, a man of equally superior intellect and character, played one of his chorale preludes on that organ; the text was "Schmücke dich, o meine Seele." The *cantus firmus* was hung with wreaths of gilded leaves, and flooded with a spirituality that prompted you to confess: "If life were to deprive me of hope and faith, this single chorale would replenish me with both."[123]

This famous excerpt reveals the full (and truly remarkable) extent of Mendelssohn's affection for this piece, one distinguished by—as Mendelssohn must have realized—an unusually lyrical hymn melody, sweet accompanimental writing in parallel sixths and thirds, beautiful ornamental figuration, and an overall mystical quality consistent with the rite of communion.[124] Schumann was impressed both by the exquisite ornamentation of the chorale tune and the work's "spiritual" quality. His reference to "that organ" strongly suggests that the performance took place at St. Thomas's.

Schumann also speaks here of Bach's "Silbermann organ," an oddity that seems to have gone overlooked in the scholarly literature. To set the record straight, no organ by Gottfried Silbermann (or any other member of that illustrious family of organ builders) was ever built in the city of Leipzig. Unless he was simply mistaken about this, Schumann must have been ruminating about the "ideal" Bach organ. His erroneous citation of the chorale title as "*meine* Seele" implies that he was relying on his memory of Mendelssohn's words and not on any musical score.

In late March 1837, immediately after concluding his second season with the Gewandhaus orchestra, Mendelssohn married Cécile Jeanrenaud. The couple spent their honeymoon in Freiburg and the Black Forest, during which time Felix composed the three preludes of what would be issued later that spring as his *Three Preludes and Fugues for the Organ.* The very title of this collection, to be sure, implies an *hommage à Bach,* as do the virtuosic pedal parts of certain movements. But it is the Prelude in C Minor that specifically reveals the influence of Bach's organ music. Like Bach's Fantasy in G Minor[125] and Prelude in E Minor, BWV 548/1, this movement begins, quite distinctively, with a fast, wide-ranging theme in the right hand, three-voice chords that alternate with rests in the left hand, and a virtual pedal point that moves in the same rhythm as the left-hand chords (see examples 1–10 and 1–11). The E-minor prelude is a particularly close match because of its opening leap in the right hand and chord progression of i–i–iv–vii°–i, which is identical to Mendelssohn's. Felix would have known this work from the print of the six preludes and fugues, BWV 543–48.

Following their honeymoon, the couple vacationed for the next few months in and around Frankfurt, often in the company of Cécile's family. During this blissful time, Felix diligently played the organ. Due to his busy schedule at the Gewandhaus, it was only during the off-season that he could devote serious attention to the instrument. Thus, over the next five years, at least, he played and composed for the organ mostly during the summer.

As far as the summer of 1837 is concerned, Mendelssohn had accepted an invitation to appear at the Birmingham Music Festival in September and knew he would be performing twice on the organ (in addition to conducting and playing the piano). On 10 July he wrote to his lawyer-friend Konrad Schleinitz that he was opening the festival with a "long" organ work by Bach.[126] Three days later, in a letter to his mother, he identified this composition as the Prelude and Fugue in E-flat Major, BWV 552, which, if considered a legitimate prelude-fugue pair, indeed ranks as one of Bach's longest organ works altogether:

Ask Fanny, dear Mother, what she would say if I were to play in Birmingham the Bach organ prelude in E-flat major [at this point, Mendelssohn notates the first two measures of the prelude] and the fugue that stands at the end of the same volume. I think she will grumble at me, but I think I would be right all the same. The prelude especially should be very accessible to the English, I would think, and both in the prelude and in the fugue one can show off the piano, pianissimo, and the whole range of the organ—and it is not a dull piece either in my view![127]

Example 1–10 Prelude in E Minor, BWV 548/1

Ever conscientious, Mendelssohn's concern was how his sister might react to his creation of a prelude-fugue pair out of two independent works. Although Bach did publish this prelude and fugue in the same collection (Part 3 of his *Clavierübung*), they are separated by twenty-five other works. The prelude stands at the very beginning, the fugue—as Mendelssohn points out in his letter—at the very end.[128] There is no proof that Bach ever intended for the two to be performed as a pair, and not until 1845, in volume 3 of the Peters edition, were they published as such. Still, Mendelssohn felt instinctively that they belonged together, definitely because of the common key but probably also because of the ease with which registration changes ("the whole range of the organ") can be made in both, due to their highly sectionalized structure. That he thought of the prelude and fugue as a self-contained entity is made clear by his final reference to them as a single work. More important, of course, is the fact that he performed them as a pair in Birmingham. He may or may not have been encouraged when Fanny wrote back: "I have very few objections to the Prelude and Fugue that you want to play in London—why not?"[129] For although he respected her opinion, she had apparently not understood his apprehension (and got the city wrong to boot). She may not have even known which prelude and fugue he meant.

Mendelssohn knew how to please his listeners. In the case of the E-flat prelude and fugue, he sensed a work that would appeal particularly to a lay

Example 1–11 Felix Mendelssohn Bartholdy, Prelude in C Minor, from *Three Preludes and Fugues for the Organ*, op. 37

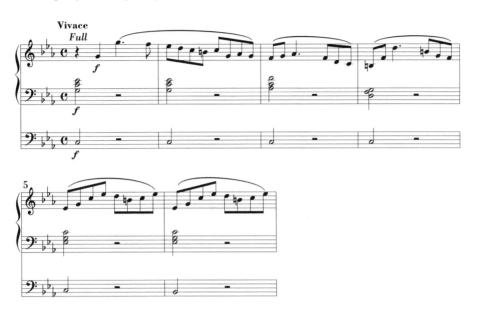

audience, if played with a panoply of organ colors. Bach himself prescribes no registration changes per se, but in the prelude he employs the markings of *forte* and *piano* for this purpose, presumably in conjunction with changes of manual. Mendelssohn had in mind something a bit more showy—and the magnificent four-manual organ by William Hill on which he played may have suggested to him all manner of razzle-dazzle. Perhaps he, like many players since, began the fugue pianissimo and built up to full organ by the end, similar to how he performed long organ chorales by Bach (in his edition of the Great Eighteen chorales, Mendelssohn advocates this "crescendo" style of registration for "O Lamm Gottes, unschuldig" and the ornamental setting of "Komm, Heiliger Geist"). Whatever the case, he must have changed manuals between the three main sections. For the echo effects in the prelude, he may have changed to a softer registration at the beginning of the first episode (see mm. 32–34 and 111–13) and then to an even softer one two bars later, where Bach writes *piano* for the first time.

Why he thought the Birminghamers would respond more favorably to the prelude is curious, considering that the fugue (known as the "St. Anne") was *the* favorite Bach organ work of English organists at this time.[130] But the prelude is certainly the flashier movement. Its ritornello proceeds with all the grandeur of a French overture, complete with fast scalar passages and trills that last over two measures at a time. One should not discount either the afore-mentioned echo effects or the three scintillating pedal runs near the end.

Reluctantly leaving behind his now pregnant wife, Mendelssohn arrived in England at the end of August. The details of his sojourn are vividly chronicled in the couple's so-called honeymoon diary. He first spent about a fortnight in London, primarily, it seems, to visit his many friends there. On 8 September he was accompanied by Klingemann and the William Horsley family to St. John's Church, Paddington, where he played "fugues by Bach and others on the organ for an hour."[131] Two days later, while playing Bach's Prelude and Fugue in A Minor for Sunday evensong at St. Paul's Cathedral, he was the victim of his celebrity:

> Cooper, the deputy of old Attwood, who had gone off on a journey, had invited me up to the organ in St. Paul's for evensong. I found a vast crowd of people gathered in the choir and elsewhere, so that I could hardly push my way through to the organ, even though the service had already ended. Every musician whom I remembered meeting in London I found again in the choir. When I had played for half an hour, and the crowd was growing rather than diminishing, I started on the great A minor Prelude and Fugue by Bach. It was going well and everything was working out successfully, when in the closing passage of the fugue, where the pedals play the rising figure alone, Cooper suddenly pulled on the assistant's bell. The weights which indicated the wind supply quickly dropped down, and the wind was gone out of the organ. Cooper ran off like a madman, quite red with anger, was away a little while, and finally returned with the news that during the performance the organ-blower, on instructions from the beadle, who had not been able to get anybody to leave the church and had been obliged to stay on longer against his will, had left the bellows, locked the door to them, and departed. Cooper wanted to fetch him back, but since I had no more time I left the organ, and had an opportunity to observe something of the "public spirit" of a crowd of Englishmen. They heaved to and fro as excited as if something important had happened. Shame! shame! was called out from all sides. Three or four clerics appeared and tore the beadle completely to pieces in front of all the people, threatening him with dismissal. Cooper helped in the chiding, and while the noisy disturbance proceeded in the church, and the people formed a jostling crowd, I left the organ and reached the open air.[132]

This infamous episode needs little amplification, except to mention that the musicians in attendance included a number of organists. One of these was Henry John Gauntlett, who in an article published five days later and titled "Mendelssohn as an Organist" gave his version of the incident:

> Just as Mendelssohn had executed a storm of pedal passages with transcendent skill and energy, the blower was seduced from his post and a farther supply of

wind forbidden, and the composer was left to exhibit the glorious ideas of Bach in all the dignity of dumb action. The entreaties of friends, the reproofs of minor canons, the outraged dignity of the organists, were of no avail; the vergers conquered, and all retired in dismay and disappointment. We had never previously heard Bach executed with such fire and energy—never witnessed a composition listened to with greater interest and gratification; and consoling ourselves with the hope that on Tuesday all might re-unite in a place where vergers are not, and under more fortunate auspices, we were hurried out of the cathedral.[133]

This "reunion" took place at Christ Church, Newgate Street, where Gauntlett was evening organist. Mendelssohn's performance there on Tuesday, 12 September, must have been one of the most satisfying of his entire career as an organist. Significantly, it also represents his first public organ recital. In his words:

At one o'clock I had to go to Christ Church to play the organ. The whole church, choir and everywhere, was stuffed full of people. Some ladies I didn't know presented me with flowers. I play a good deal and it comes off well. In the sacristy refreshments of cakes and wine were served. All the churchwardens came and expressed their thanks, and mocked the churchwardens of St. Paul's, where such a scandal was not wholly unexpected. There was no fear of such a thing with them. Old Wesley, trembling and bent, shook hands with me and at my request sat down at the organ bench to play, a thing he had not done for many years. The frail old man improvised with great artistry and splendid facility, so that I could not but admire. His daughter was so moved by the sight of it all that she fainted and could not stop crying and sobbing. She believed she would certainly never hear him play like that again; and alas, shortly after my return to Germany I learned of his death.[134]

Felix offered another account of the affair in a letter to Cécile:

I wrote to you early in the morning, and then went to play the organ. There were I suppose about a thousand people gathered together there, the church packed full. I could hardly push my way through to the organ bench, and there sat a 78-year-old organist, the most famous one here, Wesley, who though old and weak, had had himself brought there by his daughters, and at my request he sat himself at the organ bench and played, and it was so moving that his daughter burst into the bitterest tears and had to be led down into the sacristy. I played for a very long time, and there was then a sort of uproar, such handshaking and crowding around me as is only to be found in England; hands appear from all sides, and speeches from so many voices that one does not know where to turn.[135]

Thus it was not only Mendelssohn but also the elderly Samuel Wesley— a renowned improviser—who performed on this occasion. The doyen of

British organists at the time, Wesley must be considered the galvanizing force behind the English Bach revival of the early nineteenth century, and he may well have been the first in that country to play Bach's organ works. Still, his performances were hardly legitimate, mainly because most English organs then either lacked pedals altogether or contained pedalboards commencing on G that extended no farther than an octave-and-a-half. Wesley also objected to the very notion of pedaling![136] Consequently, in playing the works of his favorite composer, this leader of the "Sebastian Squad" required an assistant to render the pedal part manually. Mendelssohn's performance greatly impressed Wesley,[137] but he was by then too aged to reform his ways. He died a month later.

At the time of Mendelssohn's performance, the pedalboard of the Elliot & Hill organ at Christ Church conformed to the standard English compass of an octave-and-a-half, beginning on G.[138] Gauntlett marveled at his colleague's ability to adapt the far-flung pedal part of Bach's A-minor fugue to such a narrow scale:

> M. Mendelssohn performed six extempore fantasias, and the pedal fugue he was not allowed to go through with at St. Paul's. Those who know the wide range of passages for the pedals with which this fugue abounds, may conceive how perfectly cool and collected must have been the organist who could on a sudden emergency transpose them to suit the scale of an ordinary English pedal board. His mind has become so assimilated to Bach's compositions, that at one point in the prelude, either by accident or design, he amplified and extended the idea of the author, in a manner so in keeping and natural, that those unacquainted with its details could not by any possibility have discovered the departure from the text. His execution of Bach's music is transcendently great, and so easy, that we presume he has every feature of this author engraven in his memory. His touch is so even and firm, so delicate and *volant,* that no difficulties, however appalling, either impede or disturb his equanimity.[139]

One could easily believe that the liberties taken by Mendelssohn with the prelude also resulted from one of these "emergency" transpositions.

Another London organist who witnessed the performance at Christ Church was the nineteen-year-old Edward John Hopkins.[140] His recollection of the event constitutes the most detailed eyewitness account of Mendelssohn's Bach playing to survive. It also bears implications for how Mendelssohn played other organ fugues by Bach:

> Hopkins . . . remembered the performance of the A minor Fugue until the very end of his life. He observed that Mendelssohn took the long episode, beginning in E minor (at the end of the first pedal entry) on the Swell, returning to the Great organ when the pedal re-enters with the subject in its original key,

but transferring the inverted pedal note E (in the treble part) to the Great organ, a bar before the other parts, with fine effect.[141]

Mendelssohn would have found no instruction to change manuals anywhere in the print of the six preludes and fugues, BWV 543–48, or in any manuscript of the A-minor fugue, which suggests that he originated the now common practice of changing to an auxiliary keyboard for the lengthy *manualiter* section in the middle of the movement.[142] Few players today, however, have adopted his technique of returning to the Great by thumbing down the high E somewhere in measure 95. It is less fussy and more satisfying musically— because the high E is not interrupted in any way—for the right hand to return either at the beginning of measure 91 or in the middle of measure 101.

The following day, Mendelssohn traveled to Birmingham, where, nine days later, in the final concert of that city's music festival, he played Bach's Prelude and Fugue in E-flat Major on the massive Hill organ of the Town Hall. In a letter written several years later, he referred to this instrument as "splendid" and no doubt appreciated its full two-octave pedal compass (C–c′).[143] Yet he complained about the narrow width of the pedal keys and the instrument's heavy touch, which must have made playing a work like the E-flat extraordinarily demanding.

To make the 11:30 coach back to London—the first leg of his return trip to Germany—he was allowed to play at the very beginning of the concert, which did not start until eleven (!), and then immediately leave. His diary entry sheds no further light on how he played the work, except for his use of "full organ." But it does show that the audience responded enthusiastically:

> At eleven o'clock I started off the fourth day and the seventh performance with Sebastian Bach's Prelude and Fugue in E flat on full organ of the large instrument. At the end they waved their handkerchiefs and flourished their hats. A plump old gentleman in the audience waved his yellow handkerchief incessantly and cried out "Goodbye! Goodbye!" The hired carriage was at the door; Moore with his servant in attendance helped me inside. Gauntlett, Thomson, and many others shook my hand once again.[144]

We have already cited two of three names mentioned here: Joseph Moore, one of the organizers of the festival; and, of course, Gauntlett, who was quickly becoming one of Mendelssohn's greatest supporters and who may have attended the Birmingham festival expressly to hear him play the organ. The third name is John Thomson, a Scottish musician whom Felix had met in Edinburgh several years earlier. Thomson also reviewed the festival for the Leipzig-based *Neue Zeitschrift für Musik,* venturing that Mendelssohn had made a "solemn and meaningful farewell in a mighty fugue by Sebastian Bach."[145]

We would be remiss not to add to this documentation a report (probably by Gauntlett) that appeared in London the following year:

> Although Mendelssohn is admitted to be the greatest extempore performer on the organ in his own country, it may be worth while to inquire into the reasons which led to the sensation he produced in our metropolis, and at Birmingham. The instruments he performed on seemed to assume a new character; the *pedale* appeared with a more grand and imposing tone.... This explanation may be offered. Mendelssohn introduced Bach to the English, as an organ composer. Our native artists had known and appreciated him, as a writer for the clavichord; the forty-eight studies had developed his genius, as a profound adept in the strict school of composition; but we had yet to venerate him as the inventor of a set of totally new effects upon the organ. It was not that Wesley was unacquainted with his Fantasias, Passacaglias, Preludes, and Codas, that he did not introduce them to the English: but never having heard a German organ, with its ponderous pedale, he could not realize the inventions of the author.[146]

To elaborate somewhat on this report, there can be no question that Mendelssohn's renditions of virtuoso pedal compositions by Bach exerted a profound and lasting influence on musical life in England. It would take some time, but by 1850 English organists were expected to perform this music just as Bach intended: unassisted, and with the pedal line played by the feet. To do so properly, they required not only two-octave pedalboards but also expansive, independent pedal divisions. In collaboration with the organ builder William Hill, Gauntlett began designing such instruments for London churches as early as 1838. By 1850, and due primarily to Mendelssohn's enduring influence, this "German System" of organ building was in full swing across Britain.

Mendelssohn's trip to England in the summer of 1837 surely represents a highpoint in his reception of Bach's organ works. Two years later, he would once again immerse himself in this repertory—as a performer, composer, and antiquarian. As in 1837, he was on summer vacation with his family in and around Frankfurt, and he again devoted much of his time to practicing the organ. On 3 July he wrote to his mother that his organ playing was going so well that he would be giving an organ concert upon his return to Leipzig.[147] This letter concludes with a paragraph addressed to Fanny:

> Oh Fanny! Take a look at the Fugue No. 3 in C major from the 6 great organ preludes and fugues of Bach, published in Vienna by Riedel. I formerly did not care for it—it is in a very simple style. But look at the last four measures. As simple as they are, I feel quite in love with them and played them through for myself about 50 times yesterday. How the left hand glides and turns, and how gently it dies away at the end! It pleases me very much indeed.[148]

Mendelssohn is speaking here of the Fugue in C Major, BWV 545/2, and its position in the aforementioned print of the six preludes and fugues for organ, BWV 543–48, as published by the Viennese house of Josef Riedel. Like many other nineteenth-century musicians, he referred to these works as the six "great" preludes and fugues owing to their size, although this adjective was not used by the publisher. His assessment of the C-major fugue as "simple," which is perhaps best understood vis-à-vis the other fugues in this collection, no doubt has to do with the brevity, narrow ambitus, and slow rhythms of the subject, as well as its straightforward treatment. Why the last four bars enchanted him so is more a matter of conjecture, but the unusual block-chord harmonization of the subject in the antepenultimate measure might well have played a role (see example 1–12). Observe, too, the measure-by-measure deceleration of the left hand during the last four measures. As Mendelssohn described this effect, "gliding" and "turning" eighth notes give way to stepwise quarter notes, half notes, and finally whole notes, as the music "gently dies away." He had used similar language in 1831 to describe "Wir glauben all an einen Gott, Vater," BWV 740.

Roughly two weeks later, Mendelssohn's fugue fetish manifested itself in three organ fugues of his own composition.[149] By his very choice of this genre, of course, he was paying tribute to its undisputed master. But he may also

Example 1–12 Fugue in C Major, BWV 545/2

Example 1–13 Fugue in C Major, BWV 545/2

have fashioned the subjects of two of these fugues from specific organ works by Bach he is known to have admired. For example, the Fugue in C Major that Mendelssohn composed at this time is based on a subject remarkably similar to that of the Fugue in C Major by Bach he had just written about to Fanny (see examples 1–13 and 1–14).[150] In addition to the general metric and rhythmic similarities, both subjects begin with a half note on C, then ascend to an F that is held for three beats, then descend by step, then ascend by either a fourth or sixth, and conclude on a tied note. Both subjects also appear initially in the alto voice. In the case of the Fugue in F Minor composed four days later, Mendelssohn appears to have taken as his exemplar the Fantasy in C Minor, BWV 562/1 (see examples 1–15 and 1–16).[151] This is the same Bach work, we should remember, whose fugal theme Felix had praised in one of his letters to Hauser. In this instance, the first seven notes of Mendelssohn's theme are melodically identical to Bach's subject, and both subjects begin by lingering on the dominant pitch.

    Mendelssohn did much of his organ practice that summer on a pedal piano at the home of Friedrich Schlemmer, an amateur organist and cousin of Cécile.[152] He was also the frequent guest of Karl W. F. Guhr, director of the Frankfurt opera and a collector of Bach manuscripts. Felix may have been re-

Example 1–14 Felix Mendelssohn Bartholdy, Fugue in C Major

Example 1–15 Fantasy in C Minor, BWV 562/1

ferring to one of these sources when on 4 June he wrote to his sister Rebecka about discovering in Frankfurt some "very significant" organ works by Bach.[153] He had known Guhr for some time, but they had just become close friends.[154] In a letter to Fanny on 18 June, Felix discussed the man's extraordinary generosity toward him:

> Give me your best advice! The eccentric *Capellmeister* Guhr has become my bosom buddy; we are quite inseparable. Recently, when we were in a most pleasant and cordial mood, and I was eagerly asking him about his large cache of Bach rarities, among which are two autographs, namely, a collection of chorale preludes and the *Passacaille,* with a large fugue at the end of it [at this point, Mendelssohn notates the first measure of the Fugue in C Minor on a Theme by Legrenzi, BWV 574], he suddenly said: "You know what? Take one of the two autographs, I want to give one of them to you. You take just as much delight in them as I do; choose which one you want, the *Passacaille* or the preludes." By the way, he was not doing this just to amuse himself, because I know that he has been offered a good bit of money for these things and that he did

Example 1–16 Felix Mendelssohn Bartholdy, Fugue in F Minor

not sell them, and I myself would have paid him well if they had been for sale—and now he freely gives me one. But now the question is: what do I take? I have a much stronger inclination for the chorale preludes, because they begin with the "old year," because other big favorites [of mine] are among them, and because the *Passac.* and the fugue are already published. But you should also speak, because you also take uncommon joy in such matters. Thus you must vote, Cantor![155]

Guhr owned several manuscripts of organ works by Bach, most of which were believed to be autograph.[156] The only one of these sources to survive, however, has been shown to be in the hand of Bach's pupil Christian Gottlob Meissner. This manuscript also happens to be the first of the two mentioned by Mendelssohn in his letter and the one he ultimately chose for himself.[157] It contains roughly half of the chorale settings of the *Orgelbüchlein*, beginning with "Das alte Jahr vergangen ist" (The Old Year Has Passed). That he decided in favor of a fragmentary, nonautograph source suggests that Mendelssohn chose poorly. But the manuscript he chose against—the putative double autograph of the Passacaglia in C Minor and the Fugue in C Minor on a Theme by Legrenzi, BWV 574—evidently was not penned by Bach either.[158]

Mendelssohn already owned a manuscript of the *Orgelbüchlein*, and he must have owned both the Passacaglia and the Legrenzi fugue in printed form.[159] Accordingly, the prospect of adding new compositions to his library did not color his decision. If we take him at his word, musical taste did enter into the equation, but surely the Passacaglia was also one of his favorite pieces. About fifteen years earlier, it had served as a compositional model for his own organ passacaglia, and in 1840 he would perform the work in Leipzig as well as London. A more decisive factor might have been the sheer number of works (twenty-six) and the larger amount of music (over a hundred measures) contained in the *Orgelbüchlein* manuscript.

Still, one assumes that what really tipped the balance was the *Orgelbüchlein*'s status as an unpublished composition and Mendelssohn's desire to issue his own edition of it. He no doubt believed that an edition based on Bach's autograph would speak with great authority. Furthermore, when he finally did publish his edition, two years before his death, he used Guhr's manuscript as his primary exemplar. Why else would he have mentioned to Fanny, who probably understood all of this implicitly, that the other two works were already published?

In this letter, Felix also expresses to Fanny his affinity for the *Orgelbüchlein* setting of "Das alte Jahr vergangen ist," yet another organ chorale by Bach scored for two manuals and pedal. Fanny may well have shared her brother's admiration of this highly chromatic and melancholy piece. At any rate, her fondness of the chorale per se is attested to by the beautiful harmonization that closes her piano cycle *Das Jahr,* completed in 1841. All three chorales set by Fanny in this cycle ("Christ ist erstanden," "Vom Himmel hoch," and "Das alte Jahr") were set by Bach in the *Orgelbüchlein.* As for the other *Orgelbüchlein* chorales contained in Guhr's manuscript that numbered among Felix's "big favorites," two works come to mind: "Ich ruf zu dir, Herr Jesu Christ," the setting he had copied out for his Parisian friends in 1832; and, for reasons to be discussed later, "Durch Adams Fall ist ganz verderbt."

Before resuming his duties at the Gewandhaus in the fall of 1839, Mendelssohn participated as conductor and pianist at a music festival in Brunswick. On the second day of the festival (7 September) he managed to steal away to the city's cathedral to play the organ. His friend Henry Chorley described the scene as follows:

> I was sitting on the second morning revolving our incessant habits in my mind, and rejoicing in the rationality of a few hours' pause, when Dr. Mendelssohn kindly paid me a visit. There were some MSS. of Sebastian Bach to be inspected; there was to be organ-playing in the Cathedral: in short, it was to be one of those mornings of musical lounging and luxury, which, as regards real enjoyment of, and insight into, the art, are sometimes worth a score of formal performances. . . . The Bach manuscripts did not turn out anything very extraordinary. It was interesting to hear Mendelssohn pronouncing on their authenticity with the certainty of a Beckford, when examining a Cellini carving or jewel; though for such a thorough-going intimacy one might have been prepared by the spirit which runs through the younger composer's harmonies, especially in his later works, and by the circumstance of his being one of the finest organ-players of his time. . . . The instrument was sadly out of order; but Mendelssohn made it speak most gloriously, winding up nearly an hour's magnificent playing by one of Bach's grand fugues.[160]

The vagueness of Chorley's account, unfortunately, does not allow for these manuscripts to be identified. They may well have included the fragmentary copy of the *Orgelbüchlein* that Felix had acquired earlier that summer, in which case he would have "authenticated" the source for all those in attendance. But Chorley's negative tone ("the Bach manuscripts did not turn out anything extraordinary") suggests that Mendelssohn played from manuscripts containing unpublished works attributed to Bach and found the music to be spurious. If so, one suspects that these scores had been supplied by Friedrich Conrad Griepenkerl, for this University of Brunswick professor possessed one of the largest collections of Bach organ manuscripts in all of Germany.[161]

Less than three months later, Mendelssohn again turned his attention to editing the music of Bach. On Hauser's recommendation he had been named the new editor-in-chief of a projected complete edition of Bach's works by the Leipzig house of C. F. Peters,[162] and he had agreed to edit the organ chorales himself, no doubt eager to take full editorial advantage of his newly acquired "autograph" of the *Orgelbüchlein*. Yet not a single volume under his aegis ever appeared, due to some irreconcilable differences over editorial practice. Mendelssohn insisted on *Urtext* style, while the press inclined toward the addition of fingerings, tempo markings, and the like.

In this connection, we should consider a rather caustic letter dispatched by Mendelssohn to the press in early 1840 concerning the Prelude and Fugue in G Major, BWV 541:

> Your Excellencies will receive herewith the corrected copy of the Prelude and Fugue in G Major by Seb. Bach. You will be amazed at the number of mistakes, but I am convinced that I have not yet found all of them, since unfortunately I am not in possession of the manuscript myself and also do not know where it is, and since my handwritten copy is not entirely correct either. In any case, it is still more correct than the one which was used for the engraving, and in the doubtful places it is certainly plausible; most of the places which I have corrected are beyond doubt, however. In particular, there are a number of mistakes in the fugue which I would immediately have corrected at my own risk even without knowing the piece at all or owning a copy of it, and with regard to which old Bach would have taken you to task quite severely: you have his subject beginning with an extra eighth note once on page 7, twice on page 8, and even three times on page 9, and give it altogether dreadful middle voices and harmonies underneath, especially in the last two systems. If you can do anything by way of apology to the honorable fellow, I would be obliged.[163]

Mendelssohn's official intent here was to publish the prelude and fugue in the new Peters edition of which he was in charge. And to this end he had taken the print of the work issued by the press around 1832—which is indeed rife with errors, including all those enumerated by him—and corrected it by hand.[164] He also mentions two manuscript sources for this piece: Bach's autograph ("the manuscript"), a perusal of which he felt would expose even more mistakes in the print; and a manuscript of his own.[165] All of this implies that Felix felt a special attachment to this piece, which is undeniably one of the most exciting Bach ever wrote for the organ.

The Leipzig Bach Recital

With respect to organ playing, Mendelssohn picked up during the summer of 1840 where he had left off the previous year. On 20 June, while picnicking with members of the Leipzig *Singverein* in the village of Rötha, he performed for the group "fugues and fantasies" by Bach on one of the two organs by

Gottfried Silbermann there, probably the larger two-manual instrument at the church of St. George.[166] He must have taken great delight in performing these works on an organ built by one of Bach's own colleagues. A month later, he agreed to "perform something of Sebastian Bach's on the organ" at the Birmingham Music Festival scheduled for that September.[167]

Yet both of these performances pale beside a recital he gave that summer in Leipzig.[168] For the first and only time in his career as an organist, he offered the public a full-length, all-Bach program, played, no less, on an instrument over which the great man himself had presided a hundred years earlier. And he did so specifically to raise money for a monument to Bach in the city. Arguably, this was the most important organ performance of Mendelssohn's life. Thanks to the many organists since who have reconstructed it, this concert would also have to rank as the most famous organ recital ever given.

The instrument on which he played was the large west-end organ at St. Thomas's, built originally in the early sixteenth century and rebuilt several times since.[169] In 1840 the organ contained fifty stops spread across three manuals and pedals. Thus whatever the instrument lacked in quality, it more than compensated for in size. Nothing is known about its keyboard or pedal compass.

Four days after the fact, Felix wrote to his mother:

> On Thursday, I gave an organ concert here in the Thomas Church, from the proceeds of which old Sebastian Bach is to have a monument erected to his memory, in front of the Thomas School. I gave it *solissimo,* and played nine pieces, and at the end a free fantasy. This was the whole program. Although my expenses were considerable, I had a clear gain of over three hundred thalers. I mean to try this again in the autumn or spring, and then a very handsome memorial may be put up. I practiced hard for eight days previously, till I could scarcely stand upright, and executed nothing but organ passages along the street in my gait when I walked out.[170]

Mendelssohn had advertised his concert at some expense, but he had also managed to raise a hefty sum of money, one equal to a third of his annual salary at the Gewandhaus. He ultimately accomplished his objective not by playing another organ recital but by conducting two additional benefit concerts for voices and orchestra. The first of these, which took place at St. Thomas's on Palm Sunday 1841, was the first performance in Leipzig since Bach's lifetime of the St. Matthew Passion. The second, given at the Gewandhaus in 1843 on the very day (23 April) the monument was unveiled, featured various vocal and instrumental works by Bach.[171] This monument, which Mendelssohn helped to design, still stands today just yards from the former site of the Thomas School (which was razed in 1902). Fittingly, the east side of the structure shows an angel playing the organ.

To judge from the rave reviews of the local critics, the recital was also an artistic success. The elderly Friedrich Rochlitz, former editor of the *Allgemeine musikalische Zeitung,* was so moved that he embraced Mendelssohn afterwards and paraphrased Simeon's *Nunc dimittis:* "I can now depart in peace, for never shall I hear anything finer or more sublime."[172] (Unlike Samuel Wesley, though, Rochlitz would not die for another two years.) An anonymous critic working for the same journal opined that "through the performance of several magnificent compositions of Sebastian Bach, and through the rendition of a free fantasy, Mendelssohn once more proved himself a distinguished organist and great artist; it was a truly splendid artistic treat, for which we are all the more thankful as it is offered to us—alas!—so seldom."[173]

But the most detailed account came from the pen of Robert Schumann:

> How well Mendelssohn understands the treatment of Bach's royal instrument is generally known; and yesterday he laid before us nothing but precious jewels, in the most glorious variety and gradation, which he only prefaced, as it were, at the beginning, and concluded with a fantasy of his own. After a short introduction, he played a very splendid Fugue in E-flat Major, containing three ideas, one built upon the other; then a Fantasy on the Chorale "Schmücke dich, o liebe Seele," as priceless, deep, and full of soul as any piece of music that ever sprang from a true artist's imagination; then a grandly brilliant Prelude and Fugue in A Minor, both very difficult, even for a master of organ playing. After an intermission, these were followed by the Passacaille in C Minor (with 21 variations, intertwined so ingeniously that one can never cease to be amazed), admirably handled in the choice of registers by Mendelssohn; then a Pastorella in F Major, mined from the deepest depths in which such a composition may be found; which was followed by a Toccata in A Minor with a Prelude typical of Bach's sense of humor. Mendelssohn ended with a fantasy of his own in which, then, he showed himself in the full glory of his artistry; it was based on a chorale (if I am not mistaken, with the text "O Haupt voll Blut und Wunden") into which he later wove the name BACH and a fugal passage—the entire fantasy was rounded out into such a clear and masterly whole that, if printed, it would appear a finished work of art.
>
> A fine summer evening shone through the church windows; even outside, in the open air, many may have reflected on the wonderful sounds, thinking that there is nothing greater in music than the enjoyment of the twofold mastery displayed when one master expresses the other. Fame and honor to young and old alike![174]

Adopting a less hyperbolic tone, Schumann also reported on the concert to his fiancée Clara Wieck: "Mendelssohn's concert lasted somewhat long. But you would have taken great joy in it, especially in the Prelude in A Minor (the same one that you play from the 6 Great), which assumed on the organ a very grand, unique, and brilliant character. There might have been a total of 400 to 500 listeners."[175] Obviously, Schumann is speaking of the Prelude in A Minor, BWV 543/1, and the six "great" preludes and fugues, BWV 543–48.

Given here in facsimile and translation is the program that Mendelssohn had printed for his recital (see figures 1–3 and 1–4).[176] As Schumann pointed out, the concert began and ended with improvisations, the first of which served as a "short" introduction to the Fugue in E-flat Major, BWV 552/2. In choosing this type of extemporization, Mendelssohn was bowing to an old tradition. As early as 1770, for example, organists in Berlin are known to have improvised their own preludes to fugues by Bach, regardless of whether Bach had furnished a prelude himself.[177] (In the case of BWV 552/2, Mendelssohn wisely chose a fugue that lacks—at least in the conventional sense—a prelude of Bach's composition.) Two such introductions—to the Fugues in G Minor and E Minor, BWV 542/2 and 548/2—from the pen of A. W. Bach have survived,[178] suggesting that Mendelssohn learned this technique directly from his organ teacher. Felix might also have observed his London colleagues doing the same thing, as this had long been a practice in England too.[179] In fact, he had performed an "introduction and fugue" himself in 1833 at St. Paul's Cathedral, but in that instance he probably improvised both the introduction and fugue. The larger truth here is the emphasis that musicians have always placed on Bach as a composer of fugues (and which, if carried to extremes in the context of a prelude-fugue pair, does a great disservice to the preludes). It is not by accident that the earliest editions of the Six Great Preludes and Fugues for organ are titled *Sechs Praeludien und SECHS FUGEN*.[180] These editions include that issued by Riedel, which Felix had written about to Fanny in 1839.

The improvisation that concluded Mendelssohn's concert was no trifle. Rather, as described by Schumann, it was a contrapuntal tour de force based on one of Bach's (and Mendelssohn's) favorite hymns, perhaps in the guise of theme and variations. The insertion of Bach's name (B-flat, A, C, B-natural) toward the end suggests the influence of *Die Kunst der Fuge* and recalls Mendelssohn's improvisation of an entire prelude and fugue on BACH at the organ during his final visit to London in May 1847.[181] The final variation might well have been a fugue on the first phrase of the chorale tune, as in the first movement of Mendelssohn's sixth organ sonata.

A little-known, undated fragment in Mendelssohn's hand sheds light on how he might have commenced his fantasy on "O Haupt voll Blut und Wunden."[182] The page begins with a harmonization of this chorale and, after a two-measure interlude of unaccompanied sixteenth notes in the right hand, continues with a first variation. Any organist knows that Mendelssohn's sixth organ sonata begins in precisely this fashion, and it could well be that this fragment was intended for the same opus. Another possibility is that the page preserves actual material from the Leipzig recital.

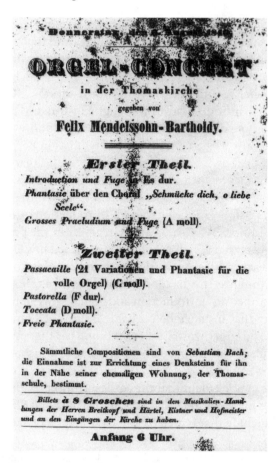

Figure 1–3 The program of Mendelssohn's Leipzig Bach recital (reprinted with the permission of Bärenreiter-Verlag)

Between these two improvisations, Mendelssohn played—probably from memory—a total of six Bach works, arranged into two groups of three (which makes for a total of eight works and thus disagrees with Mendelssohn's report, in his letter to his mother, that he played nine pieces). Within each of these groups, moreover, a relatively introspective piece stands at the center, followed by a showpiece of sorts. As if to complement this symmetry, Felix also chose repertory representing no fewer than six different compositional genres: fugue, chorale, prelude, passacaglia, pastorale, and toccata. To be sure, however, the audience that evening paid less attention to how these works were organized than to Mendelssohn's "manipulation" and "pedipulation" of them.[183] Except perhaps for the Passacaglia in C Minor, these works had been under his fingers (and feet) for years, but playing all six in succes-

Thursday, 6 August 1840

ORGAN CONCERT

in the Thomas Church

given by

Felix Mendelssohn-Bartholdy

First Part

Introduction and Fugue in E-flat Major
Fantasy on the chorale "Schmücke dich, o liebe
   Seele"
Great Prelude and Fugue (A minor)

Second Part

Passacaille (21 variations and fantasy for full organ)
   (C minor)
Pastorella (F major)
Toccata (D minor)
Free Fantasy

All compositions are by Sebastian Bach; the proceeds are
intended for the erection of a monument for him in the vicinity
of his former residence, the Thomas School.

Tickets from 8 groschen are to be had at the music shops
of Messrs. Breitkopf & Härtel, Kistner, and Hofmeister, and at
the entrances to the church.

Starting at 6:00 p.m.

Figure 1–4 The program of Mendelssohn's Leipzig Bach recital, as translated by the author

sion no doubt challenged even his technique—and necessitated marathon practice sessions, as his letter to his mother makes clear. According to one of his newspaper advertisements for the event, he considered these pieces among "the most significant" Bach ever composed.[184]

Let us take them in order. The "Fugue in E-flat Major" was of course the same fugue Mendelssohn had played in Birmingham three years earlier, BWV 552/2. (Bach wrote no other organ fugue in this key, and Schumann can be describing no other piece.) We can only assume that in Leipzig, too, Felix played each of the three main sections of the fugue on its own manual. That he chose not to play Bach's Prelude in E-flat on this occasion suggests that he had changed his mind about the viability of this prelude and fugue as a self-contained pair. He followed with a work in the same key, "Schmücke dich" from the Great Eighteen. It might seem odd that he could call such a piece a fantasy, but compared to the hundreds of chorale settings by Bach (including most of those in the *Orgelbüchlein*) where the tune is presented continuously and devoid of embellishment, this is a decidedly free arrangement. The final piece on the first half was the "grandly brilliant" Prelude and Fugue in A Minor, BWV 543, which Mendelssohn made sure to designate as one of the six "great" preludes and fugues.[185] Schumann's description implies full organ and a fast tempo.

The second half of the recital opened with the Passacaglia, or, as Felix always called it, "Passacaille" in C Minor. Schumann's report that the work was "admirably handled in the choice of registers" leaves little doubt that Mendelssohn frequently changed registrations between variations, as has long been the custom. Perhaps, then, he only gradually built up to "full organ." To conclude, Bach sets the first half of the ostinato theme as a fugue lasting over a hundred measures. Compared to the preceding twenty (not twenty-one) variations, this section of the work could easily qualify as a fantasy, as Mendelssohn characterizes it here. There is no record of his having performed the Passacaglia prior to this date.

The question raised by the next work on the program, the Pastorale in F Major, BWV 590—Bach's only work by this name—is the number of movements that were played. Only the first movement had been published by this date, which is strong evidence that it was also the only one performed. Schumann wrote that the last Bach work on the recital was a "Toccata in A Minor," but no such organ work by Bach survives. Rather, as the printed program indicates, Mendelssohn offered a toccata in D minor, which means that he played either the "Dorian" toccata (BWV 538/1) or the infamous Toccata in D Minor, BWV 565. For the same reasons discussed earlier apropos of Mendelssohn's trip to Weimar in 1830, he must have again played the latter. Schumann's response to the opening section of this work as downright comical is seriously at odds with the traditional interpretation of gloom and doom.

The Final Years

Mendelssohn would continue to champion Bach's organ works until the very end of his tragically short life. In addition to performing the music at home and abroad, he managed shortly before his death to edit and publish over sixty of Bach's organ chorales. At about this same time, he published his own Six Sonatas for the Organ, op. 65. While rightly considered a milestone in the history of organ music for its novel treatment of the instrument, this collection also represents Mendelssohn's final compositional salute to the organ music of Bach.

A month after his Leipzig recital, Felix traveled to England for the sixth time. As in 1837, his official business was the Birmingham Music Festival, where once again he was to conduct and perform as pianist and organist. On 22 September, at the opening concert, he played "a fugue" on the Town Hall organ, which had early that year been fitted with an experimental, high-pressure reed stop.[186] In view of his agreement earlier that summer to "perform something of Sebastian Bach's" and considering that his other organ performances at the festival were improvisations, we can only assume this fugue was by Bach.

Upon his return to London, he was taken by H. J. Gauntlett on 30 September to test the new organ at St. Peter-upon-Cornhill, an instrument designed by Gauntlett and built by William Hill according to the "German System."[187] No one else may have attended other than the church's organist, Elizabeth Mounsey. With Gauntlett and Mounsey on either side, Mendelssohn played two works of his own composition (the Prelude and Fugue in C Minor, op. 37, no. 1, and the Fugue in F Minor) and two by Bach: the Passacaglia in C Minor and, according to the original Grove *Dictionary of Music and Musicians,* "Bach's noble Prelude and Fugue in E Minor."[188] The latter may have been BWV 548 (the "Wedge"), the last of the Six Great Preludes and Fugues for organ, since earlier in his Mendelssohn article Grove cites Bach's other organ Prelude and Fugue in E Minor (BWV 533) as "the short E-minor." (It is also hard to accept that Sir George would have used the adjective "noble" to describe such a modest and juvenile work as BWV 533.) When, after the performance, Mounsey asked for Felix's autograph, he obliged by inscribing the ostinato theme of Bach's Passacaglia.[189]

There is no evidence of another organ performance by Mendelssohn until June 1842, during his seventh English sojourn. In addition to conducting the London premiere of his *Scottish Symphony* and performing one of his piano concertos, he played the organ at two different churches (St. Peter-upon-Cornhill and Christ Church, Newgate Street) and at Buckingham Palace, where Prince Albert returned the favor by playing for him. These performances consisted for the most part of improvisations on themes by Haydn and Handel. It is documented, however, that on 17 June Mendelssohn both extemporized and played a "prelude and fugue of Bach" on the organ at a concert of the Sacred Harmonic Society at Exeter Hall.[190] He wrote to his mother that he performed for "three thousand people, who shouted hurrahs and waved their handkerchiefs, and stamped with their feet until the hall resounded with the uproar."[191] According to Grove, the Bach work in question was the Prelude and Fugue in E-flat Major, BWV 552.[192]

It seems appropriate at this juncture to consider a further statement by Gauntlett, penned decades (23 January 1875) after Mendelssohn's death:

We knew the six Grand Fugues and the Exercises. But what Mendelssohn did was this: He brought out what Marx called the "not well-known" Pedal organ music. He was the first to play the G minor, the D major, the E major, and the short E minor, of which he gave a copy to Novello, who printed it with a note. And he taught us how to play the *slow* fugue, for Adams had played all fugues fast. I recollect Mendelssohn's saying: "Your organists think Bach did not write a slow fugue for the organ."[193]

Gauntlett addressed these remarks to his fellow organist Elizabeth Mounsey, who herself had witnessed Mendelssohn's Bach playing firsthand.[194] They concern, first of all, specific works that Mendelssohn introduced to British organists. Because the Marx/Mendelssohn edition alluded to contains exactly one work in each of the keys cited by Gauntlett, we can easily identify all four of them: the Fantasy and Fugue in G Minor, BWV 542; the Prelude and Fugue in D Major, BWV 532; the Prelude and Fugue in E Major, BWV 566; and, of course, the Prelude and Fugue in E Minor, BWV 533. Despite the lack of corroborating documentation in the case of the first three pieces, there is no reason to doubt Gauntlett's report. (One wonders, though, why the C-minor passacaglia does not appear in his list, since Mendelssohn had presumably "introduced" this work in the presence of both Gauntlett and Mounsey.) How many other Bach works did Mendelssohn play in England that we know nothing about?

Considering the great stir that Mendelssohn's Bach playing caused in England, it is inconceivable that whenever he performed a fugue there, he chose a relatively slow tempo. This great virtuoso, after all, was celebrated for his fast tempi.[195] Gauntlett's point that Mendelssohn had, for whatever reasons, a penchant for "slow" fugues must therefore apply only to certain examples. If Novello's metronome marking ($\downarrow = 88$) reflects Mendelssohn's own practice, one of these was the "short E minor."

There is no easy segue back into our narrative except to state that in the year following Mendelssohn's performance at Exeter Hall, he played a very different type of "recital" at St. Thomas's than he had in 1840. He did so primarily for the edification of his composition students at the newly opened Leipzig Conservatory. Also present was the twenty-five-year-old Charles François Gounod, who was in town specifically to make Mendelssohn's acquaintance.

A note sent by Mendelssohn on 16 May 1843 to Konrad Schleinitz, who had become the de facto administrative director of the conservatory, establishes the exact date of the performance and indicates that admission was by invitation only: "Tomorrow afternoon I am playing Sebastian Bach on the Thomas organ; other than the aforementioned Gounod, no one will be listening except whom you send . . . I think at 5, because, instead of a composition lesson, I am going to take the music students with me."[196]

Thus one of the first "field trips" that ever took place at this venerable institution was devoted to the organ music of Bach. It is not known how many of the twenty-two students at the school were enrolled in Mendelssohn's course, but it is clear beyond any doubt that he was now promoting this repertory as a music professor.

Gounod offered an account of the affair in his autobiography, albeit one that would have us believe he was the entire audience:

> Mendelssohn . . . was an organist of the first order and wished to acquaint me with several of the numerous and admirable compositions of Sebastian Bach for that instrument, over which he reigned supreme. For this purpose, he ordered to be examined and put in good condition the old organ of St. Thomas, formerly played by Bach himself; and there, for more than two hours, he revealed to me wonders of which I had no previous conception.[197]

Mendelssohn's performance, therefore, was a watershed in Gounod's Bach reception. Indeed, by the time the Frenchman returned to Paris that fall to begin his career as an organist, Bach had become one of his "gods."[198] There is also reason to believe that his *Méditation sur le 1ᵉʳ Prélude de piano de S. Bach*—that most popular of Bach adaptations—was inspired by Mendelssohn's example.[199]

It is hardly surprising that in playing for over two hours, Mendelssohn would have improvised, and in this connection we turn to a posthumous tribute to Gounod written by Charles-Marie Widor:

> Gounod often told me of that unforgettable evening in the church of St. Thomas, at Leipzig, where stands the old organ of John Sebastian Bach. The church was empty. "Stop down there," said Mendelssohn, who went up to the gallery and began to improvise on the *chorale* "Durch Adams Fall." Every one knows what an improviser he was, and that evening, whether it was owing to the fascination of the theme or the desire to captivate his single listener, he surpassed himself. For two hours the instrument vibrated as if it recognized the powerful hand of old, as if it recalled the harmonies of the Titan of music. "Great shivers ran along my spine," said Gounod, when calling to mind that unparalleled experience, "and every time I think of it I seem to feel those shivers again!"[200]

Widor's recollection would not be so important for our concerns were it not for the particular chorale cited, because without question the most famous setting of "Durch Adams Fall ist ganz verderbt" ever put to paper is that in the *Orgelbüchlein,* a piece wherein Bach portrays Adam's fall from grace not merely with a descending pedal figure but also through an extraordinary, unorthodox display of dissonance and chromaticism. The work was especially well-known in Leipzig at this time because Schumann had published it three years earlier in the *Neue Zeitschrift,* presumably, as will be explained in the second chapter of this book, after Mendelssohn had introduced him

to the *Orgelbüchlein.* All of which is to say that Mendelssohn probably got acquainted with this hymn through the *Orgelbüchlein* setting. He may even
have incorporated material from that work into his improvisation.

Six months later, Mendelssohn played Bach on this same organ for another musical tourist, the Viennese composer Johann Vesque von Püttlingen,
who in 1839 had invited Mendelssohn to conduct his oratorio *St. Paul* at a
music festival in Vienna (after accepting the offer, though, Felix ultimately
declined, and a scandal ensued).[201] Accompanied by his brother, Vesque had
traveled to Leipzig in 1843 to sample the city's musical life, which he considered the richest in all of Germany. On two separate occasions (1 November
and 4 November) Mendelssohn regaled his colleague with Bach organ fugues.
Of the latter performance, Vesque wrote: "With wonderful virtuosity, Mendelssohn played for us on the Thomas Church organ the Bach fugues in A
minor and D major, then motets and other things."[202] This can be a reference
only to the Fugue in A Minor, BWV 543/2, and the Fugue in D Major, BWV
532/2, two of Felix's favorite works.

The following year, while vacationing near Frankfurt, Mendelssohn began
to compile his magnum opus for the organ, the Six Sonatas, op. 65. The compositional influences on this magisterial collection extend from his own
piano works to the "voluntaries" of the English organ school, but none is
more palpable than the organ music of Bach. All the sonatas contain fugues,
and virtuoso pedal writing is commonplace. Consider, too, Schlemmer's report that chorales were included in the sonatas because of Mendelssohn's
"great love for J. S. Bach's works, especially the chorale preludes, and the
treatment of the chorales in the church cantatas."[203] In certain movements,
furthermore, Mendelssohn alludes to some of his favorite Bach organ works.
Just compare the French-overturish "B" section of the first movement of the
fourth sonata—singled out by Gauntlett as "a Bach prelude, and yet not
Bach"—to the ritornello of the Prelude in E-flat Major, BWV 552/1;[204] or the
fugue subject in the last movement of the fourth sonata to the "B theme" that
appears (also initially in the pedals) starting in measure 176 of the Toccata in
F Major, BWV 540/1; or the left-hand part of the first variation on "Vater
unser im Himmelreich" found in the sixth sonata to that of the first variation of the partita on "Christ, der du bist der helle Tag," BWV 766;[205] or
the pedal part of this same variation to that of the *Orgelbüchlein* setting of
"Durch Adams Fall."

Less obvious, perhaps, is the relationship between the double fugue in
the first movement of the third sonata and the Fugue in E-flat Major, BWV
552/2, a rare example in Bach of a double fugue whose second subject is introduced without any counterpoint.[206] In both of these fugues, the second
subject is played first by the left hand, simultaneously with the final cadence
of the first section; the right hand then drops out until the second statement

Example 1–17 Fugue in E-flat Major, BWV 552/2

(see examples 1–17 and 1–18). What is more, both of these second subjects employ perpetual motion in the rhythm equal to one-fourth of the pulse of the previous section. Neither is really playable on the pedals.

A final work to be considered in this context is Mendelssohn's aforementioned Fugue in F Minor for organ, which he rewrote in September 1844 for inclusion in the Six Sonatas (and, for whatever reasons, chose ultimately not to include it).[207] As examples 1–19 and 1–20 illustrate, the coda of the revised version begins with the same exotic harmonies (V_2^4 / N^6) and figuration found at the close of Bach's Toccata in F Major. Indeed, Mendelssohn's two measures are rather like Bach's in augmentation. What has never been pointed out is that this is the very passage that had so thrilled Felix when he played the toccata during his visit to Switzerland in 1831.

The Six Sonatas were published (in September 1845) by Coventry & Hollier, the same London house that in 1845–46 brought out Mendelssohn's editions of Bach's organ chorales. Charles Coventry was an enthusiastic advocate

Example 1–18 Felix Mendelssohn Bartholdy, Sonata No. 3 in A Major, first movement, from *Six Sonatas for the Organ*, op. 65

Example 1–19 Toccata in F Major, BWV 540/1

of Bach's music, and during the 1830s his firm issued three volumes of preludes, fugues, toccatas, and fantasies—almost none of which had appeared in England—under the title *John Sebastian Bach's Grand Studies for the Organ.*[208] Mendelssohn had in 1836 received a complimentary copy,[209] and three years later he expressed his high opinion of the collection to Hauser:

> If in your catalog you are also mentioning printed editions, do not forget an English one of the most important organ pieces that is very correct and good: that by Coventry and Hollier. I own in this edition the six great organ preludes and fugues, which were published originally in Vienna by Riedel (A minor, B minor, etc.), and several of the works edited by Marx, among others the G-minor fantasy and fugue.[210]

Mendelssohn cites here three of Bach's most beloved organ compositions: the Preludes and Fugues in A Minor and B Minor, BWV 543 and 544, respectively; and the Fantasy and Fugue in G Minor, BWV 542. Why he alludes to the edition he had prepared jointly with A. B. Marx merely as that "edited by

Example 1–20 Felix Mendelssohn Bartholdy, Fugue in F Minor (revised version)

Marx" is open to conjecture. Perhaps he was being characteristically modest or coy, or perhaps his relationship with Marx had so deteriorated by this date that he wished no further association with him.[211]

Mendelssohn had at some point promised to send Coventry organ works by Bach for the continuation of the *Grand Studies,* and in a letter of 8 February 1844 Coventry reminded his colleague of their agreement:

> My dear Sir, Some time since you very kindly promised through our friend Bennett you would send me some correct studies by Bach, or pedal fugues. I beg to enclose you the list of those already published [i.e., the *Grand Studies*]. I shall feel very grateful to you if you will send me some others. I want much the one called St. A[nne] that you play. I was the first who published these pedal fugues in this country about eight years since. At that time most of the organs here had but few pedals, since that time all the organs in this country have been improved, and *of course,* a greater demand for Bach. —It will give me pleasure to remunerate you in any way you think best. Hoping you will excuse my taking so much of your time, I am yours very truly —Charles Coventry.[212]

Coventry's (exaggerated) remarks about the English organs of his day echo our discussion earlier of the impact that Mendelssohn's Bach playing had on British organ building during the 1830s and 1840s. To judge from his comment about the "St. Anne" fugue, Coventry may have witnessed Mendelssohn's performance of the E-flat prelude and fugue at Exeter Hall in June 1842.

At some point, Mendelssohn dispatched this fugue to Coventry, and in late August of that year he forwarded to the publisher a large batch of mostly unpublished chorale settings, plus four free works: the Prelude and Fugue in E Minor, BWV 533; the Prelude and Fugue in D Minor, BWV 539; the Toccata in E Major (first two movements only); and the Prelude and Fugue in G Major, BWV 541. According to his cover letter, Mendelssohn had "carefully looked over and corrected" all sixty-five works.[213] The E-flat and the G major subsequently appeared for the first time in the *Grand Studies,* as Numbers 18 and 19, while the other free works sent by Mendelssohn replaced the versions that Coventry had published in the 1830s. In all three cases, Coventry had taken his original versions from *Johann Sebastian Bach's noch wenig bekannte Orgelcompositionen,* probably without the permission of either Marx or Mendelssohn.

The chorale settings, all of which were subsequently printed by Coventry & Hollier, are essentially the ones Felix had written about to Hauser in 1833. Most appeared in 1845–46 under the title *John Sebastian Bach's Organ Compositions on Corales (Psalm-Tunes) Edited from the Original Manuscripts by Felix Mendelssohn Bartholdy* (see figure 1–5).[214] Books 1 and 2 of this series contain forty-four chorales from the *Orgelbüchlein;* Books 3 and 4 contain fourteen of the Great Eighteen chorales, plus the setting of "Wir glauben

Figure 1–5 Title page of *John Sebastian Bach's Organ Compositions on Corales*, Book 1 (Bodleian Library, Oxford)

all an einen Gott, Vater" that Felix had mailed to his sisters in 1831. The remaining two works, which are the partitas on "Christ, der du bist der helle Tag" and "Sei gegrüsset, Jesu gütig," were published separately in 1846.[215]

Taken as a whole, these publications represent a milestone in the reception of Bach's organ chorales. Neither the *Orgelbüchlein* nor the Great Eighteen chorales had ever been issued as a collection, and the vast majority of the works contained in these two sets had never been published at all.[216] It is impossible to say whether the chorale partitas had been published prior to Mendelssohn's editions, since both pieces were also published in 1846 by C. F. Peters in volume 5 of that firm's edition of Bach's complete organ works. Mendelssohn's edition of the "Sei gegrüsset" partita was no doubt the inspiration behind the organ-duet version of his good friend and successor at the Gewandhaus, Niels Gade.[217]

It took the press only three months to prepare proofs of Books 1 and 2.[218] When Mendelssohn received them, he observed one general problem, which he urged Coventry to rectify:

> Pray alter the inscription which is to be found at the bottom of every page, *Bach's Fugues, &c.* Why is Bach's name always connected with Fugues? He has more to do with Psalm-tunes than with Fugues; and you call the beginning of your collection Bach's Studies, which I like much better. Pray alter this, and call it either Studies, Organ-music, or Chorales, or as you like, but *not* Fugues.[219]

Coventry heeded his editor's advice (and with good reason, since none of the forty-odd works contained in the *Orgelbüchlein* could possibly be construed as a fugue). Still, what makes this such an interesting excerpt is Mendelssohn's comments on Bach as a composer. For one thing, he absolutely bristled at the popular notion that Bach wrote fugues to the near exclusion of everything else. For another, he believed that chorale settings ("Psalm-tunes") figured more prominently in the master's oeuvre. To make such a claim—which is not without basis—Mendelssohn must have been thinking, rather along the lines of Schlemmer's testimony, not only of the organ chorales he was then editing but also of the many chorale arrangements found in Bach's vocal works.

The preface to Books 1 and 2 of the Coventry & Hollier edition, dated 17 February 1845, deserves to be quoted in full:

> The following Continuation of John Sebastian Bach's Studies for the Organ (44 Short Preludes, 16 Grand Preludes, and 2 Corales with Variations) Contains all those Organ Compositions of his on Corales (or Psalm-Tunes) which I have been able to collect and which not only bear his name, but most evidently the marks of his genius.
>
> Of the 44 Short Preludes, I am fortunate enough to possess his manuscript with the exception of but a few pages; the pieces are numbered in his own handwriting (even twice in a different way), and there can be no doubt that he intended them to form a Collection of their own; they differ entirely, in length as well as in style, from the 16 Grand Preludes. Of these last I have not seen Bach's manuscript, and do not even know whether it still exists and where, but I possess an old copy written either during his lifetime or at least very shortly after. As he used to copy his own manuscripts several times, and make different alterations in every copy, but still more as other copyists used to misunderstand his meaning, and thus transmitted many wrong passages, bars, & chords in these complicated works, it is almost always a difficult task to get at Bach's original reading in its correctness.
>
> Accordingly, I directed my attention principally to this point & tried to make this Edition deviate as little from Bach's original writing as I possibly could. I even thought it interesting to the Public, to see by his original inscriptions, how he gave now and then a direction as to stops, movement, or style of playing, but much more frequently left all these particulars to the taste and fancy of the performer.
>
> It may also be interesting to compare the Corale-Melodies of this Collection with those of the Choral-Buch (Collection of Corales), of which there exist several correct Editions.[220]

Most of Mendelssohn's remarks here serve to explain his uncompromising *Urtext* editorial style and to describe his sources. For almost fifteen years he had collected manuscripts of these works, and he was especially proud of his

Orgelbüchlein "autograph." It may seem strange that he omitted the setting of "Komm, Gott Schöpfer, Heiliger Geist" (BWV 631a) found in this manuscript, but he probably did this to avoid duplication, as his edition of the Great Eighteen includes a revised version (BWV 667) of the same work. Otherwise, he ordered the works exactly as they appeared in his exemplars, which is more or less the same liturgical-year sequence found in the actual holograph. In this regard, Mendelssohn's edition is far superior to the Peters edition published the following year.[221]

A German edition of Books 1 and 2, titled *44 kleine Choralvorspiele für die Orgel von Johann Sebastian Bach,* was published in 1845 by Breitkopf & Härtel, which in 1845–46 would issue a parallel edition of all five dozen works. In the spirit of homage, Mendelssohn refused for his name to appear anywhere in these German publications, a stipulation that forced him to "depersonalize" as well as translate the preface just quoted.[222] He also declined any honorarium.

The next edition in this series, that of the "Grand Preludes" (published by Breitkopf & Härtel as *15 Grosse Choral-Vorspiele für die Orgel von Johann Sebastian Bach*), appeared in 1846. In this case, Mendelssohn's primary exemplar contained all the Great Eighteen chorales except "Vor deinen Thron tret ich hiermit" and the two settings of "Jesus Christus, unser Heiland." At some point in the editorial process, however, he jettisoned the third setting of "Allein Gott in der Höh sei Ehr," because it had already been published.[223] This reduced the number of works from sixteen to fifteen. As it stands, the edition contains fourteen of the Great Eighteen chorales—arranged in the same order as Bach's autograph—and the miscellaneous setting of "Wir glauben," BWV 740.

Probably because he lacked the time, Mendelssohn was unable in this instance to write a preface in "good English."[224] He therefore sent the same German preface to both publishers. No doubt it was his friend Klingemann who did the English translation,[225] given here in its entirety:

> The present 15 Grand Preludes on Corales (as I already observed in my Preface introducing the 44 short Organ Preludes on Corales) are published from several old written copies, nearly concordant amongst themselves, and without any modern addition as to Time, Selection of Stops, or similar matter.
>
> With regard to the Selection of Stops, it might not be superfluous to remark in general that, for the present compositions, the superscription "Full Organ" does not always mean *all* the real Stops of an Organ; furthermore, that whenever the superscription says "for two rows of Keys and Pedal," only soft Stops ought to be used.
>
> In the Prelude No. 6, on the Corale "O Lamb of God," it appears necessary to change the Stops at the beginning of each new Verse, so that the third Verse is played with the greatest number of Stops (perhaps towards the end with full

Organ). In No. 2 also, "Come holy Ghost," I would recommend here and there to change the Stops after the termination of the different periods of the Cantus firmus, or gradually to increase the power of the Organ to the end. In No. 3, "On the rivers of Babylon," most probably only an 8 feet Pedal is meant, without any 16 feet Stops.

It need hardly be mentioned that for the Prelude No. 8, as well as for the one No. 14, no 16 feet Stop whatever must be used in the Pedal.

These remarks progress from the general to the specific. Having explained his *Urtext* editorial style, Mendelssohn warns against a too literal interpretation of *Organo Pleno* and advocates soft stops for any piece marked for two manuals. Considering that this was the first collected edition of the Great Eighteen, these instructions were probably not the least bit "superfluous," especially outside Germany. Of course, "soft" needs to be understood not as an absolute concept but as relative to "Full Organ."

Mendelssohn next comments on individual pieces, starting with "O Lamm Gottes, unschuldig." Most players today still follow his suggestion of a variation-by-variation increase in registration. He recommends the same approach for the second setting of "Komm, Heiliger Geist," probably to achieve variety in what is a very long and monotonous work. Still, whereas this sort of buildup works well for a set of three variations, adding stops between all nine phrases of the chorale seems most excessive, and it thoroughly fragments the work's structure. Mendelssohn also cautions against sixteen-foot pedal registers in "An Wasserflüssen Babylon," "Von Gott will ich nicht lassen" (Prelude No. 8), and "Wir glauben" (Prelude No. 14). His rationale in the first instance is by no means clear, but in the latter two it surely has to do with, respectively, the unusual tenor range of the pedal line and the presence of a double-pedal part (which can become easily obscured if played with low registers).

To conclude, let us consider some miscellaneous documents involving—for the most part, anyway—Mendelssohn's last two years. We begin with a letter of 14 April 1873 from Robert Franz (an organist, conductor, prolific composer of lieder, and great Bach enthusiast) to the singer Julius Stockhausen. Exactly what Franz means here by "rhythmic accent" is open to interpretation, but he is undoubtedly referring to the Fugue in A Minor, BWV 543/2:

The whole secret to the execution of [chorale melodies] lies in rhythmic accent. In no way, though, do I presume to have discovered this on my own. Rather, many years ago I once heard Mendelssohn playing Bach's great A-minor fugue on the organ, and it was on that occasion that my eyes were opened. On the organ, one can accentuate only rhythm because the notes are all the same volume.

When Mendelssohn played, you could hear the caesuras quite clearly; you could hear every voice as it entered and then disappeared from the scene.

Should it not be a thousand times easier to achieve with singing voices what was possible for this extraordinary man on the organ?[226]

As to when and where Franz witnessed this performance by Mendelssohn, there is precious little evidence to go on, merely a letter of 15 September 1845 in which Felix proposes visiting with Franz in Halle later that month, primarily to hear his orchestra there.[227] If this sojourn took place, Mendelssohn could have played the fugue for his colleague at that time. Another possibility is that Franz had heard Mendelssohn render this movement on his all-Bach recital in Leipzig five years earlier. Other organists from the surrounding area are certainly known to have attended.[228]

The remaining documents stem from the final year of Mendelssohn's life. Two concern the historian Johann Gustav Droysen, who in March 1847 found himself in utter despair over the death of his wife. Writing to Droysen a month later, Mendelssohn offered various remedies for his friend's melancholy, one of which was a Bach organ work: "If music brings you joy, you could have your local organist play you 'Schmücke dich, liebe Seele' by Sebastian Bach!"[229] Obviously, Mendelssohn was hoping that his favorite organ chorale would have the same cathartic effect on Droysen that he had discussed with Schumann.

Droysen's response to Felix's letter is also worth quoting, if only for the light it sheds on the Bach reception of another Mendelssohn: "You say you would like 'Schmücke dich, o liebe Seele' played for me. When I was in Berlin last year, Fanny invited me to a musicale. 'The Lord's Time is the Best Time' was sung—and I knew immediately what I was in store for! Now that was a sermon!"[230]

To judge from the context of Droysen's remarks, it was another composition by Bach that he had heard in Berlin, and there is no other candidate than Cantata 106, *Gottes Zeit ist die allerbeste Zeit*. Not only is the title of this work virtually the same as that given by Droysen ("Des Herren Zeit ist die beste Zeit"), but we know that Fanny led a performance of it at one of the Mendelssohn family musicales in 1835.[231] Furthermore, Felix had conducted the piece in public on more than one occasion, once as a requiem to his father. Abraham, in turn, had reacted most enthusiastically to Fanny's performance.[232] The cantata was doubtless a family favorite.

Three days after drafting this letter to Droysen, and accompanied by his young pupil Joseph Joachim, Felix traveled to England for the tenth and last time. His punishing schedule during these four weeks in London included on 5 May an organ performance at a Concert of Ancient Music organized by the Prince Consort for the Hanover Square Rooms. There, on "one of the worst [organs] in the metropolis," Felix improvised and played a Bach prelude and fugue.[233]

Table 1–1 Documented Performances by Mendelssohn of Bach's Organ Works

Date	Place	Works Performed
April 1825	Paris	Prelude in E Minor, BWV 533/1; Prelude in A Minor, BWV 543/1
13 October 1825	Berlin (Mendelssohn home)	Pastorale in F Major, BWV 590; "fugue" and "fantasia"
24 October 1828	Brandenburg (St. Gotthard's)	Prelude in E Minor, BWV 533/1; Pastorale in F Major, BWV 590; "preludes"
14 April 1829	Hamburg (St. Michael's)	unspecified
late May or early June 1830	Weimar (town church)	Toccata in D Minor, BWV 565
late August 1831	Engelberg (monastery)	"a couple of fugues"
3 September 1831	Sargans (village church)	Fugue in D Major, BWV 532/2; Toccata in F Major, BWV 540/1; Fugue in G Minor, BWV 542/2
4 September 1831	Lindau (village church)	"Schmücke dich, o liebe Seele," BWV 654
22 September 1831	Munich (St. Peter's)	"some fugues"
late September or early October 1831	Munich (St. Peter's?)	"Schmücke dich, o liebe Seele," BWV 654
27 May 1832	London (St. Paul's Cathedral)	unspecified, possibly including the Prelude and Fugue in E Minor, BWV 533
10 June 1832	London (St. Paul's Cathedral)	"fugue music," probably including the Fugue in A Minor, BWV 543/2
23 June 1833	London (St. Paul's Cathedral)	three unspecified pieces
21 July 1833	London (home of the ironmonger Friedrich Heinke)	two unspecified pieces
4 May 1834	Düsseldorf (home of the painter Wilhelm von Schadow)	"fugues"
late July or early August 1834	Werden (village church)	unspecified
after July 1835, before July 1836	Leipzig (St. Thomas's)	"Schmücke dich, o liebe Seele," BWV 654
8 September 1837	London (St. John's, Paddington)	"fugues"
10 September 1837	London (St. Paul's Cathedral)	Prelude and Fugue in A Minor, BWV 543

Table 1–1 *(continued)*

Date	Place	Works Performed
12 September 1837	London (Christ Church, Newgate Street)	Fugue in A Minor, BWV 543/2
22 September 1837	Birmingham (Town Hall)	Prelude and Fugue in E-flat Major, BWV 552
2 July 1839	Frankfurt (home of Friedrich Schlemmer?)	Fugue in C Major, BWV 545/2
7 September 1839	Brunswick (Cathedral of St. Blasius)	a "grand fugue" and other unspecified pieces
20 June 1840	Rötha (probably St. George's)	"fugues and fantasies"
6 August 1840	Leipzig (St. Thomas's)	Fugue in E-flat Major, BWV 552/2; "Schmücke dich, o liebe Seele," BWV 654; Prelude and Fugue in A Minor, BWV 543; Passacaglia in C Minor, BWV 582; Pastorale in F Major, BWV 590; Toccata in D Minor, BWV 565
22 September 1840	Birmingham (Town Hall)	"a fugue"
30 September 1840	London (St. Peter-upon-Cornhill)	Prelude and Fugue in E Minor, either BWV 533 or 548; Passacaglia in C Minor, BWV 582
17 June 1842	London (Exeter Hall)	Prelude and Fugue in E-flat Major, BWV 552
17 May 1843	Leipzig (St. Thomas's)	unspecified
1 November 1843	Leipzig (St. Thomas's)	"fugues"
4 November 1843	Leipzig (St. Thomas's)	Fugue in A Minor, BWV 543/2; Fugue in D Major, BWV 532/2
5 May 1847	London (Hanover Square Rooms)	unspecified prelude and fugue
30 August 1847	Ringgenberg (village church)	unspecified

Finally, in late summer of 1847, while vacationing in Switzerland, Mendelssohn is said to have played the organ for the very last time. This according to Henry Chorley, who on 30 August accompanied his ailing comrade to a church in the backwater of Ringgenberg, where on a "poor little organ" Mendelssohn improvised and performed "one or two movements by Sebastian Bach."[234] He would die less than three months later, at the tragically young age of thirty-eight.

Without question, Felix Mendelssohn Bartholdy was the most influential champion of Bach's organ works during the early Romantic era. Notwithstanding his activities as an editor, composer, antiquarian, pedagogue, and all-around ambassador, it was as a brilliant performer (particularly in England) that he had his greatest impact. His documented performances of this repertory—both public and private—are given in table 1–1. While this makes for a long list of over thirty items, it offers a fragmentary picture at best. Still, these data serve as a powerful reminder that Mendelssohn occupied himself with Bach's organ music his entire lifetime.

TWO

Robert Schumann

SCHUMANN'S ADMIRATION OF BACH knew no bounds. While Mendelssohn declared that Bach was "in no respect inferior to any other master, and in many respects superior to all,"[1] Schumann repeatedly proclaimed him the greatest of all composers. He may not have played the organ to any degree of proficiency, but Schumann knew Bach's compositions for the instrument better than did most organists of the day. And since he acknowledged Bach to be his most profound musical influence,[2] it comes as no surprise that Schumann modeled several of his own compositions after organ works by Bach. In the context of the nineteenth-century Bach revival, however, Schumann made his biggest contribution as editor of the *Neue Zeitschrift für Musik,* a periodical that regularly reviewed performances and editions of organ works by Bach—and where Schumann himself published a half dozen of them.

Leipzig

Schumann was probably introduced to Bach's organ works by his childhood piano teacher J. G. Kuntsch, organist at the church of St. Mary in Zwickau.[3] Still, he may not have developed a serious interest in the music until April 1832, roughly one and a half years after settling in Leipzig. For it was at this point that the twenty-one-year-old began his study of F. W. Marpurg's *Abhandlung von der Fuge,*[4] a treatise in which seven different organ chorales by Bach are excerpted to illustrate various contrapuntal procedures. Two of these chorales employ canon, a technique utilized by Schumann in many of his own compositions.

Two weeks later, Schumann noted in his diary that he and Clara Wieck (the twelve-year-old daughter of his new piano teacher) had sight-read at the piano "six Bach fugues, four hands."[5] Although he is known at this same time to have begun a rigorous investigation of the *Well-Tempered Clavier*, Schumann's reference to exactly six fugues rendered as piano duets strongly suggests that he and his future wife played that evening the Six Great Preludes and Fugues for organ, BWV 543–48. No other collection of six Bach fugues for any medium was in print at the time, and, as discussed in chapter 1, performing Bach's organ music at the piano in this way was a common practice. (Both Robert and Clara would eventually become connoisseurs of these pieces.) Giddy with inspiration, Schumann would later that same night compose the bass theme of his *Impromptus sur une Romance de Clara Wieck*, op. 5, a work replete with Bachian traits.[6]

Schumann suspended his diary from October 1832 until October 1837, and his correspondence from this period sheds no light on the subject either, but one can infer from his dealings with local organists that his involvement with Bach's organ music continued through the middle of the decade. For example, in connection with his founding of the *Neue Zeitschrift,* he had by March 1834 discovered a colleague in Carl Ferdinand Becker, organist at the church of St. Peter in Leipzig. Although Schumann would later grumble that Becker was no "great musician" and that, as a judge of compositional talent, he could not tell the difference between "Bach, Pachelbel, and himself,"[7] the organist was one of the most frequent contributors to the journal under Schumann's ten-year-long editorship (1834–44). Not only did Becker regularly play Bach's organ music, but he owned eighteenth-century manuscripts of many pieces and edited others for publication.[8]

Another organist arrived in Leipzig in the summer of 1835. His name was Felix Mendelssohn Bartholdy. Mendelssohn shared with Becker a propensity to collect and edit Bach, but he was also—as Schumann knew better than anyone—a consummate musical genius. From the time they met until Mendelssohn's death in 1847, Schumann praised his friend as one of the leading talents of that era. He also pointed to Mendelssohn as the person who "first renewed Germany's awareness of Bach."[9] Undoubtedly, therefore, Mendelssohn's enthusiasm for Bach's organ music deeply impressed Schumann. Having already discussed the famous episode involving "Schmücke dich, o liebe Seele," we will have several more opportunities later on to explore Mendelssohn's influence on Schumann in this regard.

The period from mid-March 1837 to April 1838 witnessed Schumann's encounter with a four-volume anthology of organ chorales titled *J. S. Bach's Choral-Vorspiele für die Orgel mit einem und zwey Klavieren und Pedal.* Edited by J. G. Schicht and published in 1803–6 by Breitkopf & Härtel, these four volumes were the most comprehensive print of Bach's organ chorales on the market.[10] As Schumann "studied" and "played through" Schicht's edition,[11] he learned a total of forty-three pieces: the six "Schübler" chorales; the five Canonic Variations on "Vom Himmel hoch"; ten settings from Part 3 of the *Clavierübung;* three works from the *Orgelbüchlein;* and a host of miscellaneous chorales, both authentic and spurious.

Almost a fourth of these works are trios whose three voices, for the sake of polyphonic clarity and a variegated organ sonority, are to be played on separate manuals and pedal. To judge from his still extant personal copy of Schicht's edition, Schumann believed that the first *Clavierübung* setting of "Allein Gott in der Höh sei Ehr" (BWV 675)—a work for which Bach provides no performance instructions and which is often played on one manual with no pedal—was to be played likewise, since he marked its bottom and middle voices, respectively, *s[inistra]. m[ano]. 16´* and *Ped. 4´.*[12] Schumann obviously took these indications from those provided by Schicht for the Schübler chorale "Wo soll ich fliehen hin," found four pieces earlier in the same volume.

Another remarkable statistic about Schicht's edition is that over a fourth of its contents are canons. In the case of the large *Clavierübung* setting of "Vater unser im Himmelreich," Schumann bracketed every phrase of the canon on the chorale melody, similar to how he analyzed fugues from the *Well-Tempered Clavier.*[13] Like a good theory student, he also saw fit to identify with diagonal lines an instance of parallel fifths in measure 17 of "Ach Gott und Herr," BWV 692, a work now known to be by J. G. Walther.

There can be no question that Schumann's close study of the canons found in Schicht's anthology is reflected in a letter he drafted to (his now fiancée) Clara Wieck on 18 March 1838 as well as in a diary entry he penned a few weeks later. We read in the former that he conceived "almost everything canonically" and in the latter that "the canonic spirit" pervaded all of his "fantasizing."[14] A compositional by-product of this obsession is the movement "Glückes genug" from Schumann's piano collection *Kinderscenen,* op. 15, written exactly a week before the letter to Clara.[15] This vignette offers canonic writing at the fifth between the treble and bass.

Around the time that Schumann concluded his study of Schicht's edition, he mentioned Bach's organ music in the *Neue Zeitschrift* (issue of 10 April 1838). He wrote there, while reviewing various concerts that had taken place in Leipzig the previous winter, that Beethoven's late string quartets "stand with some of Bach's choruses and organ compositions on the most extreme boundaries of all that has hitherto been attained by human art and imagination."[16] This encomium no doubt pertains to certain works contained in Schicht's anthology. Indeed, one of the most "extreme" organ pieces Bach ever wrote is the aforementioned setting of "Vater unser," a work of such contrapuntal and rhythmic complexity that one commentator has argued that two different performers are required.[17]

From early 1839 to late 1841 Schumann printed six organ works by Bach in the *Neue Zeitschrift*. To be exact, the venue was not the journal proper but a series of supplements titled "Collection of Music Pieces from Old and Modern Times" (*Sammlung von Musik-Stücken alter und neuer Zeit*). Included were the Fugue in C Minor, BWV 575 (February 1839); the *Orgelbüchlein* settings of "Ich ruf zu dir, Herr Jesu Christ" and "Das alte Jahr vergangen ist" (December 1839); the *Orgelbüchlein* setting of "Durch Adams Fall ist ganz verderbt" (June 1840); the Fantasy in C Minor, BWV 562/1 (May 1841); and the *Orgelbüchlein* setting of "O Mensch, bewein dein Sünde gross" (December 1841). Schumann had explained shortly before he began to issue the series that its main purpose was to promote previously unpublished works, including "some of the finest" by his favorite composer.[18] He presumably did most if not all the editing himself.

These six examples raise a whole host of issues, starting with why Schumann chose these particular works and how he got his hands on the music in the first place. The answer to both questions is that Mendelssohn must have played a key role. As we learned in the first chapter of this book, "Ich ruf zu dir," "Das alte Jahr," and the fantasy were among Mendelssohn's favorite Bach works, and by far the easiest way for Schumann to have gained access to the *Orgelbüchlein* was through his friend, who by the summer of 1839 owned two manuscripts of the collection. Furthermore, Schumann acknowledged Mendelssohn as one of his sources for "Das alte Jahr."

In contrast to the other five pieces, the fugue was edited quite freely. For one thing, dynamics are sprinkled throughout for the sake of an idiomatic performance at the piano, in accordance with the heading *Clavier oder Orgel*. Other emendations include a tempo marking of *Mässig* (the equivalent of "andante"), staccato dots for the countersubject, a ritard for the big cadence at measures 30–31, a ritard toward the conclusion of the pedal solo, and a marking of *Adagio* at the very end. Why this juvenilia appealed to Schumann is open to conjecture, but the appoggiatura harmonies found throughout the fantasy are consistent with his own compositional style.[19] If his organ and piano fugues are any indication,[20] Schumann would also have approved of the six lengthy pedal points.

Turning to the *Orgelbüchlein* chorales, three of them are among Bach's most intrepid works altogether. "Das alte Jahr" and "O Mensch" display an extreme use of chromaticism to depict, respectively, the passing of the old year and the agony of the Crucifixion. In "Durch Adams Fall," a threshold of dissonance rarely seen in tonal music serves as a metaphor for Original Sin. That leaves "Ich ruf zu dir," whose hymn text imparts a sense of longing that was central to the whole movement of Romanticism. All four works exude an emotionalism that would have appealed quite naturally to any member of Schumann's generation.

Mendelssohn may well have introduced Schumann to all of these settings except "Das alte Jahr," which occupies the very last page of Schicht's anthology. Still, it was Mendelssohn who enabled his comrade to print this piece according to what they both assumed to be Bach's autograph (but what was actually a manuscript in the hand of Bach's pupil, Meissner). Schumann tells us this himself, for at the top of this page of his copy of Schicht's edition he wrote "corrected by Mendelssohn according to Bach's original manuscript" (see figure 2–1).[21] Mendelssohn's corrections, which reflect the standard readings found in modern editions, are entered in light pencil and appear in almost every measure. They affect everything from pitch and rhythm to voice leading and ornamentation, and they agree completely with the readings from Mendelssohn's own edition of the *Orgelbüchlein* published in 1845. Virtually all of these corrections also found their way into Schumann's edition. A second inscription in Schumann's hand, *nicht c?*, appears at the start of the penultimate system.[22] It corresponds to a partially erased question mark that he drew beneath the second alto note of the last bar of the system. His concern obviously was the friction between the alto and soprano notes (c′ versus d′). Mendelssohn, though, did not see fit to change the passage (which is undoubtedly authentic), and Schumann therefore printed it exactly as did Schicht.

As we saw in chapter 1, Mendelssohn could not have acquired the Meissner manuscript prior to June 1839. Since Schumann did not publish "Das alte Jahr" until December of that year, it follows that Mendelssohn must have corrected his friend's copy of the work in either late summer, upon returning from Frankfurt to Leipzig, or sometime that autumn. During this same period, Mendelssohn introduced Schumann to another collection of chorales by Bach. This is documented by a letter of 10 October 1839 from Schumann to Clara Wieck that involves, among other things, the French composer and conductor Hippolyte-André(-Jean)-Baptiste Chelard:

> Yesterday morning Chelard was with me for a long time, and I played a lot of music to him, first like a pupil, but then it got better. He understands little, however, and thinks Bach an *old* composer and his compositions *old*. I told him Bach was neither new nor old, but a great deal more, namely, eternal. I really almost lost my temper over it. Mendelssohn had a bunch of *large* chorales by Bach copied for me, and I was in great ecstasy over them just when Chelard arrived.[23]

As to the identity of the works supplied by Mendelssohn, consider first that he owned exactly two manuscript collections of chorales by Bach: the

Figure 2–1 "Das alte Jahr vergangen ist," BWV 614, as published in *J. S. Bach's Choralvorspiele für die Orgel*, ed. J. G. Schicht. Robert Schumann's personal copy, with corrections in the hand of Felix Mendelssohn Bartholdy (Robert-Schumann-Haus, Zwickau, catalogue no. 11831-D1/A 4)

Orgelbüchlein and the Great Eighteen. Because Schumann would not have described the miniatures that comprise the former as "large," he must be re-ferring to the latter. Evidently, he not only revered the Great Eighteen but also played some of them for his guest (who was presumably in Leipzig to partake of the city's thriving musical scene). Schumann's complaints about the Frenchman echo what Mendelssohn had to say in 1825 about Parisian musicians and their ignorance of Bach.[24]

In May 1839, three months after Schumann had begun to publish organ works by Bach, he reviewed in the *Neue Zeitschrift* various editions of key-board music by Scarlatti and Bach, including one by Haslinger of the Six Great Preludes and Fugues for organ. His comments on the edition proper are prefaced by the most impassioned statement he ever issued regarding the supremacy of Bach's organ music. According to this panegyric, the organ works are timeless masterpieces that epitomize Bach's art:

> But it is only at his organ that he appears to be at his most sublime, most au-dacious, in his own element. Here he knows neither limits nor goal and works for centuries to come. We have to mention here a revised edition by Haslinger of six preludes and fugues originally issued by Riedel in Vienna. They are al-ready familiar to organists. Number 4 is the wonderful Prelude in C Minor [BWV 546/1].[25]

Some eight months earlier, Schumann had traveled to Vienna in hopes of securing Tobias Haslinger as the new publisher for the *Neue Zeitschrift*. His intention, ultimately, was to settle there with his bride-to-be Clara Wieck. At some point during his long (and unsuccessful) stay in the Austrian capi-tal, he seems to have mailed Clara a copy of the Six Great, which she received just before leaving Leipzig on 8 January 1839 for a six-month stay in Paris. Shortly after returning to Germany that summer, while lodging at her mother's home in Berlin, she dispatched a missive to her fiancé in which she asked: "Tell me, how does one play Bach's pedal fugues? If the pedal part is always played in octaves, are they even possible to play? (I am speaking of the 6 pre-ludes and fugues with which you sent me to Paris.)"[26]

Robert had introduced Clara to these pieces seven years earlier, when they had sight-read them together at the piano. He now armed her with the same music on the eve of her Parisian sojourn in hopes that the budding vir-tuoso would add it to her concert repertoire. Having chided her a year ear-lier for limiting herself to only one Bach work, Robert felt strongly that she should play more Bach.[27]

Clara's questions here touch on a perennial problem in transcribing organ music for the piano. Out of a desire to simulate sixteen-foot stops and achieve an idiomatic piano sonority, she was naturally drawn to the idea of playing the pedal line in octaves with her left hand. Yet she realized that this technique normally forces the right hand to take all the manual parts, a difficult circumstance in the case of a fugue with four or five independent voices. Not surprisingly, the work that poses the least difficulty in this regard is the only one of the six she is known to have played with any frequency: the Prelude and Fugue in A Minor, BWV 543. Rarely in this prelude do the feet and hands actually play at the same time, and the fugue contains an unusually long *manualiter* interlude. Clara might also have sensed that the fugue had real possibilities as a virtuoso exercise in perpetual motion. According to the organist and critic Eduard Krüger, she played it at the breakneck tempo of $\downarrow$. = 75.[28]

Under Robert's watchful eye, the A-minor prelude and fugue quickly became one of Clara's specialties. That she had by the following summer begun to play the prelude is documented by Robert's letter to her of 7 August 1840, discussed in the first chapter of this book. As for the fugue, the elderly Franz Liszt remarked to his piano pupils in 1886 that Clara had played that movement "40 years ago . . . in Leipzig."[29] Since Liszt set foot in Leipzig only twice during the 1840s, in March 1840 and December 1841, one assumes he heard Clara perform the fugue during one of these stays. Another sojourner to Leipzig around this time was Mendelssohn's friend Henry Chorley, who visited the Schumanns at their home in October 1840, a month after their wedding.[30] The Englishman later wrote about how much he had enjoyed "the *organ-playing* on the piano of Madame Schumann,"[31] likely a further reference to the A-minor. Clara's most notable performance of either movement took place on 10 July 1847 in Robert's native Zwickau, and in his presence, at a festival devoted to his own compositions. A month earlier, Robert had informed the festival's director that his wife would be rendering a "fugue by Bach in A minor, actually for organ."[32]

Interestingly, the same movement was performed thirteen years later in Zwickau at a festival commemorating the fiftieth anniversary of Schumann's birth, but under very different circumstances.[33] Robert had died four years earlier, and Clara chose not to attend because she knew her archrival Liszt would be there. For his part, Liszt played Schumann's op. 11 piano sonata. He also managed to persuade Theodor Kirchner, a member of both Schumann's and Mendelssohn's circle in the 1840s, to perform an impromptu organ concert at the church of St. Mary. In addition to improvising and playing music by Schumann, Kirchner offered "the great A-minor fugue by Johann Sebastian Bach." He may have done so in deference not only to Robert and Clara but also to Liszt, for this fugue was one of his favorites as well.

During his last four years in Leipzig (1841–44), Schumann continued to champion Bach's organ music, both as editor of the *Neue Zeitschrift* and as an independent musician with an ever-widening circle of friends and colleagues. The most cherished member of that circle was, of course, Clara, and we learn from the couple's "marriage" diaries that by the fall of 1841 they had begun to play organ works by Bach *on the organ*. Sometime between 27 September and 24 October, Robert wrote about their visit to a local church:

> We also played the organ once in St. John's Church; an awful thing to remember because we did not handle it with any accomplishment, and in the Bach fugues Clara could never get past the second entrance, as though she were standing at a wide brook [i.e., *Bach*]—but we want to try it again soon; the instrument really is just too magnificent.[34]

Whatever these fugues were, Robert's delightful pun implies that Clara's attempts at pedaling were all in vain.

She had evidently been more successful a few months earlier, while vacationing in Freiberg, a city that boasted four different organs by Gottfried Silbermann. In a diary entry of 6 July 1841, Robert described that scene as follows:

> Lest I forget the most important thing, we also looked [today] at the outstanding Silbermann organ; the organist preluded and postluded a D minor fugue by Bach in C-sharp minor, which made us laugh a great deal. Clara also played, and soon might well be the most capable player. We are also planning to take organ lessons in Leipzig.[35]

Because that date fell on an ordinary weekday (Tuesday), it would seem that the couple attended not a church service but rather a private demonstration that began and ended ("preluded and postluded") with the same Bach fugue. Evidently, the instrument on display was tuned a half step lower than normal.

Shortly after returning to Leipzig that summer, Schumann heard on 1 August an organ recital by C. F. Becker at the church of St. Nicholas, where Becker had become the regular organist.[36] According to a capsule review that appeared five days later in the *Neue Zeitschrift*, the program included music by Bach, Handel, J. L. Krebs, and Becker himself, as well as a Fugue on BACH that the performer offered as a work of Sebastian Bach. Almost certainly this refers to the latter movement of the Prelude and Fugue in B-flat Major on BACH, BWV 898, a piece known to have been played by Becker on at least one other occasion.[37] Although the anonymous reviewer praised Becker as a "highly valuable artist on his instrument," he, like most commentators since, disputed the fugue's authenticity, arguing instead that it was by one of Bach's pupils. It stands to reason that this critic was Schumann himself.

Three months later, Schumann published in the *Neue Zeitschrift* an essay on typographical errors found in musical editions of his day, including two of organ works by Bach.[38] He had this to say about the *Bureau de Musique* edition of the F-major toccata published by Peters and the Haslinger edition of the "Wedge" fugue:

In the grand and splendid *Toccata with Fugue for Organ,* two manual voices move above a pedal point in a strictly canonic sequence. Is it possible that this has been overlooked by the proofreader? For he has allowed a number of notes to stand that are not compatible with the canon. Similar oversights occur during the course of the piece in the corresponding passages on pages 4 and 5. Though these may be easily corrected, the clarification of another passage in the same piece is more difficult. My readers will no doubt remember the grandiose pedal solo; by comparing this with the corresponding passage stated a fourth lower, they will find that a number of errors have crept in. Two measures are completely missing on page 4, between measures 3 and 4; these may be seen in transposed form on page 5, system 6, second and third measures. Here, only the original manuscript could settle the matter. Perhaps Mr. Hauser of Vienna owns it; if so, he could be solicited for a comparison. No one should consider as immaterial the possession of a piece as extraordinary as this composition in its most authentic reading. To tolerate such errors would be like allowing a tear to remain in a picture, a page to fall out of a favorite book. . . .

But who, when he is reveling in Bach's harmonies, can think of everything, most of all, of errors? Thus I for years overlooked one in a Bach fugue that was very familiar to me, until a master—who certainly has an eagle eye—pointed it out. The fugue is in E minor, on a wonderful theme, and is the sixth in the Haslinger edition. If one inserts between the third and fourth measures [a whole note on f-sharp,] it will be correct. Of this there is no doubt.[39]

Schumann prized the toccata both for its introductory canon and for its pedal solo. His description of the latter as "grandiose" suggests that he had heard the work played on a full registration by a skilled organist. And one need look no further than Mendelssohn for an organist-colleague of his who had a special fondness for this movement—and who had used it on his tour of Switzerland to "tumble down the church." Schumann's only acquaintance mentioned by name in this excerpt is Franz Hauser, whom Robert had known for several years and whom he had seen intermittently during his long visit to Vienna in 1838–39. It is safe to say he was interested in Hauser, whom he described as a "strange man" and a "choleric hypochondriac (!) who always contradicts what anyone else says," mainly for his huge collection of Bach manuscripts.[40] Hauser, though, did not own the autograph of the F-major toccata,[41] so Schumann's hunch that this source may have lacked the same two bars (mm. 58–59) as the *Bureau de Musique* edition was never confirmed.

Apropos of the E-minor fugue, Schumann recognized the bold originality of the subject, a theme described by Henry Chorley as "spreading in form like a wedge" (hence the nickname).[42] If Schumann is to be trusted here, this most studious of Bach devotees had never noticed that in the Haslinger edition the subject first appears minus its fourth measure (all the other statements are complete). In Schumann's defense, though, it must be admitted that measure 3 of the theme flows quite smoothly and convincingly into measure 5, despite the repeated e's. The "eagle eye" who had discovered this mistake almost certainly was Mendelssohn.

Some five months after the publication of this essay, Schumann again referred to Bach's organ music in the pages of the *Neue Zeitschrift*. He did so in the 5 April 1842 issue, while reviewing some piano etudes by A. H. Sponholtz:

> The author of the above is an organist, and one must know this in order to fully appreciate his endeavors. His aspirations are lofty ones; he would gladly bless the whole world with his art. But his powers are still undeveloped . . . especially as regards modulatory form. For example, who likes to be thrown out of the saddle from G minor to E major in a little piece only two pages long, as in the first etude? The composer scarcely knows how to stick to any key, which is doubly surprising in an organist who must know his Sebastian Bach. . . . At our next meeting, a volume of well-executed fugues would please us more than another one full of sketches. At his royal instrument, the composer must have learned the value of clearly defined artistic form, such as that given to us by Bach in his largest as well as smallest works.[43]

The main argument of this passage is that Bach's organ works provide a model for any fledgling composer, something Schumann knew from personal experience. By "clearly defined artistic form," Schumann means not only Bach's use of clearly articulated modulation schemes but also his impeccable craftsmanship in general.[44] And Schumann is saying that this attribute presents itself in virtually all of Bach's compositions for the organ, regardless of size. In this respect, one can hardly question that the phrase "smallest works" denotes the chorales from the *Orgelbüchlein*, which are among the shortest pieces for any medium that Bach ever composed.

By assuming that any organist "must know his Sebastian Bach," Schumann is stating that Bach's music occupies a central position in the organ literature. No one would dispute this claim even today, since Bach still dominates the organ repertory like no other composer dominates any other repertory. Writing five years earlier in the *Neue Zeitschrift*, Schumann had already expressed this sentiment in decidedly stronger terms—and in a manner downright insulting to other composers of the late baroque era: "With regard to composition for organ and piano, obviously no one of [Bach's] century can measure up to him. Indeed, to me, everything else appears in comparison to the development of this giant figure as something conceived in childhood."[45]

To continue with our narrative, on 14 August 1842 C. F. Becker presented for the citizens of Leipzig his second annual summer organ recital at St. Nicholas's. Included on the program was Bach's Schübler chorale "Wa-

chet auf, ruft uns die Stimme,"[46] a work that would have held special significance for Schumann as the very first piece in J. G. Schicht's anthology. But
Schumann could not attend this performance, as he and Clara were on vacation. Shortly after returning to town on 22 August, he sent Becker an apol-
ogy: "Unfortunately, I could not attend your organ concert; I just returned a
few days ago from a brief excursion to Bohemia. I am very sorry—I would
have especially enjoyed hearing [at this point, Schumann notates the first measure of the right-hand part of "Wachet auf"]."[47]

Two days before he left on this trip, Schumann wrote two different letters in which he mentioned or alluded to organ works by Bach. One was addressed to the young J. G. Herzog, who had asked for a critique of several of
his own compositions. Schumann responded with fatherly advice and yet
another utterance about the supremacy of Bach's organ music:

> You seem to be particularly at home on the organ. This is a great advantage,
> and *the greatest composer in the world has written the majority of his most splen-*
> *did pieces for this instrument.* But the organ can also tempt one into a certain
> comfortable way of composing, because almost anything sounds good on it.
> At any rate, don't write too many small pieces. Also, try your hand at some of
> the larger forms, such as the fugue, the toccata, etc., of which Bach has left us
> the highest examples.[48]

In the other letter, Schumann praised Sebastian Bach's *Magnificat* and
disparaged the music of Emanuel Bach.[49] More to the point, he asked its recipient to "think of him" whenever he played Bach on the organ. He was writing in this instance to Eduard Krüger, a schoolteacher from East Friesland,
unabashed Bach enthusiast, and perhaps Schumann's most scholarly colleague
of all. The two had corresponded since 1838, when Krüger contributed the
first of several articles to the *Neue Zeitschrift*. Schumann may even have offered
him the editorship of the journal in late 1843.[50]

Krüger's letters to Schumann provide ample evidence of his fanaticism
for Bach. Even before he began to play the organ, Krüger thought of the composer as "a god" and the "source of all music." Sometime around his thirty-
second birthday in late 1839, he resolved to learn that "holy instrument," de-
voting himself almost exclusively to Bach's oeuvre. Apparently without the
benefit of a tutor, he made spectacular progress, and in the span of one and
a half years had mastered such demanding pieces as the Wedge fugue, the
Prelude in E-flat Major, and the Prelude and Fugue in G Major, BWV 541.[51]

Krüger has already been mentioned in reference to Clara Schumann and
the Fugue in A Minor, BWV 543/2. His only opportunity to hear her perform
this movement would have been on his brief visit to Leipzig in July 1843,
which, after years of planning, he undertook expressly to meet her husband.

During these few days, Krüger was a frequent guest at the couple's home, where he played Bach at the piano and where Clara presumably played not only the A-minor fugue but also, from the Six Great, the Fugue in C Minor, BWV 546/2. According to Krüger, she played the latter at the moderately slow tempo of $\quad$ = 85.[52]

Naturally, Krüger held forth at the organ as well. Here is an anonymous "review" that appeared later that month in the *Neue Zeitschrift:*

> We have recently gotten to know and appreciate another side of Dr. E. Krüger, to whom the *Zeitschrift* is already indebted for his many outstanding essays. He played for a few music lovers on the organs of the churches of St. Thomas and St. Nicholas, and showed himself to be a splendid performer, especially in some of Sebastian Bach's most difficult pieces.[53]

In a letter of early August 1843, Krüger thanked Schumann personally for these kind words, so there can be no question that Robert himself authored them. Clara, too, was impressed, scribbling in the couple's diary that Krüger was "a brilliant man and proficient musician, especially on the organ."[54]

Upon his departure from Leipzig that summer, Krüger received from Schumann a not insignificant farewell gift: a manuscript copy of Bach's *Die Kunst der Fuge* that Robert himself had penned as a study score some six years earlier. A missive written by Krüger to Schumann four months later implies that he may have had Robert to thank for at least one other Bach manuscript:

> "Komm, Heiliger Geist" is monstrously powerful and agitates the organ in its innermost regions, so that everything flows out of the pipes like a thick stream of lava. "An Wasserflüssen Babylon" is full of secret, delicate geniality; quiet, gentle voices of Oriental (!) childhood songs. "Schmücke dich, o liebe Seele," sentimentally fragrant with a spicy tenderness; "O Lamm Gottes, unschuldig," full of strange, unusual swells and stresses.[55]

Krüger can only be describing—in the highly romanticized language for which he was known—Bach's Great Eighteen organ chorales, specifically the first, third, fourth, and sixth works in the set. (In the case of "O Lamm Gottes," he seems to refer not to the work as a whole but to measures 135–38, where Bach singles out the word "verzagen" for intensely chromatic treatment.) As discussed earlier, none of these pieces had yet been published, but Schumann owned the entire collection in manuscript. Thus, from what is known about Krüger's circumstances, the easiest way for him to have gained access to the Great Eighteen was through Schumann, who could have engaged a local scribe to prepare a fresh copy from his manuscript. Schumann probably introduced Krüger to these incomparable works during his sojourn in Leipzig.

Schumann had by this time joined the faculty of the newly formed Leipzig Conservatory, where, under Mendelssohn's supervision, he taught composition, score reading, and piano. One of his piano pupils was Alfred Dörffel, who would go on to make a name for himself as a critic and as the editor of several volumes of the *Gesamtausgabe* of Bach's works published by the Bachgesellschaft. We have Dörffel to thank for the following account of Schumann's pedagogical methods:

> Schumann once requested that at our next lesson I was to play organ chorales by Bach, for example, "Wachet auf, ruft uns die Stimme." I was initially anxious about how to play both the pedal and manual voices as notated. I leapt as deftly and quickly as possible from the pedal notes, which I handled like short grace notes, to the notes for the left hand, and I sustained the pedal notes with the damper pedal. After sufficient practice, my execution of everything had become quite polished . . . Schumann was pleased with my *manipulation*. Schumann himself was wont to perform organ chorales at the piano this way, and he was very adept at playing these leaps.[56]

The piece cited here, of course, is the Schübler chorale by the same name, Bach's only organ setting of this hymn. Dörffel's report therefore provides additional evidence that this beautiful work was one of Schumann's favorites. It also evinces that Schumann continued to play Bach's organ chorales at the piano several years after his study of Schicht's anthology. In terms of performance practice, Dörffel is describing a technique whereby the left hand jumps as much as an octave-and-a-half from a grace note to a "melody" note played by the thumb.[57] Schumann had already utilized this technique in his own piano works. Its clearest manifestation may be seen in the seventh of his *Impromptus sur une Romance de Clara Wieck*,[58] a work that was cited earlier vis-à-vis Schumann's reception of the Six Great Preludes and Fugues for organ, BWV 543–48 (see example 2–1). Otherwise, this intriguing anecdote raises questions that can never be answered. Was Schumann forced to perform Bach's organ chorales with such emphasis on the left hand because of his notoriously crippled right hand? Did he and his students use these works expressly as technical studies for the left hand? Which chorales besides "Wachet auf" did he play or teach according to this methodology?

Dresden and Beyond

Schumann's last year in Leipzig, 1844, was one of his bleakest. On the personal side, he suffered from a variety of physical ailments as well as the mental illness that would lead to his ultimate demise. Largely because of these

Example 2–1 Robert Schumann, *Impromptus sur une Romance de Clara Wieck*, op. 5, Variation 7

maladies, he decided in June to give up the *Neue Zeitschrift* and in September to resign from the Leipzig Conservatory. When he was passed over in favor of Niels Gade to succeed Mendelssohn at the Gewandhaus, he saw no opportunity in the city to further his career. On 13 December he moved his family to the Saxon capital of Dresden.

Dresden was no "Sebastianstadt," but it had its share of Bach devotees. None was more influential than Johann Gottlob Schneider, organist of the court church. (This is the same Schneider mentioned in the first chapter of this study in reference to Mendelssohn and the D-major fugue from Book 1 of the *Well-Tempered Clavier*.) A renowned performer and pedagogue, Schneider was particularly famous for improvising in the style of Bach and for always ending his organ lessons by playing a Bach fugue or chorale setting.[59] To judge from Schumann's household records, he quickly became a good friend of Schneider and whiled away many an hour listening to the virtuoso play his church's magnificent Silbermann. Bach was doubtless standard fare on these visits.

We do not know if Schneider advised his new colleague on how to write for the organ, but on 7 April 1845, four months after the Schumanns had relocated to Dresden, Robert began drafting his first and only works for the instrument, the Six Fugues on BACH, op. 60. That January, the couple had embarked on an intense study of counterpoint, which quickly resulted in a series of preludes and fugues for piano composed by Clara on themes by her husband and Bach. Robert would follow with his Four Fugues for Piano, op. 72, and Six Studies for Pedal Piano, op. 56. After a summer hiatus, Robert's "Fugenpassion" (as he called it) returned, and by November all six of the BACH fugues had been drafted. At no other time in Schumann's life did he devote himself so zealously to contrapuntal composition, a phenomenon that was to have significant therapeutic value in his ongoing struggle with depression. Needless to say, he took Bach as his main compositional model.

Given Schumann's interest in Bach's organ music, it is not surprising that he now finally turned to the organ as a compositional medium. His interest in the instrument per se—which in and of itself stemmed directly from his study of Bach—had been growing in earnest ever since he had resolved four years earlier to take organ lessons. In July 1844 he made good on this vow, recording in his household records that he had taken his "first organ lesson."[60] (With whom he does not say.) He continued to play the instrument, if only sporadically, during his first two years in Dresden, sometimes with Clara pumping the bellows.[61]

To hone their skills as organists, the Schumanns even chose in April 1845 to rent a piano pedalboard. It sat beneath their piano through July of that year and, according to Clara, brought them "much pleasure."[62] There can be no doubt that the couple used this device to play organ works by Bach. A few days after it arrived, Robert began to compose for the instrument, and two months later he had completed not only the six Studies but also the Four Sketches for Pedal Piano, op. 58.

Because the six Studies are a series of canons, they may be seen as Schumann's creative response to the many organ canons by Bach that he had studied over the years, including the F-major toccata and roughly a dozen chorales from Schicht's anthology. Indeed, the first of the Studies may be a direct copy of the canon that opens the toccata (see examples 2–2 and 2–3).[63] Both offer in their upper two voices a canon at the octave based on the same type of sixteenth-note figuration, which in both instances leads to continuous sixteenth-note motion. Moreover, both of these canons unfold above pedal parts that rely heavily—and, in the case of the toccata, exclusively—on pedal points. But Schumann might also have been inspired here by the first of Bach's Canonic Variations on "Vom Himmel hoch,"[64] a work he knew from Schicht's anthology. This movement, too, is a trio whose upper two voices produce nonstop sixteenths in the guise of a canon at the octave (see example 1–5). Furthermore, it is in the same key as Schumann's canon.

As for the BACH fugues, the fact that they are derived from the same melodic cell suggests *Die Kunst der Fuge* as a conceptual model, as does the extraordinary complexity of Schumann's counterpoint. But Bach's organ fugues obviously served as a point of departure as well. Observe, for example, the virtuosic pedal part of the second fugue, whose figuration recalls Bach's numerous *Spielfugen* for the organ.[65] In addition, Schumann likely cribbed the subject of this fugue from the Fugue in C Minor, BWV 575, one of the Bach works published by him in the *Neue Zeitschrift* (see examples 2–4 and 2–5). Besides the BACH motive that opens Schumann's subject, what so distinguishes these two themes is the initial series of sixteenth notes, which in both instances begins with a stepwise descent and ends with a large upward leap, followed by rests. (Schumann states his series once, while Bach states his sequentially.) Both themes then conclude with the same variety of sixteenth-note figuration.

Example 2–2 Toccata in F Major, BWV 540/1

Example 2–3 Robert Schumann, Study in C Major, from *Six Studies for Pedal Piano*, op. 56

Example 2–4 Fugue in C Minor, BWV 575, as published by Robert Schumann in a supplement to the *Neue Zeitschrift für Musik* (February 1839)

Example 2–5 Robert Schumann, Fugue No. 2 on BACH, from *Six Fugues on BACH*, op. 60

In composing the final fugue of the set, Schumann apparently drew on one of Bach's most celebrated works for the organ, the E-flat fugue (the "St. Anne") that ends Part 3 of the *Clavierübung*.[66] For the only time in this opus, he presents the first three pitches of the BACH motive as a dactyl, and in ponderous 4/2 time, exactly how Bach begins his fugue (see examples 2–6 and 2–7). Also like Bach, Schumann writes an exposition of his subject in five voices—an unusually thick fugal texture—and both works wind up as double fugues, with a separate exposition of a second subject for the hands alone. It is probably no accident either that both fugues close their respective collections and that they do so with a sense of climax and grandeur. Most of the stylistic traits already mentioned contribute to this effect, as do the considerable length of both fugues and their use of full organ (which Schumann first employs to introduce his second subject). That Schumann greatly admired this Bach fugue is attested to by his review of Mendelssohn's all-Bach recital, quoted in chapter 1.

Schumann spent the last day or so of his "contrapuntal year" in Leipzig, having returned there for the first time since his move.[67] The occasion was the annual New Year's Day concert at the Gewandhaus, which in 1846 featured Clara—in the final month of her fourth pregnancy—in her husband's Piano Concerto. It was evidently during this weeklong stay that Mendelssohn presented Schumann with a copy of his edition of Bach's *Orgelbüchlein,* which

Example 2–6 Fugue in E-flat Major, BWV 552/2

had been issued some months earlier. Schumann wrote on the title page of this source that it was "received from Mendelssohn in the winter of 1845–46."[68]

In 1846 Mendelssohn's other three editions of Bach's organ chorales (those of the Great Eighteen and the partitas on "Christ, der du bist der helle Tag" and "Sei gegrüsset, Jesu gütig") rolled off the press, and he supplied his friend with fresh copies of each of these publications as well. Schumann wrote on the title pages of all three sources that they were received from Mendelssohn in the year 1846.[69] His inscription on the edition of the Great Eighteen chorales specifies October as the month of receipt, implying that Mendelssohn presented it to him in Leipzig around the time of Clara's 22 October appearance at the Gewandhaus.[70] Perhaps all three editions were presented at

Example 2–7 Robert Schumann, Fugue No. 6 on BACH, from *Six Fugues on BACH*, op. 60

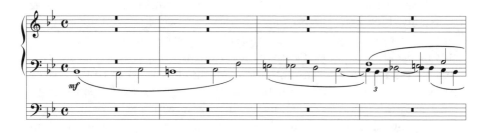

the same time. At all events, the various markings made by Schumann within these sources document his study of the music. With regard to the Great Eighteen and the two partitas, he was content merely to correct or question certain pitches.[71] But in the case of the *Orgelbüchlein,* his inscriptions betray a close analysis of Bach's counterpoint.

These inscriptions appear in four pieces, two of which, not surprisingly, are canons: "Gott, durch deine Güte" (also known as "Gottes Sohn ist kommen") and "In dulci jubilo." In both instances, Schumann provided a heading to indicate the type of canonic writing employed. For "Gott, durch deine Güte," a canon at the octave between the upper right-hand and pedal voices, he wrote *Pedal im Canon der Octava.* For "In dulci jubilo," a double canon for most of its duration, he wrote *Doppelcanon bis zum Zeichen* § ("double canon until the sign §") and inserted the corresponding segno at the end of the sixth measure of the third system, exactly where the double canon ends (see figure 2–2). The latter symbol is drawn with such precision as to suggest typesetting. Observe also the slurs inserted by Schumann to mark discrepancies between the *dux* and *comes* of the canon for the lower two manual voices (see the end of the first system, the beginning and end of the second system, and the beginning of the third system).[72] These slurs appear in two musically identical passages where the *comes* moves from d to a instead of d to c, obviously to avoid parallel octaves with the soprano. Other inscriptions made by Schumann on this page include the marking *NB* ("Nota Bene"), found beneath the third of his slurs, and the designation of *8 Fuss* for the pedal line.[73] The latter agrees with the pedal registration furnished by Mendelssohn for "Gott, durch deine Güte" as well as that furnished by Schumann himself for "O Lamm Gottes, unschuldig," a further canonic setting found seven pieces later in this edition.

In the other two works that preserve Schumann's analytical markings, he drew in brackets to mark several near instances of parallel octaves. These passages may have attracted his attention because they almost always concern the two most prominent voices: the soprano, which states the unadorned hymn tune; and the bass, which is the pedal line. As figure 2–3 shows, Schumann detected seven such passages in "Wir Christenleut," all of which would have resulted in parallel octaves were it not for an intervening eighth note in the bass voice. He marked two additional passages in "Lobt Gott, ihr Christen, allzugleich," between the soprano and bass in measure 3, and between the alto and bass in the transition from measure 6 to measure 7.

Both of these works, unlike the two canons, are entirely typical of the *Orgelbüchlein* as a stylistic entity: above motivically unified figuration in the lower three parts, the unembellished hymn melody sounds continuously in the soprano voice. In the fall of 1848, Schumann set the chorale "Freu dich sehr, o meine Seele" in this same manner for inclusion in his piano collection

Figure 2–2 "In dulci jubilo," BWV 608, as published in *44 kleine Choralvorspiele für die Orgel von Johann Sebastian Bach*, ed. Felix Mendelssohn Bartholdy. Robert Schumann's personal copy (Robert-Schumann-Haus, Zwickau, catalogue no. 11825-D1/A 4)

Album für die Jugend, op. 68 (see example 2–8). He also chose to base the motivic work of this "Figurirter Choral" on the rhetorical-musical figure known as the *suspirans,* the most common of all the accompanimental motives used by Bach in the *Orgelbüchlein.*[74] Beginning with a rest or "suspiration," the motive in Schumann's arrangement consists of four off-the-beat eighth notes. It is also confined mostly to the alto voice, which means that the lower two voices, contrary to Bach's practice, are little more than harmonic filler. Like Bach, however, Schumann produces constant motion—and forward momentum— in the rhythm one-fourth the value of the main pulse (understood here as the half note) by stating the motive more or less continuously. His adoption of the *Orgelbüchlein* as a stylistic exemplar in this instance represents but one aspect of the Bachian nature of the *Album,* for the collection also contains a canon and fugue inspired by Bach's example.[75] Furthermore, the very idea of the volume—keyboard music for children—probably comes from the *Clavier- büchlein* drawn up by Bach for his nine-year-old son Wilhelm Friedemann,[76] especially considering that the *Album* originated as a birthday gift for Schumann's seven-year-old daughter Marie.

Figure 2–3 "Wir Christenleut," BWV 612, as published in *44 kleine Choralvorspiele für die Orgel von Johann Sebastian Bach*, ed. Felix Mendelssohn Bartholdy. Robert Schumann's personal copy (Robert-Schumann-Haus, Zwickau, catalogue no. 11825-D1/A 4)

The only other bit of evidence from Schumann's Dresden period linking him to Bach's organ music is an entry into his household records dated 23 July 1850: "Early, Schneider's beautiful organ playing (Bachiana) at St. Sophie's."[77] In other words, on that Tuesday morning J. G. Schneider once again treated his famous colleague to a private Bach organ recital—however informal—in this instance on the two-manual Silbermann at the church of St. Sophie. Both Schumann and Schneider must have known this was an instrument on which Sebastian Bach himself had concertized (and on which Friedemann Bach had played many a worship service as the church's regular organist), and they must also have realized that the centennial of Bach's death—a milestone in the history of early Bach reception—was only five days away. Schumann's observance of this anniversary is well documented, for over the next five days he attended two different concerts commemorating the occasion, one at the Frauenkirche in Dresden on 25 July (which was presided over by the organist Carl Kloss and therefore presumably featured solo organ works by Bach) and another in nearby Meissen on 28 July, the actual date of the centennial.[78] He marked the latter date in his household records as the "Bach day." In light

Example 2–8 Robert Schumann, "Figurirter Choral," from *Album für die Jugend*, op. 68

of all this information, it would seem that Schumann actually solemnized the anniversary over a six-day period, beginning with Schneider's performance.

Roughly a month later, Schumann left his native Saxony to become the municipal music director of the city of Düsseldorf (the same post held by Mendelssohn). He would remain there until March 1854, at which time, after an unsuccessful suicide attempt, he checked himself into a private sanatorium at Endenich, a suburb of Bonn. It is the greatest tragedy of his short life that he would never leave this asylum. He died there on 29 July 1856, leaving behind a widow and six children. Ironically, his death date is only a day later than Bach's.

During his tenure at Düsseldorf, Schumann conducted such large-scale Bach works as the St. John Passion, St. Matthew Passion, and B Minor Mass. He also undertook a project titled "Bachiana," whereby he wrote piano accompaniments to all of Bach's compositions for solo violin and cello. Still, compared to Leipzig or even Dresden, Düsseldorf had no Bach tradition to speak of, and there is no documentation concerning Schumann's reception of Bach's organ music there except for a single letter and a catalogue of his music library.

This letter was written by Schumann in late 1852 and addressed to one Julius von Bernuth, a young admirer of his who was contemplating music as a career. Similarly to how he had responded to the young J. G. Herzog a decade earlier, Schumann suggested to Bernuth that he study Bach's organ works, particularly the "chorale preludes and the great fugues."[79] Presumably, this is yet another reference to the Six Great Preludes and Fugues.

In August 1853 Schumann had enough free time at his disposal to rearrange his extensive music library and compile a catalogue of its holdings, about five hundred titles altogether.[80] Of the forty-eight volumes containing works by Bach, one-third are editions of organ music—clear evidence that the organ works were absolutely central to Schumann's Bach reception. Presented in table 2–1 are the titles of these editions as given by Schumann, along

Table 2–1 Editions of Bach's Organ Music Contained in Schumann's Music Library

Title Given by Schumann	Contents According to BWV Number
44 kleine Choralvorspiele für die Orgel, hg. von Felix Mendelssohn-Bartholdy	BWV 599–630, 632–44 (*Orgelbüchlein*)
15 grosse Choral-Vorspiele für die Orgel, hrsg. von Felix Mendelssohn	BWV 651–63, 667, 740 (Great Eighteen Chorales)
Choralvorspiele für die Orgel, 4 Hefte	BWV 614, 633–34, 645–50, 664b, 675–84, 691–93, 697–701, 704–8, 710–11, 748, 759, 769a
Orgelkompositionen, hrsg. von Adolf Bernhard Marx, 3 Hefte	BWV 532, 533, 539, 542, 550, 565, 566, 569
Praeludien und Fugen für Orgel, 3 Bde.	unknown
Klavierübung Teil I-III	Teil III contains BWV 552, 669–89, and 802–5
Toccata und Fuge für Orgel, Nr. 2 und 3	Nr. 2 = BWV 540; Nr. 3 = BWV 538
Fantasie für Orgel	BWV 562/1?

with their contents. The order, in which chorale settings are separated from free works, is also Schumann's.

Most of these titles have already been mentioned. With respect to the first four, Schumann's personal copies of these publications have survived intact. They include, in addition to Mendelssohn's two editions (which probably not by accident head the list), the four volumes of J. G. Schicht's chorale-anthology and the three volumes of the Marx/Mendelssohn edition, *Johann Sebastian Bach's noch wenig bekannte Orgelcompositionen*.[81] For the sixth title, Schumann cited, in addition to Parts 1 and 2 of Bach's *Clavierübung*, which are for harpsichord, Part 3 of the same collection, which contains a total of twenty-seven organ works. We have alluded previously to the seventh title in conjunction with Schumann's essay on musical typos. Both its wording and numbering agree with an edition that had been issued twenty years earlier by C. F. Peters in its series *Bureau de Musique*. Collectively titled *TOCCATA ET FUGUE pour l'Orgue ou le Piano-Forte composé par J. S. Bach*, the edition consists of three volumes or "numbers," each containing a single piece. Number 2 is the Toccata and Fugue in F Major, BWV 540; Number 3 is the Dorian toccata and fugue, BWV 538. Schumann can be referring to no other edition of either work.

Thus the only titles whose identity is at all unclear are the fifth and the last. By "Fantasie für Orgel," Schumann probably meant his own edition of the Fantasy in C Minor, BWV 562/1, which he had published in 1841 in a supplement to the *Neue Zeitschrift*, and under practically the same title ("Phantasie für Orgel"). The three volumes of "preludes and fugues" allow for two possibilities. One is that Schumann is citing the *Bureau de Musique* edition of the Preludes and Fugues in A Minor, G Major, and G Minor (BWV 551, 541, and 535), a three-volume set analogous to the toccata edition just described.[82] The other possibility is that he is referring, somewhat casually, to the thirty-odd preludes, fantasies, toccatas, and fugues that had been published in the mid-1840s by Peters as volumes 2, 3, and 4 of its complete edition of Bach's organ works. Either way, Schumann's library contained well over one hundred organ compositions by Bach, many of them in two different editions.

Four months after drawing up this catalogue—and only weeks after being relieved of his duties in Düsseldorf—Schumann found himself in the Netherlands, with Clara, in the midst of a wildly successful concert tour. With Clara (pregnant yet again) at the piano and Robert at the conductor's podium, the couple were fêted wherever they appeared. While in Rotterdam, they were in the constant company of Jan Albertus van Eijken, organist at the Zuiderkerk and organ instructor at the local conservatory. On the afternoon of 9 December, Robert (and perhaps Clara as well) visited this church to hear Eijken perform. He wrote in his diary that the organist played "masterfully" on a "beautiful" instrument.[83] The session had to be curtailed due to the extreme cold, but not before the young virtuoso had rendered works by Bach, Gade, Mendelssohn, and Schumann.

Schumann must have been gratified by Eijken's performance for reasons other than vanity. For one thing, the organist was probably a long-standing acquaintance, as Eijken had been a pupil of J. G. Schneider in Dresden during Schumann's first two years there. At the very least, Schumann doubtless saw something of his old friend in the young man's playing. Furthermore, Eijken was a fellow Bach fanatic who in 1850 had co-founded the first Bach society in the history of the Netherlands and who in 1854–56 would publish organ transcriptions of works from the *Well-Tempered Clavier*.[84] Finally, Schumann's diary entry identifies the Bach piece performed by Eijken as the Fantasy and Fugue in G Minor. Schumann would have known this piece from the Marx/Mendelssohn edition, and he would surely have appreciated the fugue as a pedal showpiece par excellence (did either Schumann or Eijken realize that its subject probably derives from a *Dutch* folk song?).[85] But Schumann would have been totally captivated by the fantasy, an unrivaled specimen of rhapsodic figuration and radical, experimental harmonies.

Schumann would never forget his visit to the Zuiderkerk that wintry day. We know this from a letter he wrote at Endenich to the violinist Joseph Joachim, who had become one of the composer's closest friends. In that missive, dated 10 March 1855, Schumann first inquired whether Eijken had succeeded in his bid to become the organist of the Reformed Church in the Westphalian town of Elberfeld.[86] (In fact, he had.) Then Schumann wrote the following: "He plays splendidly. In Rotterdam I heard him play fugues by Bach as well as BACH fugues . . . on an organ that was entirely worthy of him." Schumann's pun, of course, refers to his own BACH fugues, which Eijken had performed for him that afternoon. His mention of "fugues by Bach" does not exactly square with what he entered into his diary, but that is beside the point. The point is that Bach's organ music stayed in Schumann's consciousness to the very end.

THREE

⌒

Franz Liszt

Iᴺ ᴛʜᴇ ꜰᴀʟʟ ᴏꜰ 1857, some fifteen months after the death of her husband, Clara Schumann embarked on a lengthy concert tour of Germany
and Switzerland. She performed first in Dresden and Leipzig, sharing the bill
with the violinist Joseph Joachim. At some point during their stay in Dresden, the two artists were treated to a performance by J. G. Schneider on the
sumptuous Silbermann organ at the court church, the same instrument on
which Schneider had often played for Robert Schumann. Also present was
arguably the era's most famous musical personality, who had traveled to the
Saxon capital to conduct the premiere performance of his *Dante Symphony*.[1]

We have no idea who invited Liszt to this gathering, but it seems unlikely
that either Clara or Joachim did. Clara had by this time developed a great an-
imosity toward the man as well as his music, and in one of her letters to
Joachim she went so far as to say that she detested Liszt from the depths of
her soul.[2] Joachim had likewise severed all ties to his erstwhile mentor, having confessed to Liszt two months earlier that his compositions did nothing
but antagonize him. Both Clara and Joachim found the music of Liszt vul-
gar and lacking in substance, as did such conservatives as Johannes Brahms
and the critic Eduard Hanslick. Their assaults on the so-called New German
School, as represented by Liszt and his followers, are quite notorious.

It is less well known that a small battle in "the War of the Romantics" was
fought in the Dresden court church that day, with Liszt and Joachim firing
salvos on the subject of Bach's organ works. Our source is a letter written by
Clara a week or two after Schneider's performance and addressed to her half
brother, the composer Woldemar Bargiel:

> I had a pleasant time in Dresden with Joachim, who played more beautifully
> and wonderfully than ever. . . . Liszt's meeting with him showed that they were

ill-suited to be together for a minute. . . . Once, when Schneider was playing us glorious things on the organ—the most beautiful works of Bach—and Joachim exclaimed, "What divine music!" Liszt replied, "Hm, dry as bones." Joachim answered, "Well, I must say I prefer it to jelly." Liszt then quickly disappeared.[3]

Clara evidently enjoyed telling this story the rest of her life,[4] if only because Liszt had been outwitted by one of her best friends (who, of course, was accusing Liszt of mawkishness). Still, since Schneider was an old colleague of hers, she probably took Liszt's remark as a personal affront. She might even have felt an uncomfortable sense of déjà vu, as nine years earlier in the same city she had arranged an elaborate musical dinner for Liszt, only to have the guest of honor dismiss her husband's Piano Quintet, with its fugal finale, as "Leipzigerisch." This famous put-down was Liszt's way of saying that such Leipzig-based composers as Schumann and Mendelssohn relied far too heavily on the complex, polyphonic style of a certain Leipziger from the previous century. To surmise from both incidents, Liszt eschewed Bachian counterpoint in his own compositions—because he deemed the style outmoded if not anachronistic—and felt nothing but contempt for Bach's music.

The first of these conclusions contains a grain of truth, for Liszt's compositions are relatively free of Bachian influence (although he wrote not only a fantasy and fugue for the organ but a prelude and fugue for the instrument based on Bach's very name). The second conclusion, however, is quite erroneous. True, there can be no question that Liszt championed Bach's music with far greater discrimination than did either Schumann or Mendelssohn—according to one of his pupils, he made a big distinction between Bach's "immortal" and "mortal" works.[5] But Liszt also regarded several of Bach's sacred vocal works, especially the St. Matthew Passion, among the greatest creations in all of music. As a pianist, he played and taught Bach's harpsichord works his whole life, with an emphasis on pieces that allowed for virtuosic display. He seems to have approached the organ music in much the same vein, learning only those works that he felt would make the most brilliant effect at the piano. (This penchant for virtuosity, along with certain religious factors, would help to explain Liszt's total neglect of Bach's organ chorales.) Consequently, Liszt's knowledge of Bach's organ music was rather limited. He may not really have known more than a dozen works. Yet as a concert pianist, piano transcriber, and piano teacher, he made a decisive impact on the reception of this repertory throughout the nineteenth century.

The Traveling Virtuoso

Liszt's father made sure that his son, to quote Robert Schumann, "knew his Sebastian Bach." Indeed, the boy was required every day to play and transpose (!) six different Bach fugues, presumably ones from the *Well-Tempered Clavier.*[6] Upon the family's move to Vienna in 1822, he continued to study the works of Bach under Carl Czerny, who would go on to issue a complete edition of the "Forty-Eight." A year later, the family relocated to Paris, the city that would serve as Liszt's home base over the next dozen years. Little is known about Liszt's Bach reception during this period, but surely it is significant that one of his closest acquaintances was the organist and Bach champion Chrétien Urhan.[7] Perhaps it was Urhan who introduced the youth to Bach's organ music.

Our first concrete bit of evidence linking Liszt to Bach's organ music dates from early 1836, by which time the twenty-four-year-old's life had changed dramatically: a year earlier, he had eloped to Switzerland with his mistress Marie d'Agoult, and in December 1835 she had given birth to the couple's first child, Blandine. Three months after the blessed event, Liszt was eager for his mother to see her first grandchild (his father had long since died). In anticipation that she would undertake the long journey from Paris, he wrote to her in March 1836 with the instruction that she bring along two of his musical scores: "Pack in your suitcase two volumes of music with the following titles (they are located in the same section of the library): *The Art of Fugue* by Bach and *Six Fugues with Pedal* by Bach (I am not completely sure whether I still have the latter work)."[8]

Considering that (1) no other set of six Bach fugues for any medium was in print at this time and that (2) Liszt occupied himself with this collection his entire adult life, the latter title must refer to the Six Great Preludes and Fugues for organ, BWV 543–48. Liszt's uncertainty about whether he "still" owned this edition suggests that it had been in his possession for several years. No doubt he planned on performing from (and studying) these two volumes himself, but he may also have intended to share them with his pupils at the Geneva Conservatoire. His citation of the Six Great as "fugues" rather than "preludes and fugues" accords with nineteenth-century practice.

During this period, Liszt and d'Agoult counted as two of their best friends the writer George Sand and the linguist Adolphe Pictet. Both were present in Fribourg on 15 September 1836 to hear Liszt test out the Aloys Mooser organ at the church of St. Nicholas. According to Pictet's detailed description, Liszt mesmerized his friends with a lengthy improvisation on this huge instrument, at one point "passing into the fugal style of Meister Sebastian Bach."[9] His extemporization of a fugue during this performance may be interpreted, in a very broad sense, as a kind of *hommage* to Bach's organ fugues.

We next hear of Liszt in connection with Bach's organ music three years later, at which time he and d'Agoult were living in Rome, awaiting the birth of their third child. Here is an excerpt from a letter, only recently published, that he drafted to Pictet in April 1839:

Marie told you, I believe, that I had conceived a beautiful and lasting passion for Lord Byron. But now I am experiencing another enthusiasm. Guess for whom? For Johann Sebastian Bach. Do you know his *Passion* at all well? What a masterpiece, my friend! It is truly prodigious. I recommend to you above all the opening Chorus—the exposition; the way the two Choruses and the Chorale are done is admirable. When we see one another again, I shall get you to touch and absorb these marvels. The *6 Fugues with pedal* are magnificent too. If you don't possess them, I shall send them to you.[10]

Again Liszt refers to the Six Great Preludes and Fugues for organ, and his zealous tone indicates more than a passing interest.

In the meantime, Liszt had begun to play actual *works* by Bach on the organ. On 1 May, eight days before the birth of his son Daniel, he played an unspecified Bach fugue on the organ of the church of San Luigi di Francesi at a worship service organized by the French embassy.[11] Despite his admiration of the Six Great, at no point in his life would Liszt have had the pedal technique necessary to negotiate any of these fugues on the organ. Most likely, he chose something from another of his favorite collections, the *Well-Tempered Clavier.*

The year 1839 was a milestone in Liszt's musical career, for it inaugurated an eight-year period during which he secured his reputation as the leading pianist in the world. He performed everywhere from Ireland to Turkey, establishing the concept of the piano recital as we know it today. He played the entire spectrum of the keyboard repertory as it then existed as well as a multitude of his own arrangements, the latter encompassing everything from songs by Schubert and Schumann to symphonies by Beethoven and Berlioz. He also performed his transcriptions of organ works by Bach.

Liszt is not known to have played any of his Bach transcriptions in public prior to his concerts in Greater Berlin during the winter of 1841–42. His program at the Singakademie on 5 January 1842 featured an E-minor organ fugue by Bach; four days later, in Potsdam, he played his arrangement of a Bach organ prelude and fugue in A minor.[12] As to the identity of Liszt's models here, one need look no further than the Six Great Preludes and Fugues, which begin with a work in A minor (BWV 543) and end with one in E minor (BWV 548).

"Lisztomania" was the term coined by the poet Heinrich Heine for the wildly enthusiastic public response to Liszt's performances in Berlin. The cognoscenti were impressed too. One critic wrote apropos of Liszt's rendition of the "Wedge" fugue that the artist "played a fugue with pedal by Johann Sebastian Bach, taking the two [actually three] manual voices mostly with the right, and the third [actually fourth] pedal voice with the left hand, without the use of an actual pedalboard, with a cleanliness and clarity that left nothing to be desired, only [the wish] to marvel to an even greater extent at the immense proficiency of the player."[13] This same writer praised the "clarity" with which Liszt had played Bach's Chromatic Fantasy and Fugue at his very first appearance in Berlin that season.

For reasons that must involve the gigue-like nature of the fugue subject, Liszt evidently performed the A-minor throughout this entire eight-year period. According to one report, which concerns Liszt's sojourn in Montpellier during August 1844, he sometimes resorted to gimmickry when playing the work in front of an audience. Liszt's official business in Montpellier that month was a series of public recitals, yet he found time one day to call on Jean-Joseph-Bonaventure Laurens, a painter, writer, and organist who was personally acquainted with all four composers under consideration in this book.[14] What is more, Laurens was one of the staunchest proponents of Bach's organ music anywhere in France at that time. His personal library included an early manuscript of the "Sei gegrüsset" partita, a copy of Mendelssohn's edition of the *Orgelbüchlein* received from Mendelssohn himself, the Haslinger edition of the Six Great Preludes and Fugues, and the Marx/Mendelssohn edition, *Johann Sebastian Bach's noch wenig bekannte Orgelcompositionen*. As a critic, Laurens lauded Bach's organ works as the composer's most perfect creations, just as he lamented that they were completely unknown in France because there were no French organists who could perform such demanding pedal parts.

On the whole, Liszt was warmly received. His host served him lunch and even drew his portrait. Laurens, however, also suspected that Liszt was a philistine. Writing some forty years later, Laurens's brother described the visit as follows:

> Liszt appeared in 1844 at the home of J. B. Laurens in Montpellier, with recommendations from Mendelssohn, [Ferdinand] Hiller, etc.
> — "You have the reputation," J. B. stated brusquely, point blank, "of being as big a charlatan as you are a great artist!"
> He rather brutally took the bull by the horns. Liszt did not flinch and even took on a spirit of frank and witty amiability. J. B. drew his portrait. They lunched, chatting about so many of the most interesting things and musical celebrities.
> — "I have to ask you," J. B. said at one point, "to play for me a certain piece by Sebastian Bach for organ with obbligato pedal, the first in the volume with the six fugues, the one in A minor so difficult that you are without a doubt the only person in the world who can tackle it. This is a unique opportunity for me today that I cannot pass up."
> — "Right now? . . . How do you want me to play it?"
> — "How? But . . . the way it ought to be played!"

— "Here it is a first time, as the author must have understood it, played it himself, or intended it to be played."

And Liszt played. And it was admirable, the very perfection of the classical style and exactly in conformity with the original.

"Here it is a second time, as I feel it, with a slightly more picturesque movement, a more modern style and the effects demanded by an improved instrument."

And it was, with these nuances, different . . . but no less admirable.

"Finally, here it is a third time, as I would play it for the public . . . to astonish, as a charlatan!"

And, lighting a cigar that passed at moments from between his lips to his fingers, executing with his ten fingers the part written for the pedals, and indulging in other *tours de force* and prestidigitation, he was prodigious, incredible, fabulous, and received gratefully with enthusiasm.[15]

This anecdote offers compelling testimony to Liszt's ability to play a single composition in a variety of styles.[16] It also shows, contrary to what has been printed in the secondary literature, that he was capable early in his career of performing a work with the utmost fidelity. On a more technical level, one may conclude that Liszt first rendered the piece without any crescendos or decrescendos, in simulation of the organ or harpsichord, and that he next played it with an abundance of dynamic shadings. When he played the work a third time, he doubtless subjected it to those "paraphrase" techniques for which he is justly famous, such as scales, arpeggios, trills, tremolos, and glissandos. (The clause concerning his execution of the pedal part "with his ten fingers" may refer to nothing more than octave doublings of pedal solos.) Most spectacular of all, he topped off these pyrotechnics with some literal fire in the form of a lighted cigar. Like Schumann and Brahms, Liszt was an avid cigar aficionado, so this trick may have been another of his trademarks. Indeed, he is reported to have accompanied Joachim in the last movement of Mendelssohn's Violin Concerto with a lighted cigar in his right hand the entire time![17]

Weimar

By the fall of 1847, Liszt had effectively retired as a concert pianist. Exhausted from eight years on the road, he now intended to dedicate himself to composition and conducting. An offer from the Grand Duke of Weimar to become Kapellmeister at his court made this possible, and starting in early 1848 Liszt served for thirteen years in this capacity. In 1869, after several years in Rome, he returned to Weimar, still under the duke's patronage. Until his death in 1886 he would spend a portion of each year there—the rest of his time would be divided between Budapest and Rome—primarily in the role of master teacher.

Not surprisingly, living in this small but important cultural center further stimulated Liszt's passion for the music of Bach. He was, of course, keenly aware that the master himself had lived in Weimar for several years, referring once to Bach as his "great Weimar predecessor."[18] No doubt he knew as well that Weimar was where Bach had written most of his organ music. Living in the Thuringian region of Germany, where so many of Bach's pupils had settled, also brought him into contact with various organists, especially A. W. Gottschalg, who still actively fostered the Bach-organ tradition. In addition, Thuringia was exceedingly rich in pipe organs of all types, which Liszt enjoyed playing himself. He could hardly have picked a better locale in which to pursue his interest in Bach's organ works.

TRANSCRIPTIONS

One of the first tasks undertaken by Liszt upon moving to Weimar in February 1848 was to notate and then publish his piano transcriptions of all half dozen of Bach's Six Great Preludes and Fugues for organ. Liszt remarked to his biographer Lina Ramann that this project originated in 1842,[19] probably in conjunction with his concerts in Berlin that year, but his subsequent travels may have prevented any real progress. By late 1847, during a three-month respite in Woronince (Russia) at the home of his new mistress, Princess Carolyne von Sayn-Wittgenstein, he was ready to resume work. We know this from Liszt's letter of 19 December 1847 to the publisher Carl Haslinger (who had taken over that firm after the death of his father, Tobias), in which he asks to be sent a copy of Bach's "Six Pedal Fugues" so that he might better "steep" himself in them.[20] Haslinger obliged by mailing Liszt a copy of that house's latest edition of the Six Great, one replete with added dynamics, phrasings, fingerings, and tempo indications. (Robert Schumann would have been pleased that this edition also restores measure 4 of the "Wedge" fugue.) Fortunately, this copy has survived intact, and it casts considerable light on Liszt's methodology.

Various markings made by Liszt throughout this source indicate that he used it both as a working score for himself and as a guide for his copyist Joachim Raff.[21] At the top of the first page of music, for example, Liszt wrote: "The pedal line is to be omitted throughout" (see figure 3–1).[22] This remark can only be construed as an instruction to Raff to score the entire collection on two rather than three staves. For added emphasis, Liszt also crossed out the first bar of the pedal line of the opening movement, the famous Prelude in A Minor, BWV 543/1.

Figure 3–1 Prelude in A Minor, BWV 543/1, mm. 1–14, as published in the Haslinger edition, *Sechs Präludien und Fugen für Orgel oder Pianoforte mit Pedal von Joh. Seb. Bach.* Franz Liszt's personal copy (Goethe- und Schiller-Archiv, Weimar, GSA 60/U 46)

The second, third, and fourth pages reveal that the most common type of change made by Liszt to the score of this movement is the doubling of certain pedal notes at the lower octave, a device, as discussed in the previous two chapters, that serves at once as an idiomatic piano technique and a simulation of sixteen-foot organ stops. In measures 22–24, 30–36, 38, 48–49, and 53,

Figure 3–1 ctd. Prelude in A Minor, BWV 543/1, mm. 15–25, as published in the Haslinger edition, *Sechs Präludien und Fugen für Orgel oder Pianoforte mit Pedal von Joh. Seb. Bach.* Franz Liszt's personal copy (Goethe- und Schiller-Archiv, Weimar, GSA 60/U 46)

Liszt wrote the doubled notes in the left-hand staff, thus negating the pedal line. (In measures 48 and 53, he crossed out the pedal notes in question.) For the pedal eighths and sixteenths in measures 46–52, he expedited matters with his version of an *8va* inscription.

Other markings made by Liszt on these three pages deserve comment as well. For example, in measures 33, 36, 37, and 52, he crossed out the left-hand

Figure 3–1 ctd. Prelude in A Minor, BWV 543/1, mm. 26–38, as published in the Haslinger edition, *Sechs Präludien und Fugen für Orgel oder Pianoforte mit Pedal von Joh. Seb. Bach.* Franz Liszt's personal copy (Goethe- und Schiller-Archiv, Weimar, GSA 60/U 46)

fingerings of the Haslinger edition, obviously meaning for the right hand to take these passages instead (since the left hand is to play the pedal part). Conversely, in measure 23 he preferred to play with his left hand material printed for the right, identifying the pitches in question as *h* (or b natural), *d, e,* and *f.* Observe, too, that in measures 35 and 46 he crossed out the down-

Figure 3–1 ctd. Prelude in A Minor, BWV 543/1, mm. 39–53, as published in the Haslinger edition, *Sechs Präludien und Fugen für Orgel oder Pianoforte mit Pedal von Joh. Seb. Bach.* Franz Liszt's personal copy (Goethe- und Schiller-Archiv, Weimar, GSA 60/U 46)

beat notes for the left hand, in the former instance because this note is already present in the octave duplication of the downbeat pedal note and in the latter instance because of the impossible hand reach.

It is important to understand that the version of Liszt's transcription of the A-minor prelude preserved in his personal copy of the Haslinger edition is hardly identical to the one he would ultimately publish. Rather, it is a pre-liminary effort, just as this source as a whole represents merely the first step in the notational phase of the project. In the published version, for instance, the pedal point in measures 10–21 is stated an octave lower and reiterated every two bars (presumably to compensate for the piano's inability to sustain a pitch indefinitely). In addition, the pedal passages in measures 24–32 and 40–44 are rendered in octaves, the last three left-hand sixteenth notes in mea-sures 37 and 39 are transposed down an octave for technical reasons, and the downbeat pedal note in measure 46 is left undoubled, which allows the left-hand notes to be retained, but as sixteenths rather than quarters. What is more, the published version contains almost none of the performance in-structions found in the Haslinger edition, although Liszt added his own fin-gerings in places. Most interestingly, the published version offers a funda-mentally different reading for the second soprano part in measure 25 (four sixteenths on beat two followed by an eighth note on beat three) that agrees with all the standard editions of the organ version. Therefore, Liszt must have consulted a source besides the Haslinger edition (whose reading, with its open-fifth chord on beat two, is obviously corrupt). A likely candidate is vol-ume 2 of the Peters edition of Bach's complete organ works, published in 1844.

In late October 1850 Liszt sent Joachim Raff a letter from Bad Eilsen, where Princess Carolyne was taking the waters for her rheumatism, in which he implored his young scribe to prepare a fresh copy of the Six Great: "As soon as you find the time, apply yourself to Bach's 6 pedal fugues, and please write very clearly and broadly."[23] This would seem to indicate that Liszt had by this date finished annotating his copy of the Haslinger edition and that he now expected Raff to copy from this source a manuscript containing all six works. Liszt's desire for a "broadly written" copy, which would allow him ample space for making annotations of his own, suggests that he planned on using Raff's manuscript as his new working score. No such manuscript has survived.

These works had always been published according to the alphabetical key sequence of A minor (BWV 543), B minor (BWV 544), C major (BWV 545), C minor (BWV 546), C major (BWV 547), and E minor (BWV 548). Inexplicably, Liszt chose a somewhat different order when he published his transcriptions, beginning with the A-minor prelude and fugue but ending with the B-minor. The title of this C. F. Peters print, which appeared in 1852, reads: *6 Praeludien und Fugen für Orgel . . . von Johann Sebastian Bach für das Pianoforte zu zwei Händen gesetzt von Franz Liszt*. At Liszt's request, his friend Siegfried Dehn wrote the preface, whose last two paragraphs are worth quoting in full:

> [Liszt's] genius and musical intelligence have now pointed in another direc-tion: the transcription for piano of Johann Sebastian Bach's greatest organ compositions. The connoisseur and reverer of Bach's works will be astounded

that this was possible, first how such a thing could even be conceived and then how it could be executed with such perfection. Even though the obbligato pedal has been transferred to the left hand, the essence of the other voices has not been lost—Bach's great organ fugues are authentically preserved, transcribed for the piano so as to be performed by a single player. What progress in piano playing since Bach's time, what amazing application of modern technique!

Liszt's latest work hints at a new era in the history of piano playing, and just as earlier eras were marked by the names of *Bach, Scarlatti, Clementi, and [Francesco] Pollini,* so the present one bears the name of *Franz Liszt.*[24]

These arrangements constitute a remarkable feat, for Liszt did—to paraphrase Dehn—retain the essence of the manual voices, despite the regular use of the left hand to play the pedal part, often in octaves. He succeeded not only by assigning more material to the right hand but also by rewriting passages in a variety of ways, including octave transposition. He added no material of his own composition, although he could have done so quite easily in, say, a thinly textured movement like the A-minor prelude. Moreover, he jettisoned virtually all the performance instructions found in the Haslinger edition. In other words, these transcriptions could hardly be more literal (which is surely why, forty years later, Max Reger dismissed them as "hackwork").[25] Since Liszt saw Bach as a kind of musical deity, even referring to him once as "the St. Thomas Aquinas of music,"[26] the fact that he imposed nothing of his own musical personality here suggests a reverence for the music as Bach himself had notated it. Indeed, over thirty years later Liszt commented to his piano class that it would have been "sinful" of him to add dynamic markings to the score of the A-minor fugue, since "the great Bach" had written none himself.[27] No doubt it was in this same devotional spirit that Liszt, rather enigmatically, inscribed the word *Passionsmusik* at the end of his copy of the Haslinger edition.

Liszt's transcriptions of the Six Great were quickly championed by two other members of his circle. In a letter of 15 September 1852 the elderly Carl Czerny congratulated his erstwhile pupil on a "splendid" job and informed Liszt that he played his transcriptions almost daily.[28] So impressed was Czerny that he encouraged Liszt to arrange all the preludes and fugues that Bach had ever composed for the organ. Three years later, Liszt's former student (and future son-in-law) Hans von Bülow expressed much the same sentiment, writing to Liszt about how greatly he admired these transcriptions and how "useful" they had been to him.[29] It is documented that Bülow was already concertizing with Liszt's transcription of the A-minor prelude and fugue, and a few years later he began to play those of the B-minor and E-minor as well.[30]

By 1860 Liszt had begun to heed Czerny's advice. We know this from a letter written by Liszt to Bülow late that year in which he reports nearly having completed a piano arrangement of Bach's "Great Prelude in G Minor" for organ.[31] Despite Liszt's plans at this time to publish several more transcriptions of this type, the only other Bach organ composition he is ever known to have transcribed is the *Fantasy* and Fugue in G Minor, BWV 542. It would therefore seem that he means the G-minor fantasy, a work that in certain sources is indeed titled "Prelude."[32] In the same missive, Liszt cites this movement as one of his very favorite pieces of music and one that he often played for his own enjoyment. Considering Liszt's affinity for Bach's similarly rhapsodic Chromatic Fantasy, this comes as no surprise. Here was a Bach *organ* work that could appeal just as strongly to his romantic sensibility.

Liszt's (still popular) transcription of the G-minor fantasy and fugue remained unpublished until 1872, when it appeared in the fourth edition of the piano method of Sigmund Lebert and Ludwig Stark, *Grosse theoretisch-praktische Klavierschule*.[33] Even a cursory look reveals that Liszt approached the two movements rather differently. He adapted the fugue in the same strict way as he did the Six Great, except that he "sinned" by regularly adding performance instructions. But in transcribing the fantasy, he freely inserted material of his own devising, not only harmonies of various kinds but newly composed melody lines as well. Added chords abound in both hands, and none is more striking than the secondary leading-tone seventh played by the left hand at the start of the third beat of measure 7, a passage—left unharmonized by Bach—whose figuration seems to suggest a tonic triad (see example 3–1). For the first three bars, Liszt also gives the left hand the option of playing thirty-second-note runs not found in the original, more or less in contrary motion to Bach's thirty-seconds. A further example of this type of countermelody may be seen on the first two beats of measure 7. Other highlights include a fully notated arpeggiation of the circle-of-fifths passage at measures 31–34, doubtless inspired by the middle section of the Chromatic Fantasy, and an optional reading for the pedal solo before the final cadence that ascends chromatically, via triplets, all the way to b-flat (see example 3–2). Such features adumbrate the bravura style of Liszt's piano paraphrases of Italian opera.

Example 3–1 Franz Liszt's piano transcription of the Fantasy in G Minor, BWV 542/1

Example 3–2 Franz Liszt's piano transcription of the Fantasy in G Minor, BWV 542/1

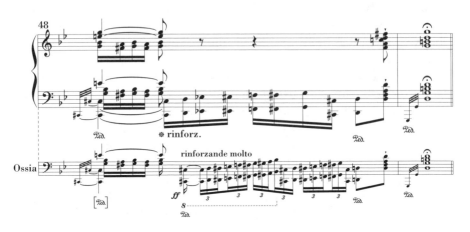

RELATIONSHIP WITH
A. W. GOTTSCHALG

That Liszt developed a serious interest in the organ shortly after settling in Weimar is attested to by his composition in the winter of 1850 of his first work for the instrument, the monumental Fantasy and Fugue on "Ad nos, ad salutarem undam" (from Meyerbeer's opera *Le Prophète*). Even if this masterpiece had not originated in the very city where Bach wrote most of his organ music, few would deny that it—or any other fantasy and fugue for the organ written in the middle of the nineteenth century—represents a kind of homage to Bach as a composer for that instrument. Of course, the same may be said of Liszt's Prelude and Fugue on BACH for organ, composed five years later. During this period, Liszt is also known to have added to his battery of keyboard instruments a three-manual *Flügelharmonium*.[34] The upper keyboard of this contraption, which was equipped with a pedalboard of one and a half octaves, was a grand piano, while the two lower manuals and pedals were a harmonium of sixteen stops. One of Liszt's visitors reported in 1854 that the virtuoso performed for him on this instrument a "fugue for organ" by Bach.

As Liszt began to compose for the organ, he naturally assimilated himself into the organ culture in and around Weimar. His circle of friends and pupils included such organists as Carl Müller-Hartung, Julius Reubke, Johann Gottlob Töpfer, and Alexander Winterberger, all of whom probably educated him about the instrument as well as its literature. But the local organist who seems to have been closest to Liszt for the longest period was Alexander Wilhelm Gottschalg.

Born in 1827, Gottschalg studied the organ with Töpfer from 1842 to 1847 at the Weimar Teachers Seminary. In 1847 he was appointed organist in nearby Tieffurt, and in 1870 he succeeded Töpfer as the organ instructor at the Seminary. After meeting in 1852, Gottschalg and Liszt became fast friends. One of their favorite activities was to explore the many fine organs that dotted the Thuringian landscape. In penning his memoirs, Gottschalg described such an excursion to the village of Dehnstedt:

> Liszt usually gave the man who operated the bellows one thaler for his work. In order that I could hear how a Bach fugue should sound, he would reach over my shoulders to play on the manuals while I would play the pedals, because he had no great fluency on them. Since he usually took very fast tempi, it was often an effort to keep up with him.[35]

Liszt also enjoyed listening to Gottschalg perform organ works by Bach on these outings, but we know from two articles published by Gottschalg in the *Neue Zeitschrift für Musik* that he objected to his colleague's old-fashioned habit of playing full organ, without any manual or registration changes. According to the first of these publications, which concerns the trend at the time toward "orchestral" organs, Liszt once heard Gottschalg employ this monochromatic registration for Bach's C-minor passacaglia and "Dorian Fantasy and Fugue." He reacted quite violently: "Do you really believe that Bach played both compositions throughout on full organ? Never and nevermore! He was much too great and sensitive an artist for that! Have you not read about how wonderfully he registered the organ?"[36] Gottschalg reports, too, that Liszt's admonition compelled him to register the fantasy and fugue in a completely different manner, obviously *with* manual and registration changes, and that shortly thereafter he played the work this way in a recital, much to the delight of his organ instructor Töpfer. In addition, he implies that it was Liszt's advice that led Töpfer to edit Bach's Passacaglia in this new fashion, with a registration change before each variation. Gottschalg published Töpfer's very influential edition in 1873 in his series *Repertorium für Orgel*.[37]

According to Gottschalg's second article, which deals with Liszt as an organist and organ composer, Liszt once heard him play Bach's "notoriously fantastic Toccata in D Minor" using full organ from beginning to end, and again he responded in no uncertain terms, complete with a reference to the Book of Revelation: "In terms of technique, it is totally satisfying, but where is the spirit? Without this, Bach is a Book of Seven Seals! Surely Bach did not play his works in such a manner; he, whose registrations were so admired by his contemporaries! When you are playing on a three-manual instrument, why should the other two manuals be ignored?"[38]

Gottschalg continues by explaining that he immediately began to experiment with a more "colorful" registration and that, a few days later, he performed the work in this new way on a recital at the Weimar town church. He states, moreover, that Töpfer was greatly pleased, even though it was Töpfer who had taught Gottschalg to play the toccata the "old, pedantic way," and exclaimed afterwards that the piece should always be performed according to Liszt's suggestions.

The "notoriously fantastic" toccata cited here by Gottschalg is doubtless the Toccata in D Minor, BWV 565, and not the so-called Dorian toccata (Bach's only other organ toccata in D minor), for he identifies the piece as contained in volume 4 of the Peters edition (the Dorian is found in volume 3) and arranged so "brilliantly" for piano by Liszt's pupil Carl Tausig (Tausig transcribed only BWV 565). Scholars have assumed that Gottschalg's earlier article refers to the Dorian toccata, Bach's only composition ever to be given this moniker. But in a footnote, Gottschalg identifies the work in question as contained in volume 4 of the Peters edition and as including pages 27–28. Since BWV 565 begins on page 27 of this volume, there is no question that Gottschalg is once again referring to this work and not the Dorian. (Besides, the Dorian represents an exceedingly rare instance in Bach's organ music where the composer himself notated numerous manual changes. Why would either Gottschalg or Töpfer have been tempted to play it on just one manual?) He erred by using the nickname of Bach's *other* D-minor toccata for organ and by calling the piece a "fantasy" instead of a "toccata." In writing these two articles, then, Gottschalg obviously furnished two slightly different versions of the same incident. It must have taken place no later than 1870, the year of Töpfer's death.

Liszt's preference for flashy registrations is entirely what we would expect from such a flamboyantly Romantic artist, regardless of whether he was merely attempting to emulate Bach's own practice. With respect to BWV 565, Gottschalg provides some fairly specific information on this subject, reporting in the earlier article that Liszt requested the organ's glockenspiel for the *prestissimo* triplets in the opening section of the work. Considering Liszt's fondness for "tinkling" bell effects in his piano music—just think of "La Campanella"—this is hardly surprising. According to the later article, Liszt instructed Gottschalg to switch to the two subsidiary manuals for the *allegro* sixteenth-note passage in measures 12–15 and to play the repeated notes in the left hand on the Quintadena, a stop that emphasizes the third harmonic.[39] With good reason, Gottschalg marveled at how "strange" this registration sounded.

Two points remain to be made about all of the foregoing. The first is that Töpfer may well have been the local organist who in 1830 witnessed Mendelssohn's aborted performance of BWV 565 at the Weimar town church: he was appointed deputy organist at the church in 1817 and principal organist in 1830.[40] The other is that Liszt's commentary on Bach's registrational bespeaks his knowledge of Bach as an historical figure. Liszt's source for this information was probably the Bach biography of J. N. Forkel, published in 1802, which remained the standard study of the composer until the appearance of Philipp Spitta's biography in 1873–79. Forkel's fourth chapter, titled "Bach the Organist," contains two references to Bach's "peculiar" yet ingenious manner of registering the instrument.[41]

Finally, Liszt and Gottschalg are known to have attended organ recitals together throughout central Germany. On 24 September 1882, accompanied by three of Liszt's pupils, they traveled to Arnstadt to hear the young Ernst Schilling play works by Bach, Krebs, Mendelssohn, and Liszt (including the Prelude and Fugue on BACH) on the very instrument presided over by the young Bach from 1703 to 1707.[42] Despite foul weather and a nasty cold, the elderly Liszt made the trip out of devotion to the performer, whom he had met in Rome and invited to Weimar that summer to participate in his master classes. According to Gottschalg's review of the performance,[43] Schilling began with the same A-minor fugue by Bach (BWV 543/2) that Liszt himself had so often played in concert. The old man may have slept right through it, however, as Liszt is reported to have "dozed some during the first part of the recital."[44]

Two years later, on 28 September 1884, Liszt and Gottschalg made another Bach pilgrimage together, this time to Eisenach for the unveiling of the Bach monument there. Although he had donated 3,000 thalers toward the statue, which beggared him for several months, Liszt was not so much as given a complimentary ticket to any part of the festivities.[45] It is unknown whether he and his entourage (which also included two of his pupils and various dignitaries from Weimar) stayed for the celebratory concert given the next day in the church where almost two centuries earlier Bach had been baptized. If so, they would have heard an organ work at least attributed to Bach whose title is printed in the program as "Toccata in D moll für Orgel."[46]

THE MASTER TEACHER

Teaching was central to Liszt's musical existence throughout his long career. Still, virtually all his piano pupils who achieved any prominence studied with the master during the latter half of his life, after he had for all intents and purposes retired as a concert pianist. The first generation of these students, which included the likes of Hans von Bülow, began to arrive in Weimar almost as soon as Liszt and Princess Carolyne had settled into the spacious house there known as the Altenburg.

Possibly the most outstanding of this group—and possibly Liszt's favorite pupil altogether—was Carl Tausig. Although only thirteen when his father brought him to Weimar in 1855, Tausig's talent was so stupendous that Liszt taught him for two solid years, even allowing the youth to live at the Altenburg as a member of the family. Tausig also transcribed for piano six organ chorales by Bach, as well as the Toccata in D Minor, BWV 565. Whereas these chorale transcriptions originated shortly before Tausig's shockingly premature death in 1871, the date of his toccata arrangement is unknown. The latter probably ranks as the most bombastic piano transcription of a Bach organ work every committed to paper, and it quickly became a favorite of concert pianists across Europe. Indeed, according to August Stradal, a pupil of Liszt's from 1884 to 1886, Tausig's toccata arrangement was at that time performed by "every" virtuoso.[47] As we will see shortly, it was also standard fare at the master classes given by Liszt in Weimar between 1882 and 1885. Liszt regarded his student's transcription as "masterful," despite Tausig's egregious realization of the three mordents at the beginning as inverted mordents (a–b-flat–a, instead of a–g–a).[48] Otherwise, one can only speculate. Did Tausig hope to emulate his teacher by transcribing an organ toccata by Bach? Did he learn any of Liszt's Bach transcriptions during his two years in Weimar? Did he get to know this toccata by hearing Gottschalg or Töpfer play it at the Weimar town church?

Tausig's chorale transcriptions are barely known, probably because of the impropriety of playing "hymn arrangements" in concert. They were published in 1873 by Adolph Fürstner (Berlin) under the title *Choralvorspiele für die Orgel von Johann Sebastian Bach für das Clavier übertragen von Carl Tausig.*[49] Tausig included some of Bach's most popular works: from Part 3 of the *Clavierübung*, the large setting of "Wir glauben all an einen Gott"; from the *Orgelbüchlein*, "Das alte Jahr vergangen ist" and "O Mensch, bewein dein Sünde gross"; from the Great Eighteen chorales, "O Lamm Gottes, unschuldig"; from the Schübler chorales, "Meine Seele erhebt den Herren"; and the miscellaneous setting of "Vater unser im Himmelreich," BWV 737.[50] Perhaps out of respect for the sacred subject matter, Tausig limited his modifications mostly to octave doublings of the pedal line. Only in verse 3 of "O Lamm Gottes" did he approach the flamboyance of his toccata arrangement. There, doublings of every sort occur in both hands (along with a steady increase in volume), even in the last thirteen measures, where the surface motion accelerates from quarter notes to eighths.

In a letter to Liszt written two months before his death, Tausig confessed a special fondness for the other Passiontide chorale from this collection: "I recently sent you by book-post [my] Bach chorale preludes. Number 3 in E-flat major is my passion. Do you not also like this sublimely sad piece?"[51] Thus, like many since, Tausig felt a special affinity for the *Orgelbüchlein* setting of "O Mensch," possibly Bach's most beloved organ chorale of all. Stricken by typhoid fever and surely suspecting that his days were numbered, he could relate all too easily to the anguish of the Crucifixion as depicted in this beautifully poignant work. Tausig dedicated his opus to none other than Johannes Brahms, a close friend from his years in Vienna (1862–64). Considering Brahms's broad knowledge of Bach's organ chorales (see next chapter), it was probably he who introduced Tausig to these six works; it could not have been Liszt. At the very least, Tausig's dedication is an acknowledgement of the reverence that he and Brahms shared for the music of Bach.[52]

All the remaining Liszt students to be considered are associated with the master's "three-fold life" (as he termed it), the period from 1869 until his death when he maintained residences in Weimar, Budapest, and Rome. To cope with the steadily increasing size of his studio, Liszt now preferred to offer group lessons using the format of the master class, a concept that he basically invented himself. In Weimar, these classes took place three times a week at Liszt's new residence there, the Hofgärtnerei (the former home of the court gardener).

In discussing these students, let us commence with Berthold Kellermann, who first came to Weimar in 1872 at the age of nineteen and returned there each year to study under Liszt until 1878.[53] On one of these sojourns, he and Liszt attended an organ recital together (location and performer unknown) featuring the Fugue in G Minor, BWV 542/2, a movement, as we have already seen, that Liszt counted as one of his favorites and one that he had many years earlier transcribed for piano. Following the performance was a scene vividly sketched by Kellermann in his memoirs:

> An organist who lacked the third finger of his right hand once gave a recital in a church, the chief item being Bach's great Fugue in G Minor. Liszt, the greatest player and connoisseur of Bach, said to me when the church was empty: "Kellermann, that missing-middle-finger trick I can do too. Look!" And before my eyes he played this difficult fugue while in *both* hands stretching out and avoiding the use of the middle finger. I then practiced it too, but found how extraordinarily difficult it was.[54]

Kellermann's report requires no explanation, but it does recall another anecdote involving Liszt, organ fugues, a handicapped performer, and one-upsmanship. According to that story, when Liszt once learned that a certain pianist (Ludwig Böhner, the real-life model for E. T. A. Hoffmann's Bach-addicted character, "Kapellmeister Kreisler") had managed to perform fugues on the organ in spite of two crippled fingers, he proceeded to play a difficult Bach fugue using only three fingers of each hand![55]

Although it is a reasonable assumption, we do not know for a fact that Liszt formally taught Bach's organ works to Kellermann or to any other pupils who came to him in the 1870s. The diaries of Carl Lachmund and August Göllerich, however, provide ample evidence of this activity during the last four years of Liszt's life. Both were regular participants in the Weimar master classes, in 1882–84 and 1884–86, respectively, and both took detailed notes on the repertory played and Liszt's comments to the performers.

These two sources document a total of fourteen performances of organ works either composed by or ascribed to Johann Sebastian Bach. In three instances, the work played is specified only to the extent that it was one of the seven transcribed by Liszt.[56] On another occasion, the nerdy Wilhelm Berger (whom Liszt had already dubbed "*Kontrapunkt*") ventured Liszt's transcriptions of the Prelude in B Minor and the "Wedge" fugue, only to be chastised for his dry, "conservatory-like" style.[57] Bach's Fantasy and Fugue in G Minor, as arranged by Liszt, was played three times, but rather sloppily in two instances.[58] One of the offenders tried to blame a particularly rough passage in the fugue on her frequent traveling, which prompted Liszt to joke that she had lost "those notes" somewhere en route. The other (a Turk by the name of Francesco Della Sudda Bey) was told by Liszt to "do his dirty laundry" at home. But Liszt did offer this student one bit of real advice, which was to play the episodes in the fugue "with an effect of casualness" and in sharp contrast to all the statements of the subject. (As we will soon see, Liszt made this same recommendation for the Fugue in A Minor, BWV 543/2.) If Liszt's transcription in its published form is any indication, he was advocating a relatively light, staccato touch for these passages, which he referred to as *Zwischenspiele* (interludes).

Otherwise, we are left with four performances of Tausig's arrangement of the Toccata in D Minor (BWV 565) and two of Liszt's transcription of the Prelude and Fugue in A Minor. Despite Liszt's admiration of Tausig's transcription, he was somewhat annoyed by its popularity. At one of his classes in 1883, he simply refused to hear it, complaining that it had already been played "three or four times" that summer.[59] The following summer, he griped that he had already heard the arrangement "at least a dozen times" but allowed it to be performed anyway.[60] Sneering at how Tausig had mishandled the three mordents at the outset, Liszt further humiliated the student (Alfred Reisenauer) by remarking that "every jackass of a modern pianist" played that transcription. Thankfully, Liszt also offered some constructive criticism, recommending that the sixteenth notes in measures 12–15 be organized into small groups rather than played continuously. (No doubt he was thinking of the four-note motive that rises sequentially in the right hand.) At one of his classes two years earlier, Liszt had suggested left-hand chords instead of repeated notes for this segment, which he believed to be most atypical of Bach.[61] Not by coincidence had Liszt focused on this same passage in advising Gottschalg how to register the toccata on the organ.

A performance of Tausig's transcription cited in neither of these diaries was that by August Stradal in late September 1884.[62] Having just arrived in Weimar, the twenty-four-year-old intended to make his master class debut with one of Liszt's own works. But after being convinced by another pupil that the master detested such flattery, Stradal settled on Tausig's arrangement, even though he considered it inferior to Liszt's transcriptions, especially those of the G-minor fantasy and fugue and the Preludes and Fugues in A Minor and E Minor. When Liszt saw the score lying on top of his Bechstein, he bellowed (again) that he had already heard that transcription "a hundred times" that year. He even demanded that the owner of the score step forward. Stradal did so, and offered to play something else instead. But when Liszt realized that the perpetrator was a newcomer, he allowed the toccata to be performed. According to Stradal's memoirs, he played "purely and cleanly," despite a bad case of nerves.

Stradal continued his studies with Liszt in Weimar, Budapest, and Rome until the master's death in July 1886. In May 1885 the two traveled together from Weimar to nearby Erfurt for a performance of Bach's B Minor Mass.[63] On the trip back—and obviously inspired by the music he had just heard— Liszt waxed nostalgic over his Bach transcriptions and maintained that it was "essential" for pianists to continue playing Bach's organ works. Realizing how many of these works were still untouched, he even went so far as to charge the younger generation with the task of transcribing *all* of Bach's organ compositions, along with the six Brandenburg Concertos, the St. John and St. Matthew Passions, and the B Minor Mass. Stradal did not take Liszt's injunction lightly. Rather, he would go on to transcribe well over one hundred organ works composed by or attributed to Bach.[64] One of these, appropriately enough, was the very toccata played by Stradal at his first master class appearance.

As for the A-minor prelude and fugue, we need to remind ourselves that this work had long been one of Liszt's favorites. That he continued playing it well into his sixties is attested to by a letter he wrote on 20 May 1877 to his friend Olga von Meyendorff. Liszt was in Hanover at this time to conduct at the annual festival of the *Allgemeiner Deutscher Musikverein,* and he was apparently hosted by the festival's organizers, Hans and Ingeborg von Bronsart. A few days earlier, the Bronsarts held a musical soiree at their home, where the guests of honor were none other than Prince Albrecht of Prussia and his wife, Princess Marie of Sachsen-Altenburg.[65] Apropos of this event, Liszt penned these lines:

> Last Thursday, Prince and Princess Albrecht spent the evening at the Bronsarts. I played several piano pieces for them—starting with the Fugue and Prelude in *A* minor for organ long ago transcribed for piano by your very humble servant [at this point, Liszt notates the first eight measures of the fugue subject].
>
> Mme Schumann having in the past been so kind as to play this transcription in public, it has been accepted as tolerable, even in the conservatories of

the *Hochschulen,* where my name is excluded and is considered an insult to sound doctrine.[66]

The reference here to Clara Schumann's "kindness" is somewhat shocking, considering her hostility toward Liszt (see the discussion at the beginning of this chapter). Furthermore, Clara herself had decades earlier transcribed this same piece and made it a staple of her concert repertory. What could have possessed her to switch to Liszt's arrangement?

Liszt participated in a very different "performance" of the A-minor fugue in Weimar at an alfresco dinner given in his honor on 7 September 1883.[67] The affair had been organized by his American pupils, including Lachmund, and featured various American dishes and decorations. Over coffee and whipped cream, one of the Americans (Arthur Bird) began to lead his fellow students in singing the subject of the A-minor fugue, knowing how fond Liszt was of this movement. According to Lachmund, the performance then evolved into a parlor game whose effect was not so unlike a medieval hocket:

> While coffee was sipped, Bird created some fun by starting those near him to singing the theme of Bach's A-minor fugue, familiar to every Lisztianer, in such a way that each sang only one note, but in correct pitch and on time, as his or her turn came. It is not easy to do; the errors and frantic efforts made by some in trying to catch the right note of the zig-zagging theme quickly enough caused much merriment. Liszt now became interested, so it was tried around the table, the Master catching his note on the fly when [his turn came].[68]

Lachmund does not indicate whether the group was able to get through all fifty-five notes of this extremely long theme. If so, the melody would have circulated around the table almost three times, with each of the twenty persons in attendance attempting at least two notes!

More to the subject at hand, Lachmund is also our source for a master class given by Liszt on 1 June 1882 at which one of the students evidently performed both the prelude and fugue. In addition, Liszt essayed the fugue himself and spoke about each movement:

> A young man had brought Bach's A-minor fugue, in the Liszt arrangement. Liszt seated himself at the grand, to illustrate to us his idea as to the proper interpretation of a Bach fugue. There was nothing of the old-fashioned stiffness of rhythm or dryness of tone one often hears in the interpretation of these fugues. There was freedom in the phrasing, as also in the cadenza-like runs [at the end of the fugue]. He made a very fine effect with the "divertimentos" (*Zwischenspiele*) which he played with lightness akin to indifference.
> "You see," he explained, "these *divertimento* measures, or little interludes, are *Nebensache* (side issues) and are intended to rest the mind for a moment,

and if you play them in this manner, with no pretense at expression, the re-entry of the theme will have a refreshing effect."

"There are two things one should always observe when playing a fugue," he continued, "that is, play just as you would at the organ, do not keep the keys down after playing them [for clarity of articulation], and play the theme at each return in the same style and rhythm, which, however, does not mean that you may not play it *piano* or *forte* at pleasure."

Of the little cadenza-like runs, he said: "Do not play these strictly in time, but with a little freedom" At the trill in the 23rd measure [of the prelude]: "One may extend this as though there were a hold on it."

It struck me that there were no expression marks in his arrangement. . . . When I expressed my regret at this, he said: "You see, I preferred to omit suggestions as to expression, rather than give the critics an opportunity to devour me and cry out at modernizing Bach; and pianists can put these in to suit their own tastes." Then, rising from his seat, he added significantly, as if he wished to go on record: "That is the way I should play Bach—and I do not think Bach would chastise me for it if he were here."[69]

According to Göllerich's diary, Liszt touched on some of these same issues at a class on 26 June 1886 that included a performance by Sophie Olsen of the A-minor fugue.[70] He expressed his particular admiration for the lengthy *manualiter* interlude in the middle of the fugue and recommended a fermata for the long, written-out tremolo (described by Lachmund as a "trill") in measure 23 of the prelude. And he once again defended the lack of dynamic markings in the published version of his arrangement: "I have indicated no *f* or *p* because the great Bach wrote none, and one may not add anything to him; that would be a sin."[71] He suggested furthermore that the fugue begin softly and that plenty of pedal be used for those passages where the organ pedal line is doubled at the lower octave.

Unfortunately—and surely to Olsen's embarrassment—Liszt also revealed the male-chauvinist side of his personality by quipping that ever since Clara Schumann had played that fugue in Leipzig forty years earlier, "all the ladies" had begun to play it. As discussed in chapter 2, Liszt was reminiscing here about his visit to the city in either 1840 or 1841. By that time, he had already gotten to know the fugue on his own, but hearing it rendered by a fellow virtuoso like Clara probably heightened his interest. Whatever the case, Liszt's lifelong advocacy of this movement—as a performer, transcriber, and teacher—is surely one reason for its enduring popularity.

FOUR

Johannes Brahms

MUSIC HISTORY HAS NEVER KNOWN a greater Bachian than Johannes Brahms. As a performer, Brahms championed Bach's music his entire life. As a composer, he regularly assimilated Bach's style into his own works, irrespective of medium or genre. And he made no secret that Bach was the composer he exalted above all others. Brahms also possessed a formidable knowledge of Bach's oeuvre.

In the domain of organ music, Brahms composed preludes, fugues, and chorale settings for the instrument that are undoubtedly modeled after organ works by Bach. He also included Bach organ works on his piano recitals. Moreover, the multitudinous inscriptions found in his personal copies of the organ-music volumes of the Bachgesellschaft edition attest to his diligent study of this repertory. Brahms's reception of Bach's organ music is evinced further by biographical information, certain theoretical documents, and his personal copy of Philipp Spitta's Bach biography.

An Overview

Brahms was introduced to the music of Bach at an early age, during his formative years in his native Hamburg.[1] Both of his piano teachers there, Otto F. W. Cossel and Eduard Marxsen, made sure the boy played Bach at his lessons, and Marxsen gave him a thorough grounding in the theory behind the music. Brahms also investigated Bach's works on his own, acquiring a number of scores in the process. Tellingly, when the fifteen-year-old gave his first solo piano recital in September 1848, his program included a Bach fugue.

The earliest evidence of Brahms's encounter specifically with Bach's organ music dates from his trip to Düsseldorf in the fall of 1853, a sojourn undertaken for the express purpose of meeting Robert Schumann (who immediately recognized the young man's genius). A few days after arriving on 30 September, Brahms performed at the home of the notary public Joseph Euler. Also present that evening was Schumann's pupil Albert Dietrich, who described the scene as follows:

> Brahms was asked to play, and executed Bach's Toccata in F and his own Scherzo in E-flat Minor with wonderful power and mastery; bending his head down over the keys and, as was his wont, humming the melody aloud as he played. He remained detached from the torrent of praise with which his performance was greeted. Everyone marveled at his remarkable talent, and, above all, we young musicians were unanimous in our enthusiastic admiration of the supremely artistic qualities of his playing, at times so powerful, or, when occasion demanded it, so exquisitely tender, but always full of character.[2]

Of course, the Bach work rendered so brilliantly by the young Brahms at this soiree was the Toccata in F Major, BWV 540/1, Bach's only toccata for any instrument in this key. He played his own arrangement, which he may never have bothered to notate. According to Max Kalbeck, Brahms's friend and first major biographer, Brahms once referred to this movement as "the heavenly barrel-organ toccata," no doubt due to its perpetual sixteenth-note motion.[3] He must also have appreciated that the toccata begins with a canon, for this was a technique that fascinated Brahms his whole life.[4] Furthermore, the opening 168 measures are rather easy to adapt to the piano. Whenever the hands play, the feet merely sustain a pedal point, which at the piano may be dispensed with altogether; otherwise, the hands are idle while the theme is stated as a pedal solo.

As discussed in chapter 2, the F-major was likewise a favorite work of Robert Schumann, who may well have attended the gathering at his friend Euler's that night.[5] Regardless, Schumann would have had many opportunities to hear Brahms play the work at his own home. Midway through Brahms's stay, another devotee of Bach's organ music paid Schumann a visit, and he was none other than the organist-painter J. J. B. Laurens, the Frenchman for whom Liszt had played Bach's A-minor prelude and fugue. We know that Laurens—a great admirer of Schumann's—painted portraits of both composers, and one can easily imagine that the three played and discussed Bach's organ works. (Clara Schumann could have contributed significantly in this regard, too.) Brahms's trip to Düsseldorf, then, can only have heightened his interest in this repertoire.

He would return there in March 1854, but under very different circumstances. A week earlier, Robert Schumann had attempted suicide, and Brahms's purpose now was to assist Clara with the running of the household. He remained intermittently throughout Robert's hospitalization, developing a strong romantic attachment to the much older woman. The two became best friends for life, and from the outset one of their mutual interests was the music of Bach.

At this time, Brahms seems to have developed a special passion for Bach's organ works. Take, for instance, the little known fact that at some point he copied out for Clara the tender "Largo e spiccato" movement from Bach's organ transcription of Antonio Vivaldi's Concerto in D Minor for Two Violins and Cello, op. 3, no. 11. As can be seen in figure 4–1, Brahms wrote in the bottom right corner of the manuscript *der lieben Clara* ("to dear Clara") and sideways in the right margin *Zum Abschied von Düsseldorf. Johannes.* ("Upon [my] departure from Düsseldorf. Johannes.").[6] To judge from the latter inscription, Brahms presented the folio to Clara on the occasion of his trip from Düsseldorf to Hamburg in the fall of 1856, a journey that closed this chapter of his life. In the top right corner, Brahms attributes the movement not to J. S. Bach or Vivaldi but to "Friedemann Bach." This is entirely expected, since during the nineteenth century this piece was ascribed to Wilhelm Friedemann Bach and known simply as his "Concerto for Organ." Brahms's orthography identifies his exemplar as the edition by F. C. Griepenkerl, published by Peters in 1844.[7] Like the F-major toccata, the first movement of this transcription begins with a fast, *manualiter* canon above a tonic pedal point.

On 11 July 1857 Brahms mailed this same transcription to his friend Joseph Joachim, so that Joachim might peruse this movement. As Brahms wrote in his accompanying letter, "I am enclosing an organ concerto by Friedemann Bach because of its beautiful Adagio."[8] Brahms and Joachim had for over a year been exchanging polyphonic compositions and exercises in hopes of improving their contrapuntal skills.[9] But Brahms obviously sent this movement, which could hardly be less contrapuntal, because of its lyrical solo line and colorful harmonies. He might also have anticipated that Joachim—one of the era's great violinists—would have enjoyed playing it.

Brahms's interest in Bach's organ music during these two and a half years may have been spurred initially by his exposure to Robert Schumann's library. He had free access to the collection, and Clara entrusted him with rearranging its contents following her move to a new apartment in June 1854, after the birth of her son Felix. A true bibliophile, Brahms wrote to Albert Dietrich about the "great delight" that Schumann's books and music gave him.[10] He could have studied numerous prints of Bach's organ works (see table 2–1), but none suggests itself more readily than Mendelssohn's edition of the *Orgelbüchlein:* Schumann marked in his personal copy seven near instances of parallel octaves in the setting of "Wir Christenleut," and Brahms cited all seven passages in his collection *Octaven und Quinten* (to be discussed later in this chapter).

Later that summer, Clara told Brahms of her desire "to learn to play the organ to such an extent that I can play Robert some of his own pieces, once

Figure 4–1 Concerto in D Minor after Vivaldi, BWV 596, third movement. Manuscript copied by Johannes Brahms for Clara Schumann (Robert-Schumann-Haus, Zwickau, catalogue no. 11509-A 1c)

he has recovered."[11] While she planned to focus on her husband's compositions, her intention merely to take up the organ again must have given Brahms
some impetus in the direction of Bach's organ works. Not coincidentally, by
November he was playing the organ himself—possibly for the very first time.
Given his already strong inclination toward Bach's music, it is easy to believe
that he tried out various organ works by the master, including even such a
virtuoso showpiece as the F-major toccata.

To what extent he practiced over the next year and a half is unclear, but
on 16 May 1856 Brahms informed Clara that he had been playing a fugue on
the organ and that he was making real headway with the instrument. This
fugue was probably one composed by Brahms himself, for by that summer
he had finished a fugue in A-flat minor for organ as well as a prelude and
fugue in A minor for the instrument (WoO 8 and 9, respectively).[12] Brahms
made sure to present Clara with autograph manuscripts of both works.

By virtue of their genre and medium, these pieces unquestionably represent an homage to Bach's organ music. And in the case of the prelude and
fugue, commentators have posited that Brahms appropriated specific organ
works by Bach as compositional models.[13] Surely one exemplar was Bach's
famous organ fugue in the same key, which, like Brahms's A-minor fugue,
includes a long *manualiter* interlude at its midpoint and a toccata-like coda
comprised largely of diminished-seventh harmonies. Most tellingly, both
codas feature in the span of two measures a torrent of pedal sixteenth notes
that arpeggiate the tonic triad from A all the way to c', and then back down
to E (see examples 4–1 and 4–2). Especially since Brahms may have encrypted
Clara's name into both movements of his prelude and fugue,[14] it bears re-
stating that Bach's A-minor fugue was one of her favorite pieces. Thus, in referring to the movement here, Brahms may have been paying tribute to Clara
as well as to Bach. One may also conjecture that the Bach "Fugue in A
Minor" performed by Brahms on 29 May 1856 at a piano recital in Cologne
was this same movement.[15]

Over the next two years, Brahms would follow with a prelude and fugue
in G minor for organ (WoO 10) and an organ prelude on the Passiontide
chorale "O Traurigkeit, o Herzeleid" (WoO 7). Both of these pieces, too, are
heavily indebted to Bachian models. For example, the otherwise unique form
of Brahms's G-minor prelude must have been suggested by Bach's G-minor
organ fantasy.[16] In both movements, rhapsodic figuration alternates with
imitative material in the order free–strict–free–strict–free, and within each
movement exactly the same themes are employed for the two imitative sections. Much of Brahms's free passagework here also appears to derive from
Bach's fantasy as well as from his G-minor organ prelude, BWV 535/1. In the
case of "O Traurigkeit," a work perhaps written as a lament on the death of
Robert Schumann, Brahms's template was furnished by the chorale preludes

Example 4–1 Fugue in A Minor, BWV 543/2

of Bach's *Orgelbüchlein,* just as we saw in chapter 2 with Schumann's "Figurirter Choral."[17] Owing to the strict four-voice texture and presence of an
obbligato pedal, Brahms hews even more closely to this design.

It may have been another fifteen years before Brahms would again write
for the organ, and by 1857 he had evidently abandoned any plans of becoming an organist.[18] Nonetheless, Clara Schumann heard echoes of Bach's organ
music in a choral work written by the budding composer in September 1858.
Brahms had mailed her his *Ave Maria,* op. 12, and fully expected a critique in
return. Clara obliged in a letter of 7 November 1859, about a month before
the work's first public performance, praising various attributes of the music
and concluding that "the mood [of the piece] always reminds me of the delightful Pastorale by Bach, which we have sometimes played together."[19]

This statement can refer to no other work than the Pastorale in F Major,
BWV 590, Bach's only composition of any kind bearing this name. Clara had
probably been introduced to the Pastorale by her husband, who in his review
of Mendelssohn's all-Bach recital had described the work as "mined from the

Example 4–2 Johannes Brahms, Fugue in A Minor, WoO 9/2

deepest depths in which such a composition may be found." She, in turn, had most likely brought the piece to Brahms's attention. That it held special significance for their friendship is implied by the memoirs of Eugenie Schumann, who reports that her mother performed the Pastorale for Brahms at their home in early October 1895, less than a year before Clara's death, on the occasion of Brahms's very last visit.[20] Clara likewise played for Brahms at that time, in addition to two of his own compositions, an unspecified organ prelude and fugue by Bach, probably the A-minor. Overcome with emotion, Brahms afterwards told Eugenie that her mother had played "quite splendidly."

A comparison between the opening measures of Brahms's *Ave Maria* and the first movement of the Pastorale will suffice to explain Clara's remark (see examples 4–3 and 4–4). Both movements are in F major and in compound-duple meter, both open with a relatively long note on f′ above a pedal point on F, and both regularly employ flowing eighth notes in parallel thirds. With respect to the long pedal points that occur throughout both movements, it is worth mentioning that the original version of Brahms's work has an organ accompaniment.[21] Did Brahms realize that the first movement of the Pastorale begins according to the same contrapuntal scheme as the F-major toccata? Both movements begin as a canon at the octave starting on f′, supported by a pedal point on F.

To focus again on Brahms's reception of this toccata, he probably played it more often than any other organ work by Bach. The printed programs of his piano recitals document one performance in the 1850s, three in the 1860s, and two in the 1870s. We also know of four performances, besides that in Düsseldorf, at private gatherings. For example, around the time of his first solo recital in Vienna, on 29 November 1862, Brahms played the toccata at the home of the Viennese lawyer Ignaz Grassl von Rechten (whose family had sought out his services as a piano teacher).[22] The family marveled at how their guest "roared through" this movement, and they were impressed as well by how "splendidly" he played Bach organ fugues. A few years later—on 7 February 1864, to be exact—Brahms performed the toccata for no less an august personage than Richard Wagner, at the latter's villa (in Penzing) on the outskirts of Vienna.[23] And in June 1865, while in Basel to attend a performance of Bach's St. Matthew Passion, Brahms played the movement for some of his acquaintances there.[24]

Finally, according to his friend Julius Röntgen, Brahms once played the F-major for "a small group of Dutch friends," including the conductor Johannes Verhulst.[25] This performance likely occurred in Amsterdam no earlier than 1877, by which time both Röntgen and Verhulst had settled in the city, but certainly no later than 1891, the year of Verhulst's death. During this

Example 4–3 Pastorale in F Major, BWV 590, first movement

period, Brahms made five trips to Amsterdam (February 1878, January 1881, January 1882, February 1884, and November 1885), and on any one of them he could have played the toccata. The elderly Verhulst praised this movement just as his comrades Mendelssohn and Schumann had done, remarking: "How far that man Bach was in advance of his own time!" Brahms simply quipped: "Of his own time? No, of all times!"

None of Brahms's performances of the F-major mattered more for his career than the one he offered at his Vienna debut. He wrote to his parents the next day that the audience had vociferously applauded every number,[26] and the event was a critical success to boot (although not every critic received Brahms's music with the same degree of enthusiasm they all showed for his playing). Writing for the *Deutsche Musikzeitung*, Selmar Bagge conceded: "We have to bestow high praise not only on [Brahms's] enormous technical attainment, but also on a performance instinct [imbued] with musical genius, on a treatment of the instrument as fascinating as it was original."[27] The same reviewer found Brahms's interpretation of the F-major toccata "peculiarly organ-like, sonorous, with great economy of dynamics, but also with a broadly dispensed sound in the main passages."[28] Judging from this description, Brahms played the toccata as if to simulate a full organ registration.

Example 4–4 Johannes Brahms, *Ave Maria*, op. 12

Twice in 1867, once in 1868, and once again in 1876 Brahms included on his piano recitals a work printed in the program as Bach's "Fantasy in G Major." This title must denote either BWV 571 or BWV 572, the only fantasias in this key composed by or attributed to Bach, and both of which happen to be for organ. To ascertain which fantasy is meant, we need only consider that (1) a critic in 1868 identified the Bach "organ fantasy" played by Brahms at a concert in Hamburg as BWV 572 and that (2) Brahms prepared a study score of the *gravement* section of this work (which will be discussed later in this chapter). There is also the fact that BWV 571 was not even available in print before 1881. One may therefore conclude that all four performances were of BWV 572.

Arrey von Dommer was the Hamburg critic who reviewed the recital given by Brahms there on 11 March 1868. In describing how the native son had performed, Dommer offered these not entirely flattering comments:

> Herr Brahms uses the pedal rather a lot, something he is admittedly forced to do by many otherwise unmanageable chords and legati in wide leaps etc. Still, his playing, as commanding as it is full-voiced, sometimes loses thereby in transparency, and runs together. That was especially the case with the Bach fantasy, originally for organ (G major, edition of the organ works by Griepenkerl and Roitzsch, Volume 4, Number 11). In the transcription of organ works for piano Herr Brahms possesses astonishing power; his excellent legato even in the most full-voiced sections and his mastery of large sonorities stand him in especially good stead there, and with their help he knows how to create the closest possible organ effect on the piano.[29]

The Viennese critic—an organist himself—had detected an "organ-like" quality in Brahms's use of an unvarying *forte* to play the F-major toccata. But Dommer sensed the instrument more in the pianist's legato touch. Since the first and last sections of the fantasy (save the final cadence) are devoid of chords per se, Dommer is obviously describing how Brahms negotiated the work's *gravement* section, which encompasses five and sometimes six voices. Contrary to the review, this thick texture did not necessarily "force" Brahms to employ the damper pedal throughout, but he would have relied on the device for the sake of idiomatic piano playing. If he played the organ pedal part as left-hand octaves, which seems likely, he would have had no choice but to engage the mechanism constantly, perhaps at the expense of clarity.

The *gravement* section of this fantasy lends itself especially well to the piano, for, despite the necessity of playing tenths with the left hand, all the material before the concluding pedal point lies within the reach of ten fingers. (Easier still on the piano is the first section, which is for manuals only.) Indeed, according to a recent edition, this pedal point was originally the only pedal passage whatsoever in this section of the work.[30] One would like to believe, though, that Brahms was drawn to the music primarily because of its luxuriant harmonies, especially those involving suspensions. To quote Brahms's pupil Florence May, "he loved Bach's suspensions,"[31] and here the technique is used often enough to suggest continuous seventh and ninth chords.

Twice in November 1867 Brahms featured on his piano recitals a Bach work listed as "Pastorale and Gigue." No composition by this name appears in the Bach canon, but the word "Pastorale," as previously mentioned, can refer only to the Pastorale in F Major, BWV 590, whose four movements include a gigue (last movement) as well as a pastorale proper (first movement). Considering that (1) these are the only movements in F major and that (2) Bach sets the gigue as a fugue, we may assume that Brahms played just these two movements as an ersatz prelude and fugue. They make for a remarkably easy piano transcription, since only the first movement even has a pedal part, and it is nothing more than a series of pedal points. This is not to imply, though, that convenience was the sole factor. As suggested earlier, Brahms may have thought highly enough of the first movement of the Pastorale to base his *Ave Maria* on it. And perhaps he heard in the gigue's theme an embellished version of one of his favorite tunes, the Christmas carol "Josef, lieber Josef, mein."[32] Others certainly have made this connection,[33] whether or not Bach himself intended it.

If the surviving documents are any indication, it was in 1867 that Brahms was most active as a public performer of Bach's organ music. In March he played the G-major fantasy, in April the F-major toccata (twice), and in November the Pastorale (twice) as well as the fantasy. It may therefore be significant that Brahms's still extant personal copy of an edition of the Prelude and Fugue in C Minor, BWV 549, bears his inscription *21 März .867*.[34] At the very least, one can imagine that in 1867 Brahms celebrated Bach's birthday (21 March) by playing this work at a private soiree. Perhaps he contemplated performing it in public, too.

Still another Bach organ work that Brahms performed at the piano is the A-minor prelude and fugue. We have already speculated that he played the fugue in recital as early as 1856, but his first documented performance (of both movements) took place nine years later, in December 1865, at a private meeting of the Cologne Musikverein.[35] Two private performances in Vienna are documented as well. The first occurred on 12 November 1882 at a private home, in the company of the pianist Karl-Heinrich Barth, who was concertizing in Vienna that month, and Maria and Richard Fellinger.[36] Barth performed first, and then Frau Fellinger summoned the courage to ask Brahms—by that time a world-renowned figure—to play something. The great man strode to the piano and dazzled his listeners with an "incomparable" rendition of the gigue-like fugue, obviously playing from memory. After this breaking of the ice, the Fellingers issued Brahms an invitation to their home, commencing what would become an exceedingly close friendship. The other private performance was witnessed by Max Kalbeck, who one day was about to enter Brahms's quarters at no. 4 Karlsgasse when he heard the beginning of the A-minor prelude emanating from the Streicher piano.[37] Kalbeck waited in silence until Brahms had finished, and then Brahms called him in, exclaiming: "Now we will play the piece properly." Performing the very substantial work a second time, Brahms "outdid himself, without showing any sign of fatigue."

This performance could not have taken place prior to 1880, the date of Kalbeck's move to Vienna. He would eventually become one of Brahms's most frequent guests, right up to the master's death in 1897. Writing about the period 1895–96, Kalbeck claimed that "almost always" when he came to call, the old man was seated at the piano playing Bach—and not just any Bach but "mostly" organ fugues.[38] We also read in Kalbeck's biography about a performance given by Brahms in June 1886, while the two men were vacationing together in Thun, Switzerland.[39] On that occasion, Brahms played at a soiree attended by Kalbeck, Friedrich Hegar (a Swiss violinist and friend of Brahms), and the conductor Karl Munzinger, and treated his audience to a "splendid toccata and fugue" by Bach, played with enough gusto to evoke the "roar" of the organ. This was probably yet another performance of the Toccata in F Major, BWV 540/1, along with its fugue.

Three additional private performances remain to be considered. One took place during the last week of January 1885, while Brahms was in Krefeld for a series of concerts.[40] At some point, following a midday meal at the home of the violist Alwin von Beckerath, Brahms played at the piano unspecified organ works by Bach (in addition to Viennese waltzes). According to Beckerath's diary, their honored guest brought to the music not a raw power but "an unending charm and grace."

A second performance dates from Brahms's visit in late May 1896 to the Hagerhof, an estate situated on the banks of the Rhine, in the vicinity of Honnef. Having just traveled to Bonn to attend Clara Schumann's funeral, Brahms journeyed on the same day (24 May) to the Hagerhof so that he might see some of his friends who had congregated there for a private music festival.[41] They included the violinist Richard Barth, the violist Alwin von Beckerath, and the banker-pianist Rudolf von der Leyen. Brahms had planned to visit only a few hours but wound up staying a full four days. Virtually all the music played, including some "Bach organ preludes and toccatas" rendered by Brahms, served as a memorial tribute to Clara. It cannot be coincidental, of course, that this repertory was especially beloved by Clara as well as by Brahms himself.

In the third performance, Brahms played organ fugues by Bach in early January 1879 at the home of his Leipzig friends, Heinrich and Elisabet von

Herzogenberg. This according to the memoirs of Ethel Smyth (the suffragist), who was then one of Heinrich's pupils. To judge from her account, Brahms may have taken special care in these movements to highlight the fugue subject when stated in an inner voice:

> I like best to think of Brahms at the piano, playing his own compositions or Bach's mighty organ fugues, sometimes accompanying himself *with a sort of muffled roar,* as of Titans stirred to sympathy in the bowels of the earth. The veins in his forehead stood out, his wonderful bright blue eyes became veiled, and he seemed the incarnation of the restrained power in which his own work is forged. For his playing was never noisy, and when lifting a submerged theme out of a tangle of music he used jokingly to ask us to admire the gentle sonority of his "tenor thumb."[42]

Brahms's hosts on this occasion were redoubtable connoisseurs of Bach's music. Among other things, Heinrich was the director of the Leipzig Bach-verein, and Elisabet was one of the group's soprano soloists. Not surprisingly, the couple's correspondence with Brahms frequently involves Bach's music, and in three instances the organ works are mentioned. For example, in a letter to Heinrich dated 21 March (again, Bach's birthday) 1882, Brahms inquired about certain volumes of the Bachgesellschaft edition he had not yet received, reporting that he already owned the volume containing the "chorale preludes."[43] More significant are two missives from Elisabet to Brahms.[44] In the first, dated 19 February 1878, she urged her former teacher to try his hand at solfège composition and informed him that she was currently using Bach's "organ sonatas" for that purpose. This is clearly a reference to Bach's six Trio Sonatas for organ, BWV 525–30. In the second letter, written on 27 March 1881, Elisabet reported on the activities of Wilhelm Rust, who had a few years earlier moved to Leipzig to assume the post of cantor at St. Thomas's. Brahms would have had a vested interest in this subject, since he had recommended Rust for the job after turning it down himself. But according to Elisabet, who loved to tease Brahms whenever possible, Rust was causing nothing but "trouble and disappointment" with what she considered his tasteless transcriptions of Bach organ works. She was aghast that Rust's music for Palm Sunday that year was to include his orchestral arrangement of Bach's "G-minor organ fugue," probably meaning the "great" Fugue in G Minor, BWV 542/2. Likewise, she frowned on Rust's choral arrangements of certain organ chorales, one of which was the miscellaneous setting of "Durch Adams Fall ist ganz verderbt," BWV 705.[45]

It is worth pointing out that both Rust and Heinrich von Herzogenberg were organists, for very few of Brahms's acquaintances played the instrument.[46] With the notable exception of Anton Bruckner, his most virtuosic organist-acquaintance may have been Samuel de Lange of Rotterdam. On 8

December 1872 the Dutchman appeared as organ soloist on a concert organized by Brahms in his capacity as artistic director and conductor of the Gesellschaft der Musikfreunde in Vienna. This unusual emphasis on organ music was due to the Gesellschaft's new Ladegast organ, a three-manual instrument that Brahms wished to showcase in all its glory. Toward this end, Lange played a Handel concerto and Bach's Prelude and Fugue in E-flat Major. Just as Mendelssohn had used the E-flat in Birmingham to show the "whole range" of that organ, so Lange must have taken advantage of the work's sectionalized structure to demonstrate various registrations. This was surely not the first time he had played the piece, as Lange was well known in his home country for his all-Bach organ recitals.[47]

About two years later, the Viennese faithful were treated to a very different interpretation of this work, when on 28 February 1875 Brahms began a concert at the Gesellschaft with Bernhard Scholz's recently published orchestral transcription of the E-flat prelude.[48] Scholz was an old friend, not to mention a fellow signatory of the infamous "Manifesto" against Liszt and the New German School presumably drafted in 1860 by Brahms himself.[49] He had also hosted Brahms as a guest performer and conductor in Breslau only weeks before the Gesellschaft concert in question, so perhaps the decision to mount the transcription was made during that visit.[50] Whatever the case, the instrumentation chosen by Scholz—two flutes, two oboes, two clarinets, two bassoons, one contrabassoon, two horns, two trumpets, three trombones, timpani, and strings—closely matches that employed by Brahms in his own orchestral works.

Enumerated in table 4–1 are all the performances of Bach's organ music that Brahms is known to have undertaken. While this list spans his entire career, it of course does not give a complete picture. Still, one pattern emerges quite clearly, and that is Brahms's preference for the "big" free works: fantasies, fugues, preludes, and toccatas. He took special pleasure in playing (and conducting) these pieces, whether in concert or at private gatherings.

Let us conclude this overview by considering Brahms's Fourth Symphony and Bach's Passacaglia in C minor. The finale of the symphony represents the earliest instance in the symphonic repertoire of a true ostinato-bass form. And it has long been established that Brahms based his ostinato theme on one from Bach's Cantata 150, *Nach dir, Herr, verlanget mich,* just as scholars have traditionally assumed that Bach's D-minor violin chaconne served as an exemplar for the overall structure of the movement. Brahms also seems to have relied heavily on Dietrich Buxtehude's E-minor organ chaconne.[51] To judge from Brahms's deployment of a theme comprising eight bars rather than the standard four, as well as his transfer of the theme into the treble register for a middle group of variations, a fourth model was Bach's C-minor passacaglia.[52] As one of Bach's most famous organ works, the passacaglia was

Table 4–1 Documented Performances by Brahms of Bach's Organ Works

Date	Place	Works Performed
early October 1853	Düsseldorf (home of the notary public Joseph Euler)	Toccata in F Major, BWV 540/1
2 February 1856	Hamburg-Altona (piano recital)	Toccata in F Major, BWV 540/1
fall of 1862	Vienna (home of the lawyer Ignaz Grassl von Rechten)	Toccata in F Major, BWV 540/1; fugues
29 November 1862	Vienna (piano recital)	Toccata in F Major, BWV 540/1
7 February 1864	Penzing (villa of Richard Wagner)	Toccata in F Major, BWV 540/1
June 1865	Basel (private performance)	Toccata in F Major, BWV 540/1
December 1865	Cologne (private performance for members of the local Musikverein)	Prelude and Fugue in A Minor, BWV 543
17 March 1867	Vienna (piano recital)	Fantasy in G Major, BWV 572
7 April 1867	Vienna (piano recital)	Toccata in F Major, BWV 540/1
22 April 1867	Budapest (piano recital)	Toccata in F Major, BWV 540/1
11 November 1867	Graz (piano recital)	Pastorale in F Major, BWV 590
12 November 1867	Klagenfurt (piano recital)	Fantasy in G Major, BWV 572
23 November 1867	Vienna (piano recital)	Pastorale in F Major, BWV 590
11 March 1868	Hamburg (piano recital)	Fantasy in G Major, BWV 572
28 February 1875	Vienna (concert by the orchestra and choir of the Gesellschaft der Musikfreunde)	Prelude in E-flat Major, BWV 552/1 (orchestral transcription by Bernhard Scholz)
21 January 1876	Amsterdam (piano recital)	Toccata in F Major, BWV 540/1
29 January 1876	Utrecht (piano recital)	Fantasy in G Major, BWV 572/1

Table 4–1 (continued)

Date	Place	Works Performed
21 February 1876	Frankfurt (piano recital)	Toccata in F Major, BWV 540/1
February 1878– November 1885	Amsterdam (private performance in the presence of Julius Röntgen and Johannes Verhulst)	Toccata in F Major, BWV 540/1
early January 1879	Leipzig (home of Heinrich and Elisabet von Herzogenberg)	fugues
no earlier than 1880	Vienna (private performance at Brahms's apartment, in the presence of Max Kalbeck)	Prelude and Fugue in A Minor, BWV 543
12 November 1882	Vienna (private performance in the presence of Karl-Heinrich Barth and Maria and Richard Fellinger)	Fugue in A Minor, BWV 543/2
25–30 January 1885	Krefeld (home of Alwin von Beckerath)	unspecified
June 1886	Thun (private performance in the presence of Friedrich Hegar, Max Kalbeck, and Karl Munzinger)	toccata and fugue (BWV 540?)
1895–96	Vienna (private performances at Brahms's apartment, in the presence of Max Kalbeck)	fugues
24–27 May 1896	vicinity of Honnef (private performances at the Hagerhof, in the presence of Richard Barth, Alwin von Beckerath, Rudolf von der Leyen, and others)	preludes and toccatas

surely known by Brahms early on, long before his composition of this symphony in the summer of 1885. Indeed, writing over fifteen years earlier to the critic Adolf Schubring, Brahms had cited Bach's passacaglia as a set of variations whose theme would allow a composer "to invent something actually new" and *in* whose theme a composer would "discover new melodies."[53] Regrettably, he never expounded on either of these ideas.

Brahms as a Scholar of Bach's Organ Works

Musical scholarship was critical to Brahms's existence, and Bach was the composer he most assiduously studied. As far as Bach's organ music is concerned, a wealth of documentation reveals Brahms's comprehensive knowledge not only of the free works but also of the chorale settings—literally hundreds of compositions. Furthermore, an investigation of Brahms's activities in this realm sheds light on his final work, the Eleven Chorale Preludes, op. 122.

THEORETICAL SOURCES

We will begin with the notion that Brahms was a theorist of Bach's organ works. The many analytical markings found in his personal copies of the organ-music volumes of the Bachgesellschaft edition certainly support this view, but these inscriptions will be considered later in conjunction with Spitta's Bach biography. Left are two documents entirely in Brahms's own hand, the famous collection that he titled *Octaven und Quinten* and his virtually unknown study score of the Fantasy in G Major, BWV 572.

The former manuscript, now readily available in facsimile, comprises eleven pages containing roughly 140 examples of parallel octaves, fifths, and related progressions discovered by Brahms in music ranging chronologically from Clemens non Papa to Georges Bizet.[54] More examples (over forty) are taken from Bach than any other composer. Brahms's aim was less to expose deficiencies in the works of the great masters than to compile interesting contrapuntal specimens. Indeed, he found many of the examples completely acceptable, an indication of his open-mindedness to the subject. (It might also be mentioned that Brahms was not above writing parallel fifths himself, as his organ compositions attest.)[55] Judging from the publication dates of his exemplars, he penned the first five pages between 1863 and 1864 and then set the manuscript aside until around 1890, at which point pages 6–8 were inscribed. Pages 9–11 appear to have originated slightly later, between 1891 and 1892.

As listed in table 4–2, a total of nine examples stem from organ works composed by or ascribed to Bach. The first seven appear on pages 1–5, the last two on pages 9–10. Thus they are separated by an interval of almost thirty years. For the first five examples, Brahms identified his exemplars as volumes

Table 4–2 Bach Organ Works Included in *Octaven und Quinten*

Work	Pagination in Manuscript	Date Entered into Manuscript	Exemplar
Fugue in C Minor, BWV 549/2	page 1	1863–64	Peters edition, volume 4 (1845)
Toccata, Adagio, and Fugue, BWV 564	page 2	1863–64	Peters edition, volume 3 (1845)
Concerto in A Minor after Vivaldi, BWV 593, last movement	page 2	1863–64	Peters edition, volume 8 (1852)
"Ach wie nichtig, ach wie flüchtig," BWV 644	page 2	1863–64	Peters edition, volume 5 (1846)
"Vater unser im Himmelreich," BWV 683	page 2	1863–64	Peters edition, volume 5 (1846)
Toccata in D Minor, BWV 565	page 3	1863–64	probably Peters edition, volume 4 (1845)
"Wir Christenleut," BWV 612	page 5	1863–64	probably Peters edition, volume 5 (1846)
Concerto in A Minor after Vivaldi, BWV 593, last movement	page 9	1891–92	Bachgesellschaft edition, volume 38 (1891)
Fugue in G Minor, BWV 535/2	page 10	1891–92	Bachgesellschaft edition, volume 15 (1867)

3, 4, 5, and 8 of the Peters edition of Bach's organ works, published between 1845 and 1852. His sixth and seventh examples are probably based on this edition as well. For the eighth and ninth examples, Brahms consulted two volumes from the Bachgesellschaft edition of Bach's complete works, published in 1891 and 1867, respectively. Except for the Bachgesellschaft volumes, none of Brahms's personal copies of these exemplars have survived.[56]

Included on pages 1–5 of the manuscript are, in the order of their appearance, excerpts from the Fugue in C Minor, BWV 549/2; the fugue from the Toccata, Adagio, and Fugue in C Major, BWV 564; the last movement of Bach's organ transcription (BWV 593) of Vivaldi's Concerto in A Minor for Two Violins, op. 3, no. 8; the *Orgelbüchlein* setting of "Ach wie nichtig, ach wie flüchtig"; the small setting of "Vater unser im Himmelreich" from Part 3 of the *Clavierübung;* the Toccata in D Minor, BWV 565; and the *Orgelbüchlein* setting of "Wir Christenleut." In the passage from the C-minor fugue, the outer parts form a parallel octave from E-flat to D between the second and third beats, despite the intervening rests (see example 4–5). Brahms, however, wrote the word *figuriert* ("figured") beside the example, meaning that it should be understood not in the context of strict voice leading but as ornamental passagework. At first glance, the excerpt from the Toccata, Adagio, and Fugue suggests a whole series of parallel fifths between the top two voices (see example 4–6). But, as Brahms's inscription *verm[inderte] Qu[inten]* connotes, the music alternates in every instance between a diminished and a perfect fifth, resulting in perfectly harmless "unequal fifths."

Following the excerpt from the Bach-Vivaldi concerto, which will be discussed shortly, we find two side-by-side excerpts from chorale preludes that apparently earned Brahms's tacit approval. In the setting of "Ach wie nichtig," parallel octaves from F-sharp to G obtain between the alto and bass on beats 3–4 (see example 4–7). The effect, though, is mitigated by a bass rest. Since elsewhere in the collection Brahms excuses parallels on the basis of intervening rests, one assumes he did so in this case, too. The excerpt from "Vater unser" implies parallel octaves from G to A between the bottom two voices on beats 3–4 (see example 4–8). But the progression is again that of unequal intervals (G to A versus G-sharp to A), and the two bass notes are separated by three rests as well.

As for the excerpts from the D-minor toccata and "Wir Christenleut," the former constitutes octave doubling rather than parallel octaves per se (see example 4–9).[57] Brahms was definitely more interested in how the arpeggiated root-position triads suggest parallel fifths every time the harmony changes. "Wir Christenleut," conversely, is a model of strict four-voice texture. As previously mentioned, Robert Schumann marked in his personal copy of the piece seven near instances of parallel fifths between the outer voices (see figure 2–3). Surely it cannot be happenstance that all seven pas-

Example 4–5 Fugue in C Minor, BWV 549/2

Example 4–6 Fugue from Toccata, Adagio, and Fugue, BWV 564

Example 4–7 "Ach wie nichtig, ach wie flüchtig," BWV 644

Example 4–8 "Vater unser im Himmelreich," BWV 683

Example 4–9 Toccata in D Minor, BWV 565

Example 4–10 "Wir Christenleut," BWV 612

sages were also referred to here by Brahms: he notated the first passage in full (see example 4–10) and wrote beside it *6 mal ähnlich wiederholt* ("repeated similarly six times"). What Brahms means by "similarly" is that the seven passages are based on essentially the same material. Unlike Schumann, though, he drew diagonal brackets between the last three pedal notes to indicate that actual parallel octaves are averted due to the intervening d.

That leaves the two excerpts entered in 1891–92, the latter of which is taken from the Fugue in G Minor, BWV 535/2 (see example 4–11). This is apparently the only one of the nine excerpts that Brahms found to be in clear-cut violation of contrapuntal practice. At issue are the parallel fifths between the inner voices during the transition from beat 2 to beat 3, something not even the most benevolent music theorist could tolerate. In this case, Brahms may have been alerted by the preface to his exemplar, which specifically mentions this passage (p. xxii).[58] The dagger drawn by Brahms beside the example probably symbolizes his disapproval. Since this is one of Bach's earliest keyboard fugues altogether—and one in which he struggles to maintain four-voice texture—the infraction may be attributed to the composer's inexperience.[59]

The remaining excerpt happens to be the same passage from the Bach-Vivaldi concerto that Brahms had entered back in 1863–64 (see example 4–12).

Example 4–11 Fugue in G Minor, BWV 535/2

Example 4–12 Concerto in A Minor after Vivaldi, BWV 593, third movement

When he first penned the example, he offered no verdict either way. But when he renotated the excerpt almost thirty years later, it carried his full endorsement. The key to understanding Brahms's change of mind lies in the excerpt from Bach's G-major harpsichord toccata that he inscribed on page 9 of the manuscript (see example 4–13). As in the concerto excerpt, the music constitutes a series of parallel-motion, first-inversion chords that could be construed as containing parallel octaves. Yet beside the passage Brahms first wrote *NB Uebermüthig u. Charakteristisch* ("NB Exuberant and Idiomatic") and then *NB Concert A moll von Vivaldi? Vielleicht* ("NB Concerto in A Minor by Vivaldi? Perhaps"). According to the first inscription, Brahms found the doubled chords in the toccata both musically compelling and appropriately textured for a keyboard instrument. The only explanation for the second inscription is that the passage reminded him of the same one from the Bach-Vivaldi concerto he had notated decades earlier, because only two examples later on the same page the latter passage reappears note for note.

Obviously, Brahms placed these two strikingly similar excerpts in close proximity so that they might be easily compared. What has never been mentioned is that his memory was likely jogged by the first volume of Spitta's

Example 4–13 Toccata in G Major, BWV 916, first movement

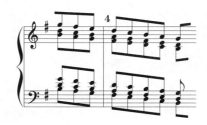

Bach biography, which Brahms had owned for almost two decades by this time. Regarding the strong stylistic affinities between this toccata movement and the concertos of Vivaldi, especially as transcribed for keyboard by Bach, Spitta writes: "The first bars of the *tutti* theme are similar in structure to those at the beginning of the second allegro movement in Vivaldi's Concerto in B Minor . . . and the heavy descending groups of chords for both hands remind us of the methods of execution which frequently occur in [Bach's] transcriptions of Vivaldi for the clavier."[60]

Beside the excerpt from the Vivaldi-Bach concerto, Brahms added a third inscription: *NB die Vorrede in der gr[ossen] Bach-Ausg[abe] hierüber ungenügend!* ("NB the preface in the great Bach edition is unsatisfactory concerning this!"). Here, he was responding to a comment found in volume 38 of the Bachgesellschaft edition, whose editor, Ernst Naumann, could abide these parallel octaves only in a melodic context. To avoid these parallels, Naumann instructed the player either to omit the upper voice, which he gave in small print as an optional part, or to omit all the harmonic material: "[In the manual], the upper voice that moves in octaves with the pedal is in small print; one can either leave it out or omit the middle voices and play in octaves only, as the original has it" (p. xlvi of the preface). A glimpse at Brahms's personal copy of this edition reveals that he initially agreed with Naumann's second option, for Brahms crossed out all the manual voices and wrote above the passage *unisono.*[61] (He also wrote *NB* beside Naumann's statement in the preface.) But after encountering the harpsichord toccata, Brahms changed his mind.

Like almost half the examples in *Octaven und Quinten,* Brahms's study score of the Fantasy in G Major, BWV 572, seems to have originated during the 1860s.[62] No doubt he prepared it in conjunction with his many performances of the piece, the earliest of which dates from 1867. Consisting of a single folio, the copy is preserved along with almost seventy others by Brahms in a collection housed today at the Gesellschaft der Musikfreunde, Vienna, under the title *Abschriften hervorragender Meisterstücke des 16.-18. Jahrhunderts zu Studienzwecken* ("Study Copies of Distinguished Masterpieces from the Sixteenth to Eighteenth Centuries").[63] To judge from certain idiosyncratic readings, Brahms's exemplar was the *Bureau de Musique* print of the fantasy issued in 1832–33 by C. F. Peters.[64] He also copied from this source the heading *Prel.[udio] quasi Fant.[asia],* a locution doubtless borrowed from Beethoven's "Moonlight" Sonata.

Brahms's score is reproduced in figure 4–2 and transcribed in the appendix to this book. It contains merely a fragmentary version of the *gravement* section of the work. Yet, contrary to what has been implied in the secondary literature, the score represents more than just an "incomplete copy," because Brahms tended to include only those passages that serve as the contrapuntal

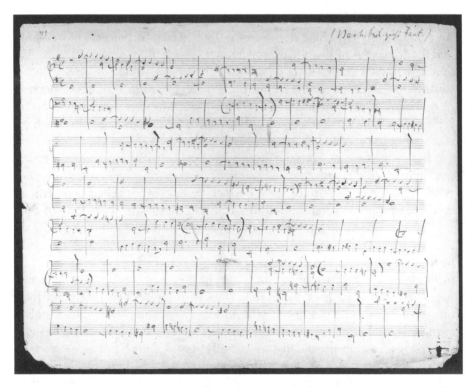

Figure 4–2 Johannes Brahms's study score (autograph manuscript) of the Fantasy in G Major, BWV 572, mm. 29–119 (*gravement* section) (Gesellschaft der Musikfreunde, Vienna, catalogue no. A 130, f. 41ʳ)

framework of the music. By stripping away the thick harmonic padding of Bach's design, he produced a reductive analysis of the highest order.

Brahms's methodology, in essence, was to notate just the statements of the principal motive and, for the sake of harmonic context, the pedal line. He succeeded in identifying virtually all the motivic statements, despite their frequency (about ninety instances, often in stretto) and the omnipresence of very similar figuration in the surrounding voices.[65] In so doing, he notated the motive in its various guises, including two statements in inversion (mm. 32–34 and 127–29). He was also perceptive enough to identify a statement at measures 83–85 wherein the motive leaps a full octave between two voices. In ten instances, he chose to mark variant motivic statements with parentheses, obviously to distinguish them from the motive in its original form. Most of these variant statements begin with an ascending second rather than repeated notes and delay the final note by means of syncopated tied notes (mm. 47–49, 74–76, 85–87, 93–95, 103–5, 127–29, 129–31, 140–42, 156–58, and 163–65). More-

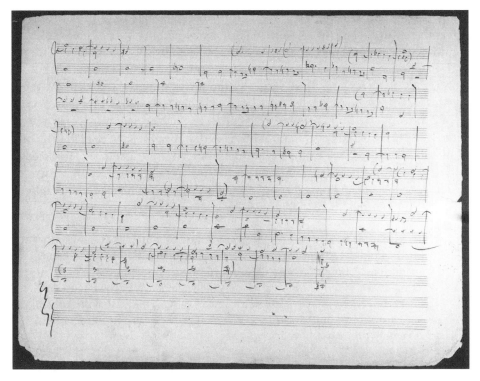

Figure 4–2 ctd. Johannes Brahms's study score (autograph manuscript) of the Fantasy in G Major, BWV 572, mm. 120–85 (*gravement* section) (Gesellschaft der Musikfreunde, Vienna, catalogue no. A 130, f. 41ᵛ)

over, the second, third, and fifth of these statements begin with a whole note, but Brahms saw fit to inscribe a half note instead, in accordance with the original form of the motive. (He made the same change in measures 34, 51, 57, and 63.) These shortened rhythms constitute a further aspect of Brahms's "reduction."[66] It is worth mentioning, too, that Brahms used a final set of parentheses for the dramatic series of left-hand parallel thirds found near the end (mm. 177–82). Last of all, diagonal slashes appear over the bar line every few measures in the manuscript. Their significance is unclear.

THE INFLUENCE OF SPITTA'S
BACH BIOGRAPHY

Brahms was personally acquainted with several of the leading music historians of his day: Friedrich Chrysander, Otto Jahn, and Gustav Nottebohm, to name but a few. He was also on friendly terms with the Bach scholar Philipp Spitta, arguably (along with Nottebohm) the foremost musicologist of the late nineteenth century. The two met in 1864 and remained in contact until Spitta's untimely death thirty years later. As demonstrated by fifty extant letters, they corresponded regularly on topics ranging from Buxtehude's organ works to Brahms's own compositions. Naturally, the music of Bach—particularly the church cantatas—was one of their favorite subjects as well.

The only one of these letters that concerns Bach's organ music was written by Spitta late in 1873. Several months earlier, Brahms had mailed him an autograph manuscript of his organ fugue on "O Traurigkeit, o Herzeleid," WoO 7 (composition date unknown), presumably in gratitude for having recently received from Spitta a copy of the first volume of his Bach biography. Spitta then offered his belated gratitude:

> When I returned from the north this past summer, I found here your beautiful organ chorale "O Traurigkeit, o Herzeleid," written out in your own hand. I would call it a "chorale fantasy," according to the terminology that I have devised myself. I find it worthy of the models of the great Seb. Bach in its art and depth, in its tenderness. . . . At the same time, it should be said that this organ piece appears to me in no way a mere copy but rather a self-reliant imitation, as one would only expect from you.[67]

Brahms would have found on page 600 of the first volume of Spitta's book an explanation, however vague, of the term "Choralfantasie." There, Spitta applies the coinage to the many chorale settings from Bach's cantatas "in which the instruments work out their own structure, while the hymn enters in the chorus of voices, controlling everything by its high moral significance and ruling in its own sphere." Brahms's version of the form comprises a three-voice fugue played by the hands, supported by a complete statement of the unadorned chorale tune in the pedals. By calling Brahms's fugue a *Choralfantasie,* Spitta was paying it the highest compliment, for on page 605 he writes that this design represents Bach's "ultimate" expression as a composer of organ chorales. According to Spitta, the form presents itself in only seven of Bach's organ chorales, all of which feature an independent polyphonic structure (such as a fugue) in the accompanimental voices. They are the miscellaneous settings of "Jesu, meine Freude," BWV 713, and "Nun freut euch, lieben Christen g'mein," BWV 734; the *organo pleno* arrangements of "Komm, Heiliger Geist, Herre Gott" and "Nun komm, der Heiden Heiland" from the Great Eighteen chorales; and the large settings of "Dies sind die heilgen zehn Gebot," "Christ, unser Herr, zum Jordan kam," and "Jesus Christus, unser Heiland" from Part 3 of the *Clavierübung.*[68] Of course, one must concur with Spitta that Brahms once again took Bach as his model here, but Brahms would eventually contextualize his work in a way never attempted by his esteemed predecessor: as the fugal movement of a prelude and fugue on the same chorale. Along with a revised version of Brahms's organ prelude on this hymn (previously discussed), the fugue was published in 1882 as the latter half of Brahms's *Choralvorspiel und Fuge über "O Traurigkeit, o Herzeleid."*

Brahms thought highly of Spitta's monumental study, which today is regarded as a landmark in the history of musicology. Indeed, he probably agreed with his friend Nottebohm that the book was "simply the best biography ever written about a musician."[69] After Spitta had mailed him a copy of volume 1 shortly after its publication in the spring of 1873, Brahms congratulated the author on his "captivating historical vignettes" and "splendid analyses," and exclaimed how long the musical community had waited for such a study.[70] Likewise, Brahms was among the first to receive from Spitta a copy of the second and final volume, immediately following its appearance in December 1879.[71]

That Brahms closely read this book is documented by the numerous markings he made in his personal copy, found at the Gesellschaft der Musikfreunde, Vienna.[72] Certain of these inscriptions pertain directly to Bach's organ works. For instance, on page 587 of volume 1, where Spitta discusses the setting of "Vom Himmel hoch" from the so-called Arnstadt Congregational Chorales (BWV 738), Brahms scribbled in the margin *B. W. Bd. 40.* This is obviously a reference to the volume of the Bachgesellschaft edition (whose actual title is *[J. S.] Bach's Werke*) where this piece is published. Since volume 40 of the set did not appear until 1893, Brahms's citation proves that he continued to consult Spitta's study decades after receiving it. To give a second example, on page 775 of the same volume Brahms drew a vertical line in the margin to mark a sentence in which Spitta claims that the subjects of Bach's organ fugues, in contrast to his harpsichord fugues, tend to begin on the downbeat. Still, the full impact that Spitta's book had on Brahms's reception of Bach's organ works can be appreciated only by comparing its text to Brahms's personal copies of the organ-music volumes of the Bachgesellschaft edition.

BRAHMS'S INSCRIPTIONS IN THE ORGAN-MUSIC VOLUMES OF THE BACHGESELLSCHAFT EDITION

As the first complete edition of Bach's oeuvre, as well as the first critical edition of any composer's complete works, this was a publication that Brahms revered. Though too young to have been involved in its conception, he became a subscriber in 1856 with volume 6 (the B Minor Mass) and two years later received the preceding five volumes as a gift from Princess Frederike of

Lippe-Detmold.[73] From 1881 on, he belonged to the advisory board, and he may even have assisted with some of the editing. To Brahms, the undertaking of this *Gesamtausgabe* ranked along with the founding of the German Empire in 1871 as the major national event of his lifetime. A pity, then, that he died only eight months before the edition was finally completed.

Brahms's personal copies of these forty-odd volumes, housed at the Gesellschaft der Musikfreunde, Vienna, provide hard evidence that he diligently studied their contents: they contain literally thousands of pencil inscriptions in his hand.[74] These markings, which typify those found elsewhere in Brahms's library of early music,[75] are mostly of an analytical nature. They give the impression of an astute scholar at work, although for Brahms the exercise was more of a hobby—and probably a welcome respite from the rigors of composing.

In all five volumes containing organ works (see table 4–3), Brahms made numerous and diverse markings. They reflect his profound understanding of Bach's art, and they often highlight aspects of the music that have never been mentioned in the secondary literature. It is no exaggeration to claim that anyone who studies these inscriptions will see Bach's organ works in a new light.

A representative sampling will be discussed here. Like any subscriber, Brahms would have received his copies hot off the press, and his routine may have been to enter a first set of inscriptions almost immediately. But he may also have continued to inscribe the volumes for as long as they were in his possession. Indeed, it can be proven that he made an annotation in volume 15, published in 1867, at least nineteen years after receiving it. In that instance, he cited a Bach cantata according to its number (152) in the Bachgesellschaft edition, although that particular volume of cantatas did not appear until 1886. The annotation, found on the first page of the Fugue in A Major, BWV 536/2, reads: *Vergl. das Concerto zur Kantate No. 152 Tritt auf d[ie] Glaubensbahn* ("Compare to the concerto of Cantata No. 152 . . ."). Thus Brahms was pointing out the close thematic correspondence between this organ fugue and the opening "concerto" movement of Bach's Cantata 152, *Tritt auf die Glaubensbahn*. One suspects he did not arrive at this comparison on his own, for Spitta had remarked on the same similarity in the first volume (p. 580) of his Bach biography.

Another inscription found in volume 15 was probably made during the early 1890s. It comprises a pair of diagonal lines drawn by Brahms to mark an instance of parallel fifths in the Fugue in G Minor, BWV 535/2, the same parallel fifths that in 1891 or 1892 he copied from this volume into *Octaven und Quinten* (see example 4–11). Given his scholarly bent and great enthusiasm for Bach's music, Brahms probably studied the Bachgesellschaft edition as a whole right up to his last days. After all, it was another heavily inscribed

Table 4–3 The Organ-Music Volumes of the Bachgesellschaft Edition

Volume Number and Date of Publication	Contents
Volume 3 (1853)	Part 3 of the *Clavierübung*
Volume 15 (1867)	trio sonatas; preludes and fugues, BWV 531-48; toccatas and fugues, BWV 564-66; passacaglia
Volume 25, part 2 (1878)	*Orgelbüchlein*, Schübler chorales, Great Eighteen chorales
Volume 38 (1891)	preludes and fugues, BWV 549-51; eight "little" preludes and fugues, BWV 553-60; miscellaneous free works, BWV 561-90; concerto transcriptions; pedal exercise, BWV 598
Volume 40 (1893)	miscellaneous chorale settings; chorale partitas

volume of this publication that was sitting open on his piano at the time of his death.[76]

Certain works are copiously inscribed, while others are entirely clean. This does not necessarily mean, however, that Brahms found the latter pieces less deserving. For example, he made no markings whatsoever in either the A-minor prelude and fugue or the G-major fantasy, two works that he regularly played. But in other works the absence of markings must represent Brahms's lack of interest. Just consider that his only inscription anywhere in the Eight "Little" Preludes and Fugues is an *NB* at the meter change before the final cadence of the E-minor fugue. What could he have learned from these works?

The Marking of Themes and Motives

By far the most common type of marking, especially in imitative textures, is a bracket used to designate a theme or motive. Normally, this symbol encloses the first few notes only, but in isolated instances it encompasses all the material. Brahms may have inserted over a thousand such brackets into these five volumes alone. They surely reflect the emphasis on imitative writing and motivic construction that so distinguishes his own compositional style.

To begin with fugues, both free and chorale-based, we see that in the Fugue in C Major, BWV 547/2, Brahms bracketed roughly a third of the fifty-plus statements of the subject, mostly those involving inversion, stretto, augmentation, or some combination of the three. (Also heavily marked are the Fugue in F Major, BWV 540/2, and the Fugue in G Minor, BWV 542/2.) In the St. Anne fugue, however, he restricted himself to the second main section, bracketing the first inverted statement of the second subject in measure 47 and the four statements of the first subject in measures 67–79. All four of these statements occur simultaneously with the second subject, in the manner of a double fugue. Likewise, in the *organo pleno* setting of "Nun komm" from the Great Eighteen, Brahms marked only the first three statements of the subject in the major mode (mm. 42–51). And in the large setting of "Wir glauben all an einen Gott" from Part 3 of the *Clavierübung*, he limited himself to the initial appearance of the quasi-ostinato bass (so described by Spitta), as stated in the pedals at measures 4–9, and the only three manual statements of the theme (mm. 76–82). The latter constitute a striking, modulatory sequence that moves via descending thirds.

To cite an example of canonic writing, another work that piqued Brahms's interest was the Canonic Variations on "Vom Himmel hoch." He made only four markings, all in Variation 4, yet they betray a sophisticated appreciation of the music. Bach's blueprint here is a canon between the soprano and bass, but the latter proceeds in augmentation, which forces the soprano to switch to new figuration midway through. This transfer occurs right after the middle C in measure 21, and Brahms drew a fermata over this note to mark the end of the canonic material in that voice. He also detected three different allusions to the chorale tune several bars later, bracketing together the last three soprano notes of measure 30 and the first five of measure 31 (= the first phrase of the chorale), then the next eight soprano notes (= the first phrase in inversion and diminution), and finally the last three alto notes of measure 31 and the first five of measure 32 (= a transposition of the first phrase). These are but a few of such allusions found throughout the movement.[77]

In analyzing Bach's organ chorales, Brahms encountered imitative forms other than fugue and canon. For example, the second setting of "Komm, Heiliger Geist" from the Great Eighteen provided a specimen not only of the ornamental chorale but also of the chorale motet, a design wherein each phrase of the hymn melody serves as a point of imitation. In this extraordinarily long work, Brahms marked the first imitative statement of every phrase save the first and last. His comprehensive knowledge of Lutheran hymnody was doubtless of great assistance.[78]

In other settings, Bach employs the technique of pre-imitation, whereby each phrase of the chorale, before being stated in relatively long notes, is the subject of imitation in rhythms either two or four times as fast. Two prominent examples are the double-pedal arrangement of "Aus tiefer Noth" from Part 3 of the *Clavierübung* and the setting of "Vor deinen Thron" from the Great Eighteen. In the first work, Brahms marked at least one statement within each point of imitation. In the second, he bracketed every imitative statement of the last phrase.

The forty-six chorales that make up the *Orgelbüchlein*, conversely, allowed for an investigation of Bach's handiwork on a much smaller scale. In these miniatures, the chorale normally appears as a continuous melody in the soprano, without any interludes whatsoever, and the lower voices tend to be based on one or two specific motives, often in imitative texture. Brahms marked these accompanimental motives, usually bracketing at least two imitative statements, in eight different works: "Vom Himmel kam der Engel Schar"; "Christum wir sollen loben schon"; "Helft mir Gotts Güte preisen"; "Das alte Jahr vergangen ist"; "Christus, der uns selig macht"; "Da Jesus an dem Kreuze stund"; "Christ ist erstanden"; and "Dies sind die heilgen zehn Gebot." It is probably no accident that "Helft mir" and "Dies sind" are listed by Spitta as two of only three works in the *Orgelbüchlein* where the primary motive is drawn from the chorale tune itself (vol. 1, pp. 590–91). Spitta's influence also suggests itself in how Brahms marked the *Orgelbüchlein* setting of "Herr Jesu Christ, dich zu uns wend." On page 592 of volume 1, Spitta characterizes this piece as one in which "the canonic bass spins out the [chorale] melody in diminution." For his part, Brahms bracketed every phrase of the chorale proper, as found in the soprano part, and every diminution statement in the pedals.

In the case of the G-minor fantasy, Brahms saw fit to analyze Bach's use of invertible counterpoint by numbering the respective themes. The passage involved, which adheres strictly to four-voice texture, first appears at measures 9–14 and then, transposed up a fifth, at measures 25–31. For both statements, Brahms numbered the three themes played by the hands and bracketed the sequential pedal figuration (see figure 4–3). Between the two statements, Bach employs every possible permutation except 2–1–3, using no permutation more than once. As numbered by Brahms, the order is: (first statement) 1–3–2, 3–2–1, 1–2–3; and (second statement) 2–3–1, 3–1–2.

Another fascinating instance concerns the large setting of "Christ, unser Herr, zum Jordan kam" from Part 3 of the *Clavierübung*. There, Brahms numbered the different segments of the ritornello, whose flowing tenor line was taken by Spitta as a depiction of that holy river (see figure 4–4). Using Arabic and Roman numerals interchangeably, and writing in very faint blue pencil, Brahms entered on the first page the following numbers: in measure 1, "1"; in measure 2, "II"; in measure 4, "3"; in measure 6 (third beat), "1"; in measure 8, "1"; in measure 10, "II"; in measure 12, "III"; and in measure 15, "I." His analysis reveals a tripartite design usually attributed to Antonio Vivaldi, and appropriated by Bach in so many of his compositions: the first segment (m. 1) grounds the tonality with tonic and dominant harmonies; the second (mm. 2–3) entails a circle-of-fifths sequence; and the third (mm. 3–6) brings things to a satisfying close with an authentic cadence. A further Vivaldian trait underscored by Brahms's numbering scheme is Bach's tendency, as the piece unfolds, to freely manipulate the segments and separate them from each other. But these "liberties" are admittedly dictated somewhat by the *pedaliter* chorale tune.

Figure 4–3 Fantasy in G Minor, BWV 542/1, mm. 1–11, as published in the Bachge-sellschaft edition. Johannes Brahms's personal copy (Gesellschaft der Musikfreunde, Vienna)

As he studied two of Bach's settings of "Allein Gott in der Höh sei Ehr," BWV 711 and 717, Brahms placed vertical strokes over the thematic notes that embody the actual hymn melody (see examples 4–14 and 4–15). Both themes represent embellished versions of the opening phrase. In the first work, Brahms marked notes 1, 4, 5, 12, and 13, the equivalent of the first four notes of the chorale, plus a passing tone between the second and third notes; in the second, he included all eight notes of the phrase by marking the first note of every triplet grouping.

Figure 4–4 "Christ, unser Herr, zum Jordan kam," BWV 684, mm. 1–15, as published in the Bachgesellschaft edition. Johannes Brahms's personal copy (Gesellschaft der Musikfreunde, Vienna)

Markings of this sort are otherwise found only in the slow movement of the second Trio Sonata (see figure 4–5). At the very beginning of the middle system, Brahms first wrote *NB* and then placed vertical strokes over notes 1, 2, 5, 7, 9, and 11, beaming them together at the top like a grouping of six eighth notes. These inscriptions make little sense until they are compared to those found in measure 24 (the last measure on the page). There, following another *NB,* as well as a bracket for the anacrusis, Brahms notated directly above the pedal eighth notes a version of the same passage consisting of twelve sixteenths. (In addition to what appears to be merely a stray mark at the top of the staff between measures 15 and 16, the only other inscription on the

Example 4–14 "Allein Gott in der Höh sei Ehr," BWV 711

page is a double bar at the end of measure 8 that signals a restatement of the opening bars in the dominant key.) Clearly, these sixteenth notes correspond to those printed in measure 1, while the six notes marked there correspond to the six pedal notes printed in measure 24. In both measures, therefore, Brahms's score contains both the original version of the main theme and that simplified for the sake of pedaling. His intention, presumably, was to test the compatibility of his alternative readings with the other two voices, a process that on the first beat of measure 24 exposes blatant parallel octaves between the outer voices. Bach, then, had reasons besides ease of performance in choosing the simplified version of the theme here.[79]

The Marking of Musical Form

These volumes also contain many inscriptions in Brahms's hand that have to do with the various forms employed by Bach in his organ works. Brahms analyzed these structures, with an eye to formal anomalies, primarily with three distinct markings: (1) a double bar, to mark the end of a section; (2) a repeat sign, to indicate a restatement; and (3) *d. c.*, for a da capo return.

Only a few such annotations appear in the preludes, toccatas, fantasies, and fugues.[80] The most significant is a *d. c.* marking found toward the end of the Wedge fugue (measure 172, beat 4), at which point Bach begins a repeat of the opening fifty-nine bars that by measure 178 becomes a note-for-note restatement. Brahms certainly realized the rarity of da capo fugues within

Example 4–15 "Allein Gott in der Höh sei Ehr," BWV 717

Figure 4–5 Trio Sonata No. 2 in C Minor, BWV 526, second movement, mm. 1–24, as published in the Bachgesellschaft edition. Johannes Brahms's personal copy (Gesellschaft der Musikfreunde, Vienna)

Bach's oeuvre (and in general), just as he must have appreciated the hidden nature of the return. Indeed, the manner in which Bach overlaps the final episode with this repeat may constitute a unique instance in his music.[81]

By far the greatest concentration of these markings occurs in the fast movements of the Trio Sonatas, where Brahms concerned himself with distinguishing between ritornello statements and episodic material. Accordingly, in the first movement of the second sonata, he marked the end of the first three ritornello statements with a double bar (mm. 8, 22, and 38) and the beginning of the second and third statements with an "X" (mm. 17 and 31). Near the end of the last movement of the third sonata (m. 145), he wrote *d. c.* where the note-for-note restatement of the opening ritornello commences, and he numbered sequentially the three big episodes that start in measures 37, 73, and 108.

Double-bar symbols and repeat signs appear in nine different chorale settings, including the partita on "O Gott, du frommer Gott." In the highly fragmented final variation of this work, Brahms marked the conclusion of the antepenultimate and penultimate sections (mm. 25 and 35) with a double bar. For the *organo pleno* setting of "Komm, Heiliger Geist" from the Great Eighteen, he provided a repeat sign before the first pedal note in measure 52, as well as double-bar symbols in the pedal line at the end of measures 43 and 86. All three markings demonstrate that measures 55–86 are an exact restatement of measures 12–43, even though Brahms's repeat sign occurs three bars early, to coincide with the beginning of the chorale phrase. (The two double bars mark the end of the repeated passage.) This sort of large-scale repetition—a feature made possible by the extraordinarily repetitive chorale tune—is encountered in no other organ chorale by Bach.

The remaining seven works come from the *Orgelbüchlein*. In the case of "Helft mir Gotts Güte preisen" and "O Mensch, bewein dein Sünde gross," Brahms drew repeat signs in measure 4 (beat 4) and measure 6 (beat 4), respectively, thereby highlighting two rare examples in which Bach varies the repeat of the *Stollen*. "Herr Gott, nun schleuss den Himmel auf" is a barform chorale whose *Stollen* is restated note for note. Yet in the Bachgesellschaft edition—as in the Neue Bach-Ausgabe—the repeat is written out in full rather than indicated by a repeat sign. Here, too, Brahms furnished a repeat sign precisely where the restatement begins (measure 7, beat 1).

Brahms's tendency to mark atypical repeats is documented by three other *Orgelbüchlein* arrangements not in bar form. Two are "Das alte Jahr vergangen ist," whose first two phrases are melodically identical, and "Christus, der uns selig macht," whose third and seventh phrases are the same. In the first work, Brahms wrote a repeat sign at the beginning of the second phrase (measure 3, beat 1), while in the second he placed an "X" at the beginning of the two phrases in question (measure 6, beat 4, and measure 17, beat 4). In both instances, Bach employs different accompanimental figuration, and in "Das alte Jahr" he varies the ornamental solo line as well. In "Herr Jesu Christ, dich zu uns wend," the issue was an unnecessary, note-for-note repeat of the last two phrases. Again, the Bachgesellschaft edition prints the repeat in full, and once again Brahms furnished a repeat sign where the repeat begins (measure 12, beat 2).

That leaves "In dir ist Freude," a fantasy-like work remarkable for its free treatment of the hymn melody. Although the tune appears more or less complete in the soprano, the individual phrases are fractured, ornamented, and unnecessarily restated. In analyzing this piece, Brahms's first and fundamental task was locating the chorale tune, which he accomplished by notating each of the six musical phrases at the appropriate junctures. As can be seen in figure 4–6, he inscribed the first two phrases on the first page, using whatever empty space was available. The phrase used for the first two lines of text, and manipulated by Bach for the first twelve bars, is written in the empty top staff of the first measure; that used for the third line, and alluded to by Bach in measures 13–16, is written in the empty bottom staff of the last measure. Observe, too, Brahms's double bar at the beginning of the penultimate measure, to mark the end of the first section, and his bracket over the first two

Figure 4–6 "In dir ist Freude," BWV 615, mm. 1–13, as published in the Bachgesellschaft edition. Johannes Brahms's personal copy (Gesellschaft der Musikfreunde, Vienna)

alto notes in the last bar, where Bach begins an embellished statement of the second phrase.

Brahms inscribed "In dir ist Freude" to the very end. He placed repeat signs in measures 18 and 51—none are printed in the score itself—to mark the restatements of measures 1–12 and 39–50, respectively, and he inserted a double-bar symbol in measure 30 to mark the end of the repeat there. Moreover, he bracketed segments of the chorale tune as found in the soprano voice at measures 30, 40, 44, and 48, and as found in the pedal part at measure 34. Finally, as a point of reference, he notated the third phrase of the chorale in the empty bottom staff of measure 40 and the three remaining phrases in the empty middle staff of measures 44–45. The work is sui generis, and Brahms knew it.

The Marking of Rhythmic, Harmonic, Melodic, and Contrapuntal Irregularities

Brahms's interest in musical anomalies extended well beyond aspects of form. Contrapuntal oddities, for example, are the very basis of his collection *Octaven und Quinten*. In his personal copies of vocal music by Bach, Gabrieli, and Schütz, he marked irregularities of rhythm, harmony, melody, and counterpoint.[82] He did so as well in the organ-music volumes of the Bachgesellschaft edition.

Two-against-three rhythms may be a veritable cliché in Brahms's compositions, but they are relatively rare in Bach. It must have delighted Brahms, therefore, when he discovered several instances of the technique in two of Bach's organ chorales. One is the *Orgelbüchlein* setting of "Herr Gott, nun schleuss den Himmel auf," a work characterized by constant eighth-note triplets in the pedals and, in the last six bars, eighth-note duplets in the manual voices. Brahms signified the initial occurrence of these duplets, in measure 19, by drawing two statements of the rhythm above the preceding beat.

The other chorale is that on "Vom Himmel hoch" from the Arnstadt Congregational Chorales. In his copy of Spitta's Bach biography, as discussed earlier, Brahms identified this piece according to its volume number in the Bachgesellschaft edition. Further evidence that he felt a special affinity to the work is provided by the many inscriptions he made in the volume itself. In this setting, Bach employs eighth-note duplets almost exclusively. Only on the first three beats of the alto voice in measure 12 do eighth-note triplets appear, and they are all stated against duplets in the pedals (see example 4–16). Brahms acknowledged these triplets by writing "3" beneath the first two sets. He obviously understood the sixteenth-note sextuplets in the tenor here to be in sync with the duplets, for beneath the second and fifth sixteenths on the first beat he wrote "3" as well, indicating a binary division of the beat.

Example 4–16 "Vom Himmel hoch, da komm ich her," BWV 738

Likewise, he marked as triplets the last nine tenor sixteenths in measure 8. Yet he also marked as a triplet the three tenor notes that comprise beat 2 of measure 7 (and that alternate with the alto to form a virtual set of sixteenth sextuplets), indicating a ternary division of the beat. To judge from these markings, Brahms was fully aware that the shifting contours of the sixteenth-note figuration throughout the work imply a series of hemiola rhythms.[83] For example, the descending scalar sixteenths on the first two beats of measure 3 suggest a ternary division (♩♩♩♩♩), while the ascending arpeggiated sixteenths on the last two beats suggest a binary division (♩♩♩♩♩). Brahms's attention to this matter is almost expected, considering that hemiola technique is a trademark of his own compositions.[84]

As far as harmony and melody are concerned, two examples of unorthodox chromaticism are marked. One occurs in the *Orgelbüchlein* chorale, "Christe, du Lamm Gottes," a work that contains some of the most dissonant harmonies Bach ever conceived (see especially mm. 5–6 and 10–11). As described by Spitta, these "most peculiar and melancholy harmonies" create an "unforgettably profound and truly musical" impression (vol. 1, p. 591). Presumably in response to Spitta's gloss, Brahms located an instance in measure 10 where a C in the lower tenor part sounds simultaneously with a C-sharp in the alto; he marked both notes with an "X." In the slow movement of the sixth Trio Sonata, Brahms's attention was drawn to measure 24, where a quarter-note trill on C-sharp played by the left hand leads to a C-natural; at the midpoint of the very long trill line, he wrote *NB*. This measure concludes a passage (mm. 21–24) of exceptional artistry.[85]

An additional harmonic irregularity was detected by Brahms in the Fugue in F Minor, BWV 534/2. Spitta criticized this movement for its lack of a coherent structure (vol. 1, p. 582), and scholars have recently questioned whether Bach could even be the composer.[86] In this same critical spirit, Brahms identified a solecism at measures 87–88 where two second-inversion chords appear in succession (see beat 4 of measure 87 and beat 1 of measure 88); beneath each of the chords, he wrote $^6_4$. Why Bach did not place the first of these chords in root position is impossible to explain.[87]

In four cases, not surprisingly, Brahms also identified or alluded to parallel fifths and octaves. Those involving the Fugue in G Minor, BWV 535/2, and the last movement of the Bach-Vivaldi Concerto in A Minor have already been discussed, both in conjunction with *Octaven und Quinten*. Another work represented in that collection is the *Orgelbüchlein* setting of "Wir Christenleut," which, as previously mentioned, contains seven instances of would-be parallel octaves. Brahms marked the first of these instances (see example 4–10) in the Bachgesellschaft edition with a pair of diagonal lines between the outer voices. He marked in identical fashion an egregious example of parallel fifths printed in the penultimate measure of the partita on "Christ, der du bist der helle Tag," where the two left-hand voices form parallel perfect fifths between the second and third beats (see example 4–17). Brahms may have interpreted this infraction as a youthful indiscretion on Bach's part, but a better possibility is that Bach intended an E-flat for the first upper note (see the Neue Bach-Ausgabe), a reading that yields perfectly acceptable unequal fifths. This, at any rate, is the reading found in the earliest extant manuscript, a source unavailable to Ernst Naumann when he prepared volume 40 of the Bachgesellschaft edition.[88] It stands to reason that Brahms did not discover this passage until he saw it in this very volume, which did not appear until 1893. Had he found it any earlier, he might have included it in *Octaven und Quinten*.

Comparative Readings, Suggested Readings, and Corrections

As Brahms studied these tomes, he made certain inscriptions in the music that are best described as editorial. In two instances, he marked discrepancies between different versions of the same work, allowing for early and revised readings to be viewed simultaneously. Several other times, he questioned the validity of a passage by suggesting an alternate reading. He also corrected typographical errors.

As a point of departure, let us consider two of the Great Eighteen chorales: "O Lamm Gottes, unschuldig" and the first setting of "Jesus Christus, unser Heiland." They both contain an exceptionally large number of markings in Brahms's hand, and it is probably no coincidence that Spitta described both works at considerable length and in glowing terms (vol. 1, pp. 601–4). In fact, the biographer devoted twice as much space to the latter work as to any other Bach organ chorale, save the Canonic Variations on "Vom Himmel hoch" and

Example 4–17 Partita on "Christ, der du bist der helle Tag," BWV 766, final variation, as printed in the Bachgesellschaft edition

the partita on "Sei grüsset." He regarded the piece as one of Bach's "grandest and most profound creations."

In marking "Jesus Christus, unser Heiland," Brahms bracketed a total of twenty-seven thematic and motivic statements, including the veiled entrance of the final chorale phrase in the left hand at measure 38. His analysis may have been facilitated by Spitta's two musical examples, each of which illustrates a particular accompanimental motive. A footnote printed on the first page of the score ("Siehe die ältere Lesart im Anhange Seite 188.") directs the user to the appendix for the early version of the work. But it would appear that when Brahms first compared the two versions, he found precious little that was different, for he wrote beneath the footnote, as if thoroughly annoyed, *durchaus gleichlautend!* ("absolutely identical!"). He eventually discovered discrepancies in the alto voice at measures 36 and 50, and he entered the readings from the early version here into the score of the revised version. Had he looked harder, he would have found additional discrepancies in measures 16 (bass), 18 (bass) 28 (tenor), 31–32 (alto), and 34 (tenor).

The situation with "O Lamm Gottes," which Spitta proclaimed "a marvel of profoundly religious art," is similar, although its two versions disagree to a far greater extent, especially in verse 2. Brahms bracketed numerous motivic statements in verses 1 and 3, and notated in measure 49 a discrepant reading from the early version. In the score of the early version itself, furthermore, he marked a host of passages where the two versions deviate from one another. In no instance, though, did he actually notate a revised reading.

In three other cases, Brahms politely suggested with a question mark and an alternate reading of his own that certain pitches in the Bachgesellschaft edition might be erroneous. For example, in measure 29 of the Prelude in C Minor, BWV 546/1, he proposed that the A's played by the right hand on the last two beats should be A-flats (to form a Neapolitan sixth), in agreement with virtually all the other statements of this episodic figure.[89] Likewise, in measure 21 of the first movement of the Pastorale (BWV 590), he suggested that the left-hand system should read f'–e'–d' on the last beat, since all the other statements of this idea—presented for the first time in measure 7—end with a stepwise descent. (One may assume that Brahms performed this movement on his piano recitals according to his reading.) Finally, in measure 28 of the miscellaneous setting of "In dich hab ich gehoffet, Herr," BWV 712, he questioned the absence of a right-hand G-sharp on the last beat, because a sharp here would produce a more focused (leading tone to tonic) progression into the next chord.

Brahms encountered a different circumstance in measure 64 of the Fugue in C Minor, BWV 537/2, as edited by his colleague Wilhelm Rust. Reasoning that Bach intended sequential material in both the alto and tenor voices, Rust devised a reading for the alto that closely matches the previous bar.[90] Unconvinced, Brahms crossed out Rust's reading (which is distinguished by its small print) and entered the reading from volume 3 of the Peters edition, one of his exemplars for *Octaven und Quinten*.

Nor was Brahms entirely happy with how Rust edited the G-minor fantasy. At the beginning of the third beat of measure 15, where Rust prints d'', Brahms wrote *(e)*, and in measure 42, beat 2, where Rust prints an A-natural for the antepenultimate note in the right hand, Brahms wrote *(c)*. Brahms also inscribed a natural sign above Rust's concluding G-minor chord, revealing his preference for a Picardy-third ending. In all three instances, Brahms took his readings from volume 2 of the Peters edition. This is not to imply, though, that the Bachgesellschaft edition is necessarily inferior. In fact, the E printed in measure 15 of the Peters edition makes no sense harmonically, which explains why the pitch was changed to D when the whole set was later revised and reissued.[91] The Neue Bach-Ausgabe offers yet another reading, an F-natural, to agree with the analogous passage at measure 44.

The Marking of Ornamentation

Brahms took a lively interest in Bach's ornaments.[92] It comes as no surprise, then, that he concerned himself with this matter as he perused the organ-music volumes of the Bachgesellschaft edition. For instance, at the beginning of the Fugue in E Minor, BWV 533/2, he wrote *NB* at exactly the same height in the score as the two mordents in the first bar. He did so, obviously, because both ornaments are printed in parentheses as editorial suggestions, which is how Rust chose to print every statement of the fugue subject in this movement. Brahms would have known this fugue as published in volume 3 of the Peters edition and would therefore have been accustomed to seeing

Example 4–18 Fugue in E Minor, BWV 548/2

these parentheses only in the two pedal statements of the subject. He may have been familiar with these ornaments, too, because of Spitta's rather detailed discussion of them (vol. 1, p. 402). Quite correctly, Spitta advocates that the middle note should be played as an A-natural rather than A-sharp.[93]

The only other work in which Brahms marked ornamentation is the so-called Wedge fugue, BWV 548/2. Here, he was struck by the inconsistent notation of the countersubject: although its antepenultimate bar normally commences with eighth-note appoggiaturas and quarter notes, four times it begins instead with straight eighth notes (see mm. 47, 91, 110, and 219). To compare these two different styles of notation, Brahms inscribed the word *vide* (Latin for "see"), writing *vi–* in measure 8 and, on the facing page, *–de* in measure 47 (see examples 4–18 and 4–19). Similarly, he wrote *NB* in measures 91 and 110 to mark the second and third instances of straight eighths. In all three cases, he bracketed the eighth notes as well. Especially since the primary source for this edition is an autograph, Brahms may have thought that Bach was demonstrating precisely how these ornaments should be realized. But, as Rust explains in his preface (p. xxxiii), Bach's hand breaks off after measure 20, before any of the eighth-note statements appear. According to recent research, it was the Gräfenroda cantor J. P. Kellner who helped Bach com-

Example 4–19 Fugue in E Minor, BWV 548/2

plete this manuscript.[94] These eighth notes, then, may be Kellner's realization, not Bach's.

Fingerings

The extremely large size of these volumes would have precluded Brahms's use of them in concert. (Besides, he seems to have performed from memory.) Still, he no doubt played from them in the privacy of his apartment. As he practiced, he found it expedient to jot down a few fingerings. In the Wedge fugue, for example, he wrote the number "5" above the right-hand E on the third beat of measure 59. This half note is surrounded on either side by sixteenth notes—the first occurrence of these rhythms anywhere in the movement—and some performers choose to play the first three sixteenths in the middle staff here with their right hand as well. Brahms's fingering suggests that he played the passage exactly this way. Otherwise, he would have taken the E with his thumb.

Brahms also inserted three fingerings into the last movement of the Pastorale, all of which occur in conjunction with the inversion of the fugue subject. The first two fingerings, *3* and *1*, are found above the first and fourth notes, respectively, of the upper part in measure 28, where the right hand plays the inverted form of the subject for the first time. The third fingering is a "1" that appears above the fourth note in the upper staff at measure 33, where the right hand plays the inverted subject a second time. In both of these analogous passages, the thumb is presumably to be crossed under the third finger, allowing the same hand position to be used until the end of the bar. Brahms made only one other marking in this work, a "suggested reading" found in the first movement. The fact that his inscriptions are limited to just the first and last movements supports the hypothesis, advanced earlier, that his public performances of the Pastorale included these two movements only.

Miscellaneous Annotations

To conclude this discussion, let us consider three miscellaneous inscriptions. Two of them are merely Brahms's identification of the cantatas from which Bach fashioned two of the Schübler chorales. Both times, Brahms cited the cantata according to its number in the Bachgesellschaft edition. In volume 25, part 2, at the beginning of "Wachet auf, ruft uns die Stimme," he wrote *No. 140*, and at the beginning of "Kommst du nun, Jesu, vom Himmel herunter," *No. 137 (alt u. Violino solo).* In the latter instance, therefore, he also identified the cantata movement involved, an aria for alto and obbligato violin.

The third inscription is found in volume 38, at the beginning of the Fugue in B Minor on a Theme by Corelli, BWV 579. It reads: *Siehe Corelli S. 142 (op. III, Son. 4)*. Here, then, Brahms identified not only the model itself (Arcangelo Corelli's Trio Sonata in B Minor, op. 3, no. 4, second movement) but also where the model could be located in a modern edition (on pages 142ff. of *Denkmäler der Tonkunst,* volume 3). This same information is contained in a footnote on page 423 of the first volume of Spitta's Bach biography. Brahms owned this edition of Corelli's chamber music, which was prepared by his friend Joseph Joachim, but made nary a mark in it.[95]

BRAHMS AS SCHOLAR-COMPOSER: THE ELEVEN CHORALE PRELUDES, OP. 122

Brahms's response to Bach's organ music manifests itself most significantly in his very last work, the Eleven Chorale Preludes, op. 122. Composed in May and June of 1896, these pieces reflect Brahms's musical outlook (and personality) in various ways. Moreover, the compositional models of the collection are exceedingly diverse, ranging from Brahms's late piano miniatures to Bach's passion settings. But this opus is nothing if not a tribute to Bach as the undisputed master of the organ chorale. It has long been established that, with respect to technique and form, Brahms used the *Orgelbüchlein* as a kind of blueprint,[96] and scholars have identified specific works from Bach's collection that probably factored in this process. Nonetheless, we are in a position to investigate this matter anew, having just seen how Brahms analyzed over a dozen *Orgelbüchlein* chorales in terms of their motivic structure, form, rhythmic design, and harmonic style. We have also witnessed Brahms grappling with these same issues (and more) in numerous organ chorales by Bach not included in the *Orgelbüchlein*. Some of these works appear to have served Brahms as exemplars, too.

The two numbers from Brahms's opus that most visibly bear the stamp of the *Orgelbüchlein* are "Herzliebster Jesu" and the first setting of "Herzlich tut mich verlangen." In both works, within the context of three manual voices and an obbligato pedal part, the chorale tune sounds continuously in the soprano, supported by unified motivic figuration beneath. What is more, both derive their accompanimental figuration from the *suspirans* (discussed in chapter 2 with regard to Schumann's "Figurirter Choral"), the most common accompanimental motive used by Bach in the *Orgelbüchlein*. Brahms departs somewhat from Bach's template by regularly stating the motive in the soprano voice as well, but this allows him to maintain continuous motion in the rhythm one-fourth the value of the main pulse, another essential ingredient of the *Orgelbüchlein* as a stylistic entity.

As he composed "Herzliebster Jesu," Brahms appears to have borrowed from two *Orgelbüchlein* chorales in particular. Consider, for example, the striking similarity between the tritone motive in the pedal line of Brahms's setting and the diminished-seventh motive used by Bach in the pedal part of "Durch Adams Fall ist ganz verderbt."[97] Both motives proceed in the same rhythm (♪ ♩) and in the same downward motion, and both involve dissonant intervals consistent with the pathos of their respective chorale texts. (As Spitta points out, Bach's motive is obviously a symbol for Adam's fall from grace.) In addition, Brahms tends to cadence with the same type of *suspirans* motive (ascending second—descending fourth—ascending second) found throughout the *Orgelbüchlein* setting of "Nun komm, der Heiden Heiland."[98] In both works, the motive usually begins in one of the upper voices and descends ultimately into the tenor, in the tradition of *style brisé*.

It may be said that three other numbers from Brahms's collection at least approximate the style of the *Orgelbüchlein,* since in all three the hymn melody appears more or less continuously in the soprano, above motivically unified accompanimental voices. For example, the first arrangement of "O Welt, ich muss dich lassen" deviates from Bach's design only by virtue of its slightly thicker texture (four rather than five voices) and tiny interludes between phrases. In fact, Brahms may have loosely modeled this piece after the *Orgelbüchlein* setting of "O Lamm Gottes, unschuldig," as both works are based on slurred "sigh" motives and are in the same key.[99]

Brahms's setting of "O wie selig seid ihr doch, ihr Frommen" fails to meet Bach's criteria only because it lacks a pedal line. Brahms, though, does conclude with an actual pedal point, exactly as Bach does in the second setting of "Jesus Christus, unser Heiland" from the Great Eighteen chorales. In no other organ chorale by Bach is the use of pedal delayed in this fashion, a circumstance that becomes all the more suggestive when one considers Brahms's unusually thorough analysis of this work in his copy of the Bachgesellschaft edition (in which he bracketed over forty thematic and motivic statements).

Third, Brahms's arrangement of "Schmücke dich, o liebe Seele" may be entirely *manualiter* and scored for only three voices, but it corresponds to a small group of *Orgelbüchlein* settings whose main accompanimental motives are based on the first phrase of the chorale. As mentioned earlier, two of these settings are "Helft mir Gotts Güte preisen" and "Dies sind der heilgen zehn Gebot," the accompanimental motives of which Brahms made sure to bracket in his copy of the Bachgesellschaft edition. One can only assume that in composing such a work himself, Brahms was inspired specifically by these two specimens of organic unity.

Three other works from Brahms's collection also seem to be influenced by organ chorales that he analyzed in the Bachgesellschaft edition. To begin with the setting of "Herzlich tut mich erfreuen," its opening bars correspond to the ritornello of Bach's miscellaneous setting of "Allein Gott in der Höh sei Ehr," BWV 711 (see example 4–14). Like Bach, Brahms commences his setting with fast and essentially monophonic figuration in the left hand that embellishes the first phrase of the chorale. Furthermore, both composers choose dance-like triple meter, make prominent use at the outset of downward arpeggiation—compare especially Bach's arpeggiated tenths in measures 1–2 with Brahms's in measure 1—and highlight the notes of the chorale proper by placing them in the top register. (Brahms treats the next two phrases of his chorale tune in this same manner.) Enhancing these similarities is the fact that both chorale melodies are in the major mode and begin with basically the same contour (they both start on the first scale degree and then move up a third).

Brahms's second setting of "Herzlich tut mich verlangen" implies Bach's influence, first of all, because the chorale tune is stated consistently in an inner voice: virtually no composer except Bach adopted this scheme for organ chorales consisting of only one movement.[100] More specifically, Brahms includes a passage of intense chromaticism redolent of two of the Great Eighteen chorales: "O Lamm Gottes, unschuldig" and the first setting of "Jesus Christus, unser Heiland."[101] As previously discussed, Brahms copiously inscribed both of these works with regard to their polyphonic structure, just as he closely compared their early and revised versions. Each contains a single, overtly chromatic passage inspired by a particular line of the chorale text, and in both instances the chromaticism (and resulting dissonance) serves as a metaphor for suffering. In Brahms's work, the chromaticism is also undoubtedly text-related, but instead of depicting a specific line, it symbolizes the theme of earthly misery that runs throughout the text.

Examples 4–20 and 4–21 give the concluding bars of the two passages by Bach; example 4–22 illustrates Brahms's passage, which comprises only one measure. In all three excerpts, a relatively fast chromatic line in descending motion sounds above a pedal point constituting the final note of a phrase of the chorale, and the line is harmonized in parallel sixths by another manual voice. Brahms's passage is especially close to that from "O Lamm Gottes," since both passages begin in effect as a series of first-inversion triads (due to harmonization by parallel fourths as well as sixths) and end with a half cadence.

Finally, because of its fantasy-like orientation and *manualiter* disposition, Brahms's arrangement of "O Gott, du frommer Gott" may be grouped together with three *manualiter* settings by Bach in which the chorale tune is handled with remarkable freedom: the final variation of the partita on "O Gott, du frommer Gott"; the miscellaneous setting of "Christ lag in Todesbanden," BWV 718; and the so-called fantasy on "Jesu, meine Freude," BWV 713. In his copy of the Bachgesellschaft edition, Brahms analyzed all three

Example 4–20 "O Lamm Gottes, unschuldig," BWV 656

works, the first with respect to form, the second and third with respect to themes and motives.

Brahms's modus operandi here is to freely embellish each phrase of the chorale, usually via constant eighth-note figuration, before presenting it out-right. Each of these embellished statements, in turn, consists of two distinct halves, the latter of which "echoes" the first by presenting basically the same material on a softer registration (and obviously on a different manual) and at a different pitch level, usually the octave. Such echo effects are integral to Bach's partita movement—which probably not by accident is based on the same chorale as Brahms's setting—and of the *Abgesang* of his "Christ lag" setting.[102] Bach, though, subjects his chorale tunes to constant embellishment and fragmentation. In fact, only at the end of "Christ lag" does either melody appear unaltered. The final phrase proper sounds three times in succession, and for the third statement the pedals are engaged for the first time. In no other organ chorale by Bach that Brahms would have known are the pedals delayed in this way.[103] It scarcely seems accidental, therefore, that Brahms also

Example 4–21 "Jesus Christus, unser Heiland," BWV 665

Example 4–22 Johannes Brahms, "Herzlich tut mich verlangen," op. 122, no. 10

reserves the pedals for the final phrase of his setting, even if he uses them not for the chorale phrase itself but for a countermelody.

Brahms's presentation of the chorale melody in this work is distinguished by its migration between voices. It begins in the soprano, moves to the tenor at the onset of the *Abgesang,* shifts to the alto at the end of the antepenultimate phrase, and then returns to the soprano. As if to guide the player through this maze of transfers and interludes, Brahms prefaces each phrase with the heading *Choral,* a designation found in no other work from this opus. Both these headings and the migratory pattern itself recall the third Bach setting in our group (BWV 713), which Brahms heavily inscribed. In setting the *Stollen* of this chorale, Bach, too, begins and ends with the melody in the top voice, and he also states it in the middle and bottom voices. Furthermore, each phrase is preceded by the heading *Choral,* a designation seldom encountered in an organ chorale by Bach.[104] It should also be mentioned that organ chorales featuring a migratory cantus firmus are quite rare per se and that rarer still are such works in which the chorale tune appears in an interior voice.[105] All of the above points to a very close relationship between these two works.

The "fantastic" element in Bach's arrangement of "Jesu, meine Freude" is how in setting the *Abgesang,* he changes meters and merely paraphrases all the material to the end. Interestingly, in the fifth movement of Bach's famous motet on this chorale (BWV 227), the melody is handled in much the same way.[106] Since Brahms studied this motet movement in order to determine its precise relationship to the hymn tune,[107] his knowledge of this motet may well have sparked his interest in the organ chorale.

A general anomaly of Brahms's collection is his predilection to state identical portions of the chorale melody in different ways. We see this most clearly in how he varies the restatement of the *Stollen* in "Schmücke dich, o liebe Seele," "Es ist ein Ros' entsprungen," and the first setting of "Herzlich tut mich verlangen." But this tendency is equally pronounced in both settings of "O

Welt, ich muss dich lassen," a tune whose repetitive design is virtually the same as bar form. In the version used by Brahms, the first two phrases are basically identical to the fourth and fifth, although they are sung to different words.

Brahms's encounter with Bach's organ chorales unquestionably pushed him in this direction. In his copy of the Bachgesellschaft edition, for example, he made sure to mark the only two passages in the entire *Orgelbüchlein* where Bach varies the restatement of the *Stollen,* and he marked two additional passages from that collection in which two melodically identical chorale phrases are set to different figuration. Furthermore, three other Bach settings that we have already posited as compositional models for Brahms's opus likewise feature a varied restatement of their *Stollen.* They are the settings of "Christ lag in Todesbanden" and "Jesu, meine Freude" just discussed, and verse 3 of "O Lamm Gottes, unschuldig" from the Great Eighteen chorales.

Remarkably, Brahms also repeats the *Abgesang* of "Es ist ein Ros' entsprungen," and in the same varied manner as the *Stollen,* with the first phrase shifted from the soprano into one of the inner voices. The resulting binary form (AABB), so characteristic of baroque dance movements, is almost unheard of for a chorale setting. Still, one model would have been provided by the *Orgelbüchlein* chorale "Herr Jesu Christ, dich zu uns wend," whose final two chorale phrases are unnecessarily restated. When he analyzed this work in the Bachgesellschaft edition, Brahms specifically marked this repeat.[108]

To conclude, the point needs to be made that Brahms's collection is also a deeply personal commentary on death whose biographical model seems to have been not the *Orgelbüchlein* but the Great Eighteen chorales. Pessimistic by nature his whole life, Brahms during his last years became obsessed with the subject of mortality—both his own and that of his colleagues. As early as 1890, he declared that his activities as a composer were over, and the following year he drew up a will. Then, with the premature passing of Elisabet von Herzogenberg in 1892, death began to invade his circle of friends. The contralto Hermine Spies succumbed in 1893 at the shockingly early age of thirty-six, and during a three-month period in 1894 Brahms lost three of his oldest comrades: Spitta, Hans von Bülow, and the surgeon Theodor Billroth. Especially devastating was Clara Schumann's death in May 1896, by which point Brahms himself was exhibiting unmistakable symptoms of liver cancer, the same illness that had claimed his father. He died from the disease less than a year later, at the age of sixty-three.

Given these dire circumstances, it is of obvious significance that most of the settings from Brahms's opus deal directly with the topics of death and dying. (The same is true of Brahms's penultimate work, the *Vier ernste Gesänge,* op. 121, composed just a few weeks earlier.) And it would appear that the idea of expressing his grief through the archaic genre of the organ chorale came to Brahms through his musicological studies, for he would have read in Wilhelm Rust's preface to volume 25, part 2, of the Bachgesellschaft edition (p. xx) that Bach compiled the Great Eighteen at the very end of his life, in the midst of a lengthy illness.[109] Therefore, Brahms's decision to author a set of organ chorales as he felt his own life slipping away may be seen as an attempt to emulate Bach biographically as well as musically.

Brahms would also have read in Rust's preface and in Spitta's Bach biography (vol. 2, pp. 759–60) that the Great Eighteen setting of "Vor deinen Thron tret ich hiermit" was Bach's "swan song" (as Rust called it), which the blind composer dictated on his deathbed. Although the text of this hymn constitutes a summary of the Christian faith, its opening line ("Before your throne I now appear") doubtless implies death as its subject matter.[110] This work, then, may have played a special role in Brahms's conception. Brahms's collection represents the most profound response to Bach's organ works in the whole history of music.

APPENDIX

Johannes Brahms's Study Score
of the Fantasy in G Major, BWV 572

Johannes Brahms's study score of the Fantasy in G Major, BWV 572, mm. 29–185 (*gravement* section) (Transcribed from the autograph manuscript, Gesellschaft der Musikfreunde, Vienna, catalogue no. A 130, f. 41)

Notes

Chapter 1

1. Over a dozen new organ works by Mendelssohn have surfaced in recent years. They are published in Little 1987–90 and Albrecht 1993–94.

2. My coverage of Mendelssohn's life, especially with respect to dates, is based on Todd 2001.

3. Werner 1963, pp. 7–10; and Wollny 1993.

4. Wollny 1993, p. 653.

5. Schünemann 1928.

6. Neumann 1962, p. 140.

7. Todd 1983, p. 56.

8. Sieling 1995, pp. 88–92 and 141–56; and Sieling 1999, pp. 306–10.

9. Cited in Sieling 1995, pp. 148–50. Translation from Little 2005, p. 75.

10. *von Freudenberg auf der Aka- / demie erhalten, und abge- / schrieben d. 9ten Dec. 1811*. See Kilian 1978–79, p. 106. According to Klein 2003, p. 24, this manuscript must have originated between September 1821 and March 1822, despite the date provided by Mendelssohn. Therefore, its actual date would appear to be 9 December *1811*.

11. Sieling 1995, pp. 148–50.

12. Boyd 1999, pp. 562–72.

13. Elvers and Ward Jones 1993.

14. There is no evidence that Bach himself ever organized these six pieces into any kind of group. Rather, this idea seems to have originated within Kirnberger's circle at Berlin. See Kilian 1978–79, pp. 15–16 and 256–57.

15. Furthermore, Levy apparently gave her manuscript of the Trio Sonatas to Mendelssohn at some point. See Kilian 1988, pp. 48–49.

16. Todd 1983, pp. 80–81.

17. A lost piece for his sister Fanny's wedding that was later incorporated into the Sonata in A Major, op. 65, no. 3.

18. Grossmann-Vendrey 1969a, p. 179.

19. Letter of 13 September 1822. See E. Wolff 1907, pp. 7–8; and Selden-Goth 1972, p. 28. According to Ramann 1880–94, vol. 1, p. 372, Franz Liszt played this same instrument thirteen or fourteen years later.

20. Letter of 20 April 1825. See Todd 1983, p. 5; and Weissweiler 1997, pp. 38–40.

21. In addition to Beethoven, the other musicians cited in Mendelssohn's letter are George Onslow, Antoine Reicha, and Pierre Monsigny, a prolific composer of comic operas.

22. See the postscript of Felix's letter to his father of 11 December 1831 (New York Public Library, No. 142).

23. Entry of 13 October 1825. See Cox 1907, p. 173.

24. Felix mentions this instrument in a letter to his mother of 25 March 1825. See Elvers 1984, p. 40.

25. Kilian 1988, p. 178.

26. Sieling 1995, pp. 152–53.

27. Letter of 3 October 1829. See Citron 1987, pp. 91–92.

28. This is the same conclusion reached (without any discussion) in Klein 2001b, p. 180. Incidentally, Fanny's only pastorale is for piano and dates from 1846. No such work by Felix survives.

29. Grossmann-Vendrey 1969a, p. 181.

30. Elvers 1984, pp. 59–61; and Little 1994, pp. 275–76.

31. Elvers 1984, p. 105.

32. Ibid., pp. 107–8.

33. Letter of 9 June 1827. See Coleridge 1887, p. 291.

34. Letter of 10 June 1831. See Coleridge 1887, pp. 451–52.

35. The Fugue in G Minor, BWV 542/2, and the Canonic Variations on "Vom Himmel hoch." See Weiss 1983, pp. 351–52.

36. Letter of 22 June 1830. See Schulz 1971, pp. 133–34. Translation adapted from Selden-Goth 1972, pp. 81–82.

37. See Bötel 1984, p. 39; Pape 1988, pp. 25–27; and David and Mendel 1998, pp. 500 and 539.

38. See especially P. Williams 1981. An entire book devoted to this issue is Claus 1995. For a recent argument in favor of the work's authenticity, see C. Wolff 2002.

39. Crum and Ward Jones 1980–89, vol. 2, pp. 32–33.

40. Very possibly Johann Gottlob Töpfer, who was appointed deputy organist at the town church in 1817 and principal organist in 1830. Töpfer was already something of an expert on organ construction by the time of Mendelssohn's visit, and he would eventually be regarded as the foremost German authority on the subject. See Chorzempa and Bähr 2001.

41. Kobayashi 1973, pp. 11–12.

42. Kilian 1978–79, pp. 85–87.

43. According to the travel diary kept by Mendelssohn during his Viennese sojourn, he played the organ on 24 September and 2 October. No further information is provided. See Zappala 2002, pp. 728 and 730.

44. Wüster 1996, pp. 58–63.

45. A modern edition of this work is Lehmann 1983.

46. Wüster 1996, p. 434.

47. Kilian 1978–79, p. 257.

48. Crum and Ward Jones 1980–89, vol. 2, p. 33; and Löhlein 1987, p. 185 (where the date is given incorrectly as 26 December). Hauser inscribed this source: *für Felix M. / Wien d. 11 Dec. 30 Hauser.*

49. "Lieber Hauser! Wenn ich an Sie schreibe so muss ich schon nicht anders als mit Dank anfangen; da haben Sie mir wieder einen göttlichen Choral v. Bach geschickt und selbst geschrieben, und das Ganze sieht so zierlich und nett u. doch gelerht aus, wie mein Zimmer in der Bärenmühle; Sie wissen ja, welche Freude mir das muss gemacht haben." Letter of 30 January 1831. See Kobayashi 1973, p. 20; and Löhlein 1987, p. 185.

50. Kobayashi 1973, p. 20.

51. Mendelssohn based his edition on the manuscript sent to him by Hauser. See Löhlein 1987, p. 193.

52. Letter to Goethe of 28 August 1831. See Schulz 1971, p. 193.

53. Ibid.

54. Letter of 3 September 1831. See Mendelssohn Bartholdy 1861, pp. 265–67. For facsimile reproductions of the two musical inserts, see Sutermeister 1958, pp. 243 and 245.

55. Sieling 1999, pp. 307 and 337, n. 42.

56. Crum and Ward Jones 1980–89, vol. 2, p. 33.

57. Werner 1963, pp. 530–31.

58. Grossmann-Vendrey 1969a, p. 181.

59. Letter of 22 September 1831. See Elvers 1984, pp. 147–48.

60. Letter of 6 October 1831. See Mendelssohn Bartholdy 1861, pp. 277–78.

61. Letter of 5 September 1831. See Mendelssohn Bartholdy 1861, p. 270.

62. Elvers 1984, p. 18.

63. Herz 1985, pp. 99–100.

64. Bormann 1926, p. 143.

65. Kilian 1978–79, pp. 254–55.

66. Letter of 14–17 November 1831. See Elvers 1984, pp. 148–49.

67. All four versions are published in Weinberger 1986.

68. P. Williams 1980–84, vol. 2, pp. 289–90.

69. The most detailed argument against Bach's authorship is Tittel 1966, pp. 130–33.

70. On Schelble's print, whose publication date is unknown, see Kobayashi 1973, p. 272.

71. Crum and Ward Jones 1980–89, vol. 2, pp. 35–36; and Kilian 1978–79, pp. 254–55.

72. "Beckchen paukt mit Virtuosität das Pedal ... u. ich stärke mein Herz zuweilen daran. Der alte Bach würde sich todtlachen, wenn er das sehen könnte." Letter of 29 July 1829, published in Weissweiler 1997, p. 85.

73. Letter of 4 June 1839 (New York Public Library, No. 406). In this letter, Mendelssohn reports on having discovered in Frankfurt some "very significant" organ works by Bach and mentions to Rebecka how he looks forward to playing them in this manner with her.

74. Griepenkerl and Roitzsch 1844–52, vol. 1, p. iv.

75. "Vorläufig bitte ich Dich liebe Fanny, folgende Stücke aus unsrer Sebastian Bachsmappe: Toccata aus d moll, Toccata aus f dur, Praelud. u. Fuge aus e moll, Fantasie aus g moll, Prael. u. Fuge aus g dur, Prael. u. Fuge aus d moll, jedes von diesen Stücken *zweimal* abschreiben zu lassen, aber wo möglich ganz correct, und dann ein Exemplar der Sammlung an Schelble in Frankf., das zweite an mich hierher für Hiller zu schicken, wenn es nicht zu voluminös ist per Post. . . . Hiller will sie à tout prix haben; er und Kalkbrenner spielen die gedruckten Orgelstücke hier bei Gelegenheit." This passage comprises a postscript to a letter of 11–14 December 1831 written by Felix to his father (New York Public Library, No. 142). Cited in Grossmann-Vendrey 1969, p. 48, but with many inaccuracies.

76. Contrary to Mendelssohn's belief, the Prelude and Fugue in E Minor, BWV 533, was almost certainly in print by this date. It appeared in 1831 or 1832 in the Mannheim publication, *Orgel-Journal*. See Schmieder 1990, p. 503; and Little 2005, p. 75.

77. Crum and Ward Jones 1980–89, vol. 2, p. 32. These sources contain the Prelude and Fugue in G Major, BWV 541; the "Little" Fugue in G Minor, BWV 578; the Prelude and Fugue in E Major, BWV 566 (first two movements only); and the Prelude and Fugue in D Minor, BWV 539.

78. Letter of 29 July 1829. See Weissweiler 1997, p. 85.

79. Letter of 8 November 1830. See Mendelssohn Bartholdy 1861, p. 52.

80. Jourdan 1998, pp. 98–99 and 126; and Elvers 1984, pp. 75–76.

81. Thistlethwaite 1990, pp. 22–23.

82. Ward Jones 1997, pp. 99–100.

83. Jourdan 1998, p. 178.

84. Edwards 1895, p. 8; Edwards 1896, p. 724; Edwards 1900, p. 791; and Jourdan 1998, p. 180.

85. Atkins 1957, p. 253.

86. See, respectively, Lampadius 1876, p. 18; and Rockstro 1884, p. 48.

87. Unpublished letter to Madame C. Kiené of 28 July 1832 (private possession).

88. Jourdan 1998, p. 180. Similarly, the organist H. J. Gauntlett recalled that Mendelssohn was the first in England ever to play Bach's "short" E-minor prelude and fugue. See Edwards 1896, p. 724. Gauntlett uses the moniker "short" here in contradistinction to the much longer Prelude and Fugue in E Minor, BWV 548. Another common nickname for BWV 533 among English speakers is "Cathedral," presumably because of Mendelssohn's performances of the work at St. Paul's.

89. Novello 1833.

90. The contents of various Bach-organ manuscripts known to have been in Mendelssohn's possession toward the end of his life are listed in Crum and Ward Jones 1980–89, vol. 2, pp. 32–35.

91. Letter of 6 May 1832 (written in English). See Edwards 1896, p. 724; and Little 2005, p. 75.

92. Little 2005, p. 76.

93. "Ich denke zugleich an die Bachschen Stücke, die wir zusammen spielten, und muss Dir noch sagen, dass ich noch ein ganzes Heft unbekannter Sachen in derselben Art von ihm hier gefunden habe, und dass sie nun alle zusammen bei Bre-

itkopf und Härtel erscheinen sollen. Es sind himmlische Sachen darunter, ich denke Du wirst Dich damit freuen." Letter of 10 August 1832. See Moscheles 1888, p. 32; and Löhlein 1987, pp. 65–66.

94. This unpublished letter is the property of the Library of Congress. It was Joseph Moore, a friend of Mendelssohn and one of the organizers of the Birmingham Music Festival, who delivered the parcel.

95. According to Temperly 2001, p. 151, Attwood "was not himself a great executant on the organ."

96. Little 2005, pp. 76–77.

97. "Weil ich heut als Sühnopfer noch nicht etwas schicken kann, woran ich selbst arbeite, so muss der alte Bach mein Schild und Schutz sein, und so schreibe ich auf der nächsten Seite ein kleines Stück, welches ich hier vor 14 Tagen zufällig habe kennen lernen. . . . Die Oberstimme ist abermals ein ausgeschmückter Choral und wird auf der Orgel mit etwas stärkeren Registern gespielt, auf Clavier müsste man sie in Octaven spielen, oder am besten wär es glaub ich, wenn Herr Baillot die Oberstimme auf seiner Geige sänge, und dann das Clavier richtig drunter fortginge." Letter of 4 September 1832, cited in Löhlein 1987, p. 65. The phrase "mein Schild und Schutz" in the first sentence is probably a pun on Psalm 119:114 ("Du bist mein Schutz und mein Schild").

98. Stinson 1996, pp. 161–66 and 175–79.

99. Cooper 1983, pp. 109, 138, and 221; and Hiemke 1999, pp. 33–34.

100. Letter of 12 January 1833. See Grossmann-Vendrey 1969a, pp. 209; and Kobayashi 1973, pp. 199–200. Hauser's thematic catalogue represents the oldest one in existence devoted to Bach. See Kobayashi 1973, p. 197.

101. Letter of 19 January 1833. See Grossmann-Vendrey 1969a, p. 209; and Kobayashi 1973, p. 201. See also Kobayashi 1973, pp. 204–8; Grossmann-Vendrey 1969a, p. 213; and Crum and Ward Jones 1980–89, vol. 2, pp. 32–33.

102. Letter of 20 February 1833. See Grossmann-Vendrey 1969a, p. 210; and Kobayashi 1973, p. 203.

103. "Mir sind in Deinem Catalog einige Stücke aufgefallen, deren Themas so schön sind, dass ich sie gerne haben möchte, und da sie meist für die Orgel sind und ich in London in St. Paul oft spiele, wie Du weisst, möchte ich sie gerne mit dorthin nehmen; also will ich Dich fragen, ob Du mir dieselben (besonders die Orgelstücke) womöglich sogleich willst copiren lassen und herschicken. Denn Morgen über 14 Tage (den 14ten) reise ich ab so Gott will. Es sind folgende Stücke: Fantasie für Orgel c moll, Choralvorspiele zu Ach Herr mich armen Sünder,—Ach Gott erhör mein Seufzen,—Christ lag in Todesbanden,—Herr Jesu Christ dich zu uns wend,—Zeuch ein zu deinen Thoren." Letter of 30 March 1833, cited in Grossmann-Vendrey 1969a, p. 183, but without any reference to the incipit provided by Mendelssohn for the C-minor fantasy. I first became aware of the incipit upon examining the original manuscript of this letter at the Staatsbibliothek zu Berlin (no shelf number).

104. See the edition of Hauser's catalogue in Kobayashi 1973, pp. 234, 254–55, and 271.

105. Emans 1997 and Weinberger 1986.

106. Interestingly, five of the six works contained in J. N. Schelble's aforementioned edition of organ chorales by Bach are of this type. The inclusion of "Schmücke dich" in this collection suggests Mendelssohn's influence.

107. Little 1987–90, vol. 1, p. vii and vol. 5, p. vi; Jourdan 1998, pp. 175–76; and Klein 2001a.

108. "Heute früh Felix Orgel in St. Pauls gespielt, wozu, da die Balgentreter schon fort waren, Klingemann und noch 2 Gentlemen deren stelle vertraten. Felix spielte eine Introduction und Fuge, improvisirte und dann ein coronation anthem von Attwood mit diesem vierhändig, und dann 3 Sebastiane. Es klang sehr gut, die Kirche war leer, nur 2 Besucherinnen des Philharmonic hatten sich versteckt, um zu hören." See Klein 2001a, p. 87.

109. Edwards 1905, p. 720.

110. These are Attwood's only extant coronation anthems. See Temperly 2001.

111. Mendelssohn's three trio-fugues, written when he was only eleven, should not be considered in this context. Their outrageously virtuosic and unidiomatic pedal parts were doubtless never intended to be performed as such.

112. Edwards 1895, pp. 42–44.

113. Kilian 1988, p. 192.

114. Klein 2001a, p. 108.

115. Stauffer 1980, pp. 98 and 122, gives the composition date as no later than 1700–06.

116. See Mendelssohn's letter to his mother of 6 May 1834 (New York Public Library, No. 192).

117. See Mendelssohn's letter to his family of 4 August 1834, published in Mendelssohn Bartholdy 1863, pp. 48–52.

118. Kobayashi 1973, p. 23.

119. Grossmann-Vendrey 1969a, p. 185.

120. Krause 1982 and Rosenmüller 2000.

121. Krause 1970, pp. 78–80; and Rosenmüller 2000, p. 188.

122. Bischoff 1997, p. 499, nn. 326, 327, and 331.

123. Translation based on Pleasants 1965, p. 93. On the date of Schumann's cemetery expedition, see Bischoff 1997, pp. 431–32. Schumann used phraseology similar to that found at the beginning of this passage in a letter to Mendelssohn of 22 October 1845: "In Bach's music I always imagine him sitting at the organ, but in yours I think more of a St. Cecilia touching the keys." See Jansen 1904, p. 251. Four years earlier, Schumann had written to his friend G. A. Keferstein that he would like nothing better than to hear Bach play the organ. See Jansen 1904, p. 181.

124. Stinson 2001, pp. 80–82.

125. Bötel 1984, p. 99.

126. "Auch Orgel muss ich zweimal spielen und eröffne das ganze Fest mit einem langen Sebastian Bach." See Grossmann-Vendrey 1969a, pp. 130–31.

127. Mendelssohn Bartholdy 1863, p. 145. Translation based on Ward Jones 1997, p. 174.

128. According to Crum and Ward Jones 1980–89, vol. 3, p. 8, Mendelssohn owned the 1804 print of this collection, published by Hoffmeister.

129. Citron 1987, p. 240.

130. See the data given in Thistlethwaite 1990, pp. 172–77. As was pointed out in the first English edition of the fugue (1827), the primary subject is melodically identical to the opening phrase of the hymn tune "St. Anne," and the fugue has been known by this nickname ever since. See Edwards 1896, p. 723.

131. Ward Jones 1997, p. 98. According to Charles Edward Horsley, who would later study privately with Mendelssohn in Leipzig, it was on this modest instrument that "many happy afternoons were spent in hearing his [Mendelssohn's] interpretation of Bach Fugues." See Horsley 1872, p. 353.

132. Ward Jones 1997, pp. 99–100. The deputy organist mentioned by Mendelssohn was George Cooper (d. 1843). The ascending pedal figure to which he refers is presumably that in measure 144.

133. Gauntlett 1837, p. 9.

134. Ward Jones 1997, p. 103.

135. Ibid., p. 192. Felix's letter, which has not survived, was apparently written a day or two after he left London for Birmingham on 13 September. Cécile quoted from it in a letter to her mother-in-law of 21 September.

136. Thistlethwaite 1990, pp. 14–15 and 172–77.

137. Pearce 1909, pp. 28–29.

138. Ward Jones 1997, p. 103, n. 1.

139. Gauntlett 1837, p. 10. According to Gauntlett 1902, Mendelssohn liked to refer to organs with such limited pedalboards as "crippled."

140. Also in attendance, according to Gauntlett 1902, was Mendelssohn's dear friend Ignaz Moscheles. But it is hard to accept Gauntlett's claim that Moscheles did not know beforehand that Mendelssohn even played the organ!

141. Pearce 1910, p. 24.

142. Furthermore, in his own C-minor fugue, which, as discussed earlier, appears to be modeled after Bach's A-minor fugue, Mendelssohn indicates (through dynamics) that the two manual episodes are to be played on an auxiliary manual.

143. Thistlethwaite 1990, pp. 127–35; Ward Jones 1997, p. 106, n. 4; and Polko 1869, p. 205.

144. Ward Jones 1997, p. 115.

145. "Heute Morgen nahm er in einer gewaltigen Sebastian Bach'schen Fuge einen ernsthaften und bedeutenden Abschied." See Thomson 1837, p. 119. On the identification of Thomson as the author of the review, see Fuchs 1982, p. 223, n. 86.

146. Review of various organ publications in *The Musical World* 8 (1838), pp. 101–2. The "forty-eight studies" referred to are obviously the forty-eight preludes and fugues of the *Well-Tempered Clavier.*

147. Mendelssohn Bartholdy 1863, p. 202.

148. Ibid.

149. For particulars, see Little 1987–90, vol. 1, pp. xiii–xiv.

150. On this point, see also Todd 2003, p. 377.

151. Hilse 1998, p. 7.

152. Rothe and Szeskus 1972, p. 148.

153. This unpublished letter is No. 406 of the Mendelssohn letters owned by the New York Public Library.

154. As late as 31 January 1839 Mendelssohn described his "personal acquaintance" with Guhr as "slight." See Polko 1869, p. 168.

155. Mendelssohn Bartholdy 1863, pp. 191–92; and Weissweiler 1997, pp. 308–9. Regarding the last word in this excerpt, "Cantor" was one of Felix's nicknames for his favorite sibling—and the moniker undoubtedly refers to Bach. See Citron 1987, p. xliii.

156. Kilian 1978–79, p. 248.

157. Löhlein 1987, pp. 50–51, 66–67, and 228; and Kobayashi 1973, pp. 204–9.

158. Kilian 1988, pp. 129–33.

159. The Passacaglia was first issued around 1834 by F. P. Dunst, the Legrenzi fugue in 1831 by Tobias Haslinger. Mendelssohn's copy of the Dunst print survives today in the Bodleian Library, Oxford. See Kilian 1988, p. 125; Kilian 1978–79, p. 257; and Crum and Ward Jones 1980–89, vol. 3, p. 9. The many corrections and revisions inscribed by Mendelssohn into this source may have been copied from Guhr's "autograph."

160. Chorley 1854, pp. 37–39. As his travel journals attest, the writer William Beckford (1760–1844) was something of an expert on Renaissance art.

161. Kilian 1978–79, pp. 233–35.

162. Lehmann 1997.

163. Letter of 6 January 1840. See Elvers 1984, pp. 207–8.

164. On this print, see Kilian 1978–79, pp. 260–61.

165. Unbeknownst to Mendelssohn, the autograph was owned at the time by J. F. Naue, director of music at the University of Halle. See Kilian 1978–79, p. 33.

166. See Mendelssohn's letter to his mother of 22 June 1840 (New York Public Library, No. 438); and Dähnert 1971, pp. 197–98. Mendelssohn also owned a booklet commemorating the onehundredth anniversary of the construction of these instruments. See Ward Jones 1985, p. 314, no. 190.

167. Polko 1869, p. 203.

168. For a detailed discussion, see Pape 1988.

169. P. Williams 1980–84, vol. 3, pp. 131–34; and Schrammek 1983. The instrument was dismantled and replaced in 1889.

170. Letter of 10 August 1840. See Mendelssohn Bartholdy 1863, p. 232.

171. Mendelssohn had also planned to "let loose" with Bach organ works at St. Thomas's as part of the unveiling ceremony, but there is no evidence he did so. See Grossmann-Vendrey 1969a, pp. 213–24.

172. Polko 1869, p. 73. Over fifty years earlier, Rochlitz had witnessed another momentous musical event in the history of the Thomas Church, for he was one of the choristers there when, in 1789, Mozart first encountered Bach's motet "Singet dem Herrn ein neues Lied." See Blume 1950, p. 27.

173. Werner 1963, p. 318.

174. David and Mendel 1998, pp. 502–3. Schumann's review appeared in the 15 August 1840 issue of the *Neue Zeitschrift für Musik*.

175. "Mendelssohn's Concert dauerte etwas lang. Du würdest aber grosse Freude daran gehabt haben, namentlich an dem Präludium in A Moll (dasselbe, das Du spielst von den 6 grossen), das ganz gross und einzig und brillant sich aus nimmt an der Orgel. Es mochten im Ganzen 400–500 Zuhörer sein." Letter of 7 August 1840. See Weissweiler 1984–2001, p. 1062.

176. According to Pape 1988, p. 19, n. 49, all that survives of this program today is a photograph.

177. P. Williams 1963, pp. 147–48.

178. Sieling 1995, pp. 151–52; and Sieling 1999, p. 307.

179. P. Williams 1963, p. 148.

180. Kilian 1978–79, p. 256.

181. Grossmann-Vendrey 1969a, p. 190.

182. Todd 1995; and Todd 2003, pp. 401–2. For a reconstruction, see Albrecht 1993–94.

183. In describing Mendelssohn's organ playing, his pupil C. E. Horsley wrote that: "I have heard most of the greatest organists of my time . . . but in no respect have I ever heard Mendelssohn excelled either in creative or executive ability, and it is hard to say which was the most extraordinary, his manipulation or pedipulation." See Horsley 1872, p. 353.

184. An ad that ran in the 29 July 1840 issue of the *Leipziger Tageblatt* began: "Der Unterzeichnete beabsichtigt, Donnerstag den 6. August Nachmittags um 6 Uhr in der Thomaskirche ein Orgel-Concert zu geben, worin er mehre der bedeutendsten Bach-Composition vortragen wird." For a facsimile reproduction, see Pape 1988, p. 12.

185. Three years earlier, in his honeymoon diary, he had also referred to this work as the "great" A-minor prelude and fugue.

186. Grove 1880, p. 277; and Thistlethwaite 1990, pp. 132–33.

187. Thistlethwaite 1990, pp. 215–22; and Edwards 1905.

188. Grove 1880, pp. 274 and 277.

189. This fragment, which today is preserved in the church's organ gallery, also bears Mendelssohn's signature and the inscription: *St. Peter's Cornhill / 30 Sept. / 1840.* For a facsimile reproduction, see Edwards 1905, p. 719.

190. This according to a review in the 23 June 1842 issue of *The Musical World.*

191. Letter of 21 June 1842. See Mendelssohn Bartholdy 1863, p. 317.

192. Grove 1880, p. 280.

193. Edwards 1896, p. 724. By "Exercises," Gauntlett probably means Part 3 of the *Clavierübung,* literally, "Keyboard Exercise." The reference in the penultimate sentence is to Thomas Adams, one of the most prominent British organists of the first half of the nineteenth century.

194. Mounsey, too, was impressed by how slow Mendelssohn played Bach. Apropos of his performances at St. Peter-upon-Cornhill, she commented: "I remember how—according to my experience—he played Bach *slower* than I expected . . . instead of rattling off the semiquavers he made them flow impressively and seriously." See Thistlethwaite 1990, p. 520.

195. Werner 1963, pp. 261–62; and Lehmann 1997, p. 94.

196. "Morgen Nachmittag spiele ich Seb. Bach auf der Thomasorgel; ausser besagtem Gounod soll niemand zuhören, als wen Du schickst . . . Ich denke um 5, statt der Compositionsstunde wärs passend, da nähm' ich die Musikschüler gleich mit." See Grossmann-Vendrey 1969a, p. 189.

197. Gounod 1895, p. 152.

198. Ibid., pp. 156–57.

199. Hiemke 1999, p. 44; and Seaton 2001, p. 680.

200. Bovet and Widor 1893, pp. 839–40.

201. Werner 1963, pp. 327–31.

202. "Mendelssohn spielte uns in der Thomaskirche Orgel vor; die Bach'schen Fugen in A moll und D dur, dann Motetten und anderes in wunderbarer Virtuosität." See Vesque von Püttlingen 1887, pp. 64 and 66.

203. Letter to the organist F. J. Sawyer of 28 March 1884. See Sumner 1962.

204. Edwards 1901, p. 795; and Sabatier 1982, p. 54.

205. Grossmann-Vendrey 1969b, p. 193.

206. Sabatier 1982, p. 54. The only other such fugue by Bach known to this author is the Fugue in C Minor on a Theme by Legrenzi, BWV 574.

207. Parkins and Todd 1983.

208. Kilian 1978–79, p. 271; and Little 2005, pp. 77–78.

209. Crum and Ward Jones 1980–89, vol. 3, pp. 5–6.

210. "Wenn Du in Deinem Catalog auch der gedruckten Ausgaben erwähnst, vergiss nicht eine englische, der hauptsächlichsten Orgelstücke, die sehr correct und gut ist: bei Coventry u. Hollier. Ich besitze in dieser Ausgabe die 6 grossen Orgelpräludien u. Fugen, die in Wien bei Riedel zuerst erschienen (a moll, h moll etc) mehrere der von Marx ebenfalls edirten u. a. die g moll Fantasie u. Fuge." Letter of 21 October 1839. See Kobayashi 1973, pp. 204–6.

211. On the demise of Marx's and Mendelssohn's friendship, see Sposato 2004, pp. 257–58.

212. Little 2005, p. 78. The mutual friend referred to by Coventry is the composer William Sterndale Bennett.

213. Polko 1869, p. 216; Ward Jones 1992, p. 252; Grossmann-Vendrey 1969a, p. 195; and Little 2005, p. 78. On 8 August 1845 Mendelssohn returned to Coventry the proofs for the G-major prelude and fugue, with a note that he had corrected them according to volume 2 of the Peters edition of Bach's complete organ works, which had just been published. See Polko 1869, p. 219; and Little 2005, p. 79.

214. According to Polko 1869, p. 217, Mendelssohn formulated this title himself. Apropos of figure 1–5, the word that appears in small print near the bottom, directly beneath the horizontal line, is "Hunter," the name of the engraver of the title page. My thanks to Peter Ward Jones for this information.

215. For full bibliographical information, see Elvers 1960.

216. On the early publication history of the *Orgelbüchlein* and Great Eighteen, see, respectively, Stinson 1996, pp. 154–55; and Stinson 2001, pp.116–17.

217. Ludwig 1996.

218. Grossmann-Vendrey 1969a, p. 195.

219. Letter of 17 December 1844. See Polko 1869, p. 217; and Little 2005, p. 78. Coventry's inscription recalls his letter to Mendelssohn of 8 February 1844, in which he refers to any free organ work by Bach as a "pedal fugue."

220. In this final sentence, Mendelssohn cites the collection best known to English speakers as Bach's "371 Four-Part Chorales."

221. Stinson 1996, pp. 160–61.

222. He had evidently proposed this same condition to Coventry, only to be vetoed. See Elvers 1968, pp. 147 and 149.

223. In the four-volume anthology *J. S. Bachs Choral-Vorspiele für die Orgel mit einem und zwey Klavieren und Pedal*, published in 1803–6 by Breitkopf & Härtel. See Crum and Ward Jones 1980–89, vol. 2, p. 33.

224. Letter to Coventry of 20 March 1846. See Polko 1869, p. 219.

225. In a letter of 15 February 1845, Mendelssohn had asked this longtime resident of London to proofread his preface to Books 1 and 2 of the Coventry & Hollier edition and to translate all the chorale titles as well. See Klingemann 1909, pp. 303–4.

226. "Im rhythmischen Akzent liegt das ganze Geheimnis des Vortrags dieser Musik. Keineswegs masse ich mir an, dasselbe aus eigenen Mitteln gefunden zu haben; ich hörte vor vielen Jahren einmal Mendelssohn die grosse Bachsche a-moll-Fuge auf der Orgel spielen. Bei der Gelegenheit ist mir der Star gestochen worden. Auf der Orgel kann man nur den Rhythmus markieren, weil die Töne keinen Unterschied der Stärke zulassen. Mendelssohns Spiel verstand es nun hinlänglich die Cäsuren . . . deutlich zu machen—man hörte jeden Eintritt einer neuen Stimme ebenso gut wie das Verschwinden derselben vom Schauplatz. Was diesem ausserordentlichen Manne auf der Orgel möglich war, sollte es mittels der Singstimmen nicht tausendmal leichter zu erzielen sein?" See Wirth 1927, p. 370.

227. Elvers 1984, p. 235.

228. Pape 1988, pp. 28–29.

229. "Musik gäbe Dir eine Freude, und Du könntest Dir von Deinem dortigen Musiker 'Schmücke Dich, liebe Seele' von Sebastian Bach vorspielen lassen!" Letter of 5 April 1847. See Wehmer 1959, p. 104.

230. "Du sagst mir, Bach's 'Schmücke dich, o liebe Seele' möchtest Du mir vorspielen. Als ich im vorigen Jahre in Berlin war, hatte Fanny mich zur Musik eingeladen. 'Des Herren Zeit ist die beste Zeit' wurde gesungen—und ich wusste schon, was mir bevorstand! War das eine Predigt!" Letter of 1 May 1847. See Wehmer 1959, p. 107.

231. Citron 1987, pp. 161, 164, n. 4, 176, and 177, n. 16.

232. See Abraham's letter to Felix of 10 March 1835, published in Mendelssohn Bartholdy 1863, pp. 83–88. See also Werner 1963, pp. 285 and 296.

233. Todd 2003, p. 547.

234. Chorley 1854, vol. 2, pp. 395–96.

Chapter 2

1. Letter of 18 January 1838 to the directors of the Lower Rhine Music Festival. See Mendelssohn Bartholdy 1863, p. 164.

2. Letter to Carl Kossmaly of 5 May 1843. See Jansen 1904, p. 228.

3. My discussion of Schumann's life is based primarily on Daverio 2001.

4. Bischoff 1997, p. 430.

5. "Abends riss ich mit Clara sechs Bachhische Fugen ab, vierhändig a vista prima." Entry of 29 May 1832. See Eismann and Nauhaus 1971–82, vol. 1, p. 400.

6. Daverio 1997, pp. 107–9.

7. Letter to Eduard Krüger of 15 June 1843. See Jansen 1904, p. 192.

8. For a complete list of music edited by Becker, see Rosenmüller 2000, pp. 137–55.

9. Plantinga 1967, p. 88.

10. For particulars on this edition, see Klotz 1957, p. 53.

11. Eismann and Nauhaus 1971–82, vol. 2, pp. 34, 40, 41, 53, and 55.

12. For some general remarks on this source, which preserves several such inscriptions in Schumann's hand, see Bischoff 1997, pp. 447 and 499, n. 328.

13. See the photograph in Bischoff 1997, p. 429.

14. Daverio 1997, pp. 164–65.

15. Eismann and Nauhaus 1971–82, vol. 2, p. 52.

16. "Rückblick auf das Leipziger Musikleben im Winter 1837/1838," *Neue Zeitschrift für Musik* 8, no. 27, p. 116; reprinted in R. Schumann 1854, vol. 3, p. 53.

17. Keller 1967, p. 280.

18. "But we shall also be mindful of earlier times. More specifically, there are many unprinted works of J. S. Bach still awaiting publication, and some of the finest of these are already in our possession." See Plantinga 1967, p. 89. In fact, though, only in the case of "Durch Adams Fall" and the fantasy did Schumann's editions constitute a first printing. On the publication dates of the other four works, see Kilian 1978–79, p. 272; and Löhlein 1987, p. 109.

19. P. Williams 1980–84, vol. 1, p. 205.

20. Keil 1973, pp. 117–18.

21. *Von Mendelssohn nach Bach's / Originalschrift corrigirt.* (Similarly, Schumann's edition of "Das alte Jahr" contains the footnote: *Nach dem Original Manuscript gedruckt.*) The heading provided by Schicht translates as "with the cantus firmus embellished and in the highest voice."

22. My thanks to Gerd Nauhaus for his help in deciphering and authenticating Schumann's script.

23. C. Schumann 1885, p. 306.

24. It should also be mentioned that a manuscript of "Wir glauben all an einen Gott, Vater," BWV 740, is known to have circulated within Schumann's circle. On this point, see Emans 1997, p. 82. Since Mendelssohn would later publish this work along with fourteen of the Great Eighteen chorales, it presumably belonged to the manuscript containing the Great Eighteen chorales that Mendelssohn arranged to be copied for Schumann.

25. "Am herrlichsten, am kühnsten, in seinem Urelemente erscheint er aber nun ein für allemal an seiner Orgel. Hier kennt er weder Mass noch Ziel und arbeitet auf Jahrhunderte hinaus. Wir haben hier einer neuen Ausgabe von 6 früher bei Riedel in Wien schon erschienenen Präludien und Fugen zu erwähnen, die Haslinger neu ausgelegt. Den Organisten werden sie bekannt sein: Nr. IV ist das wundervolle Präludium in C-Moll." *Neue Zeitschrift für Musik* 10, no. 39 (14 May 1839), pp. 153–54; reprinted in R. Schumann 1854, vol. 3, p. 95.

26. "Sag mir doch, wie spielt man denn die Fugen von Bach mit Pedal? das Pedal soll doch immer in Octaven sein, dann sind sie ja aber nicht möglich zu spielen? (ich spreche von den 6 Präludien und Fugen die Du mir mit nach Paris geschickt.)" Letter of 11 October 1839, published in Weissweiler 1984–2001, p. 738. On Clara's visit to Paris, see Reich 1985, pp. 89–96.

27. Bischoff 1997, pp. 441 and 443. The one Bach work regularly played by Clara at that time was apparently the Fugue in C-sharp Major from Book 2 of the *Well-Tempered Clavier*.

28. Krüger 1844, pp. 121–22.

29. Jerger 1975, p. 151.

30. Eismann and Nauhaus 1971–82, vol. 2, p. 112.

31. Chorley 1854, vol. 2, p. 51.

32. Letter to C. E. Klitzsch of 10 June 1847. See Jansen 1904, p. 270.

33. Loos 2002, p. 415.

34. Nauhaus 1993, p. 112.

35. Ibid., pp. 92–93.

36. Schumann's household record for this date contains the entry "Orgelconc. v. Becker." See Eismann and Nauhaus 1971–82, vol. 3, p. 189.

37. Fuchs 1982, pp. 222–23; and Krause 1982, p. 92.

38. "Ueber einige muthmasslich corrumpirte Stellen in Bach'schen, Mozart'schen und Beethoven'schen Werken," *Neue Zeitschrift für Musik* 15, no. 38 (9 November 1841), pp. 150–51; reprinted in R. Schumann 1854, vol. 4, pp. 59–66.

39. Translation based on K. Wolff 1946, pp. 53–54.

40. Schumann's diary entry of 15 October 1838 reads: "Hauser, ein merkwürdiger Mensch, eine Art cholerischer Hypochonder. Er . . . widerspricht immer gerade dem, was der Andere vertheidiget." See Eismann and Nauhaus 1971–82, vol. 2, p. 75.

41. This holograph has evidently been lost since the eighteenth century. See Kilian 1978–79, p. 403.

42. Chorley 1854, vol. 1, p. 327.

43. "Der Verfasser ist Organist, man muss dass wissen, um sein Streben mehr schätzen zu lernen. Es drängt und treibt ihn in die Höhe; er möchte die ganze Welt mit seiner Kunst beglücken. Aber die Kräfte sind noch unentwickelt . . . namentlich in der modulatorischen Form. Wer wird z. B. in einem kleinen 2 Seiten langen Stück aus G-Moll sich gleich aus dem Sattel und nach E-Dur werfen lassen, wie in der 1sten Etude? So vermag der Verfasser fast in keiner die Tonart festzuhalten, was an einem Organisten, der doch seinen J. Seb. Bach kennen muss, doppelt wundert . . . es würde uns ein Heft wohlgesetzter Fugen bei der nächsten Begegnung mehr erfreuen, als ein zweites voll Skizzen. An seinem königlichen Instrumente muss er ja den Werth ausgeprägter Kunstform, wie sie Bach im Grössten und Kleinsten giebt, zu würdigen gelernt haben." *Neue Zeitschrift für Musik* 16, no. 28, pp. 110–11; reprinted in R. Schumann 1854, vol. 4, pp. 115–16. The works under review were Sponholtz's *Charakteristische Etuden*, op. 16.

44. Eight years earlier, in his article on Bach for the *Damenkonversationslexikon*, Schumann had referred to the composer's "consummate mastery of [his] craft" as well as his great expressivity. See Bischoff 1997, pp. 453–56; and Plantinga 1967, pp. 87–88.

45. "Kann sich freilich, was Orgel- und Claviercomposition anlangt, Niemand seines Jahrhunderts mit ihm messen, ja will mir Alles andere, gegen seine ausgebildeten Riesengestalten gehalten, wie noch in der Kindheit begriffen erscheinen." *Neue Zeitschrift für Musik* 6, no. 10 (3 February 1837), p. 40; reprinted in R. Schumann 1854, vol. 2, p. 197.

46. Krause 1982, p. 92.

47. Letter presumably of late August 1842. See Jansen 1904, pp. 218–19 (where the date is given incorrectly as 13 August).

48. Letter of 4 August 1842 (emphasis added). See Jansen 1904, p. 217.

49. Ibid., p. 218.

50. Boetticher 1941, p. 232. The following discussion of Krüger and Schumann is based on Boetticher 1941, pp. 228–32; Boetticher 1979, pp. 99–101; and Martin 1959, pp. 411–15.

51. In late summer or early fall of 1842, Krüger performed these works in recital. A decidedly enthusiastic review appeared in the 18 October 1842 issue of the *Neue Zeitschrift*.

52. Krüger 1844, p. 121.

53. "Hrn. Dr. E. Krüger, dem die Zeitschrift schon so viele gediegene Aufsätze verdankt, haben wir jüngst auch von anderer Seite kennen und schätzen gelernt. Er liess sich vor einigen Musikfreunden auf den Orgeln der Thomas- und Nicolaikirche hören und zeigte sich als trefflicher Spieler namentlich in mehreren der schwierigsten Stücke von Seb. Bach." *Neue Zeitschrift für Musik* 19, no. 6 (20 July 1843), p. 24.

54. Eismann and Nauhaus 1971–82, vol. 2, p. 267.

55. "Komm heiliger Geist ist ungeheuer kräftig und regt die Orgel im tiefsten auf, dass alles aus den Pfeifen hervorströmt wie ein dichter Lavastrom. An Wasserflüssen Babylon ist voll heimlicher zarter Gemütlichkeit, stille sanfte Stimmen aus morgenländischen Kindheitsliedern. Schmücke dich, o liebe Seele sentimental duftig mit würziger Innigkeit, O Lamm Gottes unschuldig voll seltsam ungewohnten Schwellens und Drängens." Excerpt from a letter of 12 November 1843, cited in Boetticher 1941, p. 231.

56. "Schumann gab mir einst auf, ihm Choralvorspiele von Bach für Orgel (z. B. Wachet auf, ruft uns u. s. w.) 'das nächste Mal' vorzuspielen. Ich war anfänglich in Verlegenheit, wie ich es ausführen sollte, um die Töne des Orgelpedals und Alles so, wie geschrieben stand, auf dem Claviere wiederzugeben. Ich sprang so geschickt und schnell als möglich von den Pedaltönen, die ich wie kurze Vorschläge behandelte, auf die Noten für die linke Hand über, indem ich jene durch Niedertreten des Pedalzuges im Klange festzuhalten suchte. Nach hinlänglicher Übung brachte ich das Ganze zu einem ziemlich abgerundeten Vortrage, der allerdings bei dem vielen Springen von den tiefen Tönen in die Mittelstimme herein nicht sehr fliessend ausfallen konnte. Schumann war mit meiner Manipulation zufrieden. Ich gewahrte, dass Schumann selbst auf diese Art die Orgelvorspiele auf dem Claviere auszuführen pflegte, und dass er in jenem Springen sehr geschickt war." See Jansen 1883, p. 73.

57. Coincidentally enough, one assumes, the composer Granville Bantock adopted this same technique in measures 13–17 of his piano transcription of this chorale. See *A Bach Book for Harriet Cohen* (Oxford University Press, 1932).

58. Leipold 1954, p. 54.

59. Gehring et al. 2001, p. 553.

60. Eismann and Nauhaus 1971–82, vol. 3, p. 367.

61. See the summary in Rossner 1997, pp. 40–42.

62. Litzmann 1902–8, vol. 2, pp. 131–32.

63. Bischoff 1997, p. 451.

64. Werbeck 1995.

65. For a discussion of this fugue type, see Stauffer 1986, pp. 134–38.

66. Leipold 1954, pp. 155–56.

67. Eismann and Nauhaus 1971–82, vol. 3, p. 410.

68. *Von Mendelssohn erhalten im Winter 1845/46.* See Bischoff 1997, p. 499, n. 326.

69. Ibid., p. 499, nn. 327 and 331.

70. A letter written by Clara to Robert the day before the concert effectively proves that Robert attended this performance. See Weissweiler 1984–2001, pp. 1227–28.

71. As pointed out, at least with respect to the "Sei gegrüsset" partita, in Bischoff 1997, n. 331.

72. At the beginning of the third system, Schumann originally notated the slur an octave too high. Another point to be made about figure 2–2 is that Mendelssohn erroneously added a second pedal voice in the last two bars, when he should have assigned these notes to the left hand.

73. Schumann likewise added the letters *NB* in measure 16 of "Gott, durch deine Güte," directly beneath the pedal line on the second beat, presumably because of the dissonant harmony.

74. Stinson 1996, pp. 67–68.

75. On the canon and fugue, see Appel 1998, p. 156.

76. Knechtges 1985, p. 165.

77. "Früh Schneider's schönes Orgelspiel (Bacchiana) in d. Sophienkirche." See Eismann and Nauhaus 1971–82, vol. 3, p. 533.

78. Ibid.

79. Letter of 17 October 1852. See Jansen 1904, p. 361.

80. Daverio 1997, p. 453; Eismann and Nauhaus 1971–82, vol. 3, p. 632; and, especially, Bischoff 1997, pp. 482–85.

81. Conspicuously absent from the list are Mendelssohn's two editions of chorale-partitas by Bach (BWV 766 and 768), which, as previously discussed, Schumann had received from Mendelssohn himself. Also missing is the Haslinger edition of the "Six Great."

82. For particulars on this print, see Kilian 1978–79, p. 261.

83. See Eismann and Nauhaus 1971–82, vol. 2, pp. 442–46, esp. 444.

84. See Boyd 1999, pp. 396–97. For a recent discussion of Eijken's arrangements from the *Well-Tempered Clavier,* see Busch 2002.

85. On the origins of the subject, see P. Williams 1980–84, vol. 1, pp. 119–20. The G-minor fantasy and fugue may have been one of Eijken's signature pieces, since he is known to have performed it on various public organ recitals. See Bokum 1971, pp. 94–99; and Heinemann 1995, p. 66, n. 72.

86. Jansen 1904, p. 405.

Chapter 3

1. According to Burger 1989, p. 206, Liszt arrived in Dresden on the first of November and left on the eighth, a day after the symphony was performed.

2. Walker 1988–97, vol. 2, pp. 340–51.

3. Letter of 15 November 1857. See Litzmann 1902–8, vol. 3, p. 28. In a letter to the conductor J. O. Grimm written on the twelfth or thirteenth of that month, Joachim reported that Schneider had played in a thoroughly "crystalline" manner for two full hours. See Joachim and Moser 1911–13, vol. 1, p. 460.

4. For example, in 1895, the year before her death, Clara told her grandson Ferdinand about the incident. See F. Schumann 1917, p. 88.

5. Stradal 1929, p. 73.

6. Heinemann 1995, pp. 28–32. My discussion of Liszt's life is based on Walker 1988–97.

7. On Urhan's Bach reception, see Walton 2001.

8. « Mettre dans votre malle 2 cahiers de Musique dont voici le titre (ils se trouvent tous les deux au même rayon de Bibliothèque) *L'Art de la Fugue* de Bach, *Sechs Fugen mit Pedal von Bach* (je ne suis pas très sur d'avoir encore ce dernier ouvrage). » See Hamburger 2000, pp. 99–102. Liszt was surely disappointed that his mother, for whatever reasons, never made the trip.

9. Smith 1986, p. 68; and Heinemann 1995, p. 4.

10. A. Williams 1998, p. 105. The *Passion* setting cited by Liszt, obviously, is Bach's St. Matthew Passion.

11. Ramann 1880–94, vol. 1, p. 518.

12. Heinemann 1995, p. 42.

13. "Eine Fuge mit Pedal von Joh. Seb. Bach spielte Liszt, und zwar die beiden Manualstimmen meistens mit der rechten, die dritte Pedalstimme mit der linken Hand, ohne Gebrauch eines wirklichen Pedals, mit einer Sauberkeit und Klarheit, die nichts zu wünschen übrig, nur die immense Fertigkeit des Spielers in noch höherm Grade bewundern liess." Excerpt from an anonymous review published in the *Allgemeine musikalische Zeitung,* cited in Heinemann 1995, p. 53.

14. See Herrmann 1965; and Hiemke 1999, p. 44.

15. Liszt se présente, en 1844, chez J. B. Laurens à Montpellier, avec des recommandations de Mendelssohn, Hiller, etc.
— «Vous passez, l'apostrophe J. B. à brûle-pourpoint, pour un aussi grand charlatan que grand artiste!».
C'était assez brutalement attaquer le taureau par les cornes. Liszt ne broncha pas et se mit même sur le pied et dans le courant d'une franche et spirituelle amabilité. J. B. dessine son portrait. On déjeune en causant de tant de choses et de célébrités musicales des plus intéressantes.
— «J'ai à vous demander, dit à un moment J. B., de me faire entendre une certaine pièce de Sébastien Bach pour orgue avec donc pédalier obligé, la première du Cahier des six fugues, celle en la mineur d'une difficulté que vous seul au monde sans doute devez pouvoir aborder. C'est aujourd'hui pour moi une occasion unique que je ne veux pas laisser passer».
— «Tout de suite . . . Comment voulez-vous que je vous la joue?».
— «Comment ? Mais . . . comme on doit la jouer!».
— «La voici, une première fois, comme l'auteur a dû la comprendre, l'exécuter lui-même ou vouloir qu'elle soit exécutée».

Et Liszt de jouer. Et ce fut admirable, la perfection même du style classique et voulu en tout d'original.

—«La voici, une seconde fois, comme je la sens, avec un peu de pittoresque de mouvement, l'esprit plus moderne et les effets propres à l'instrument perfectionné». Et ce fut, avec ces nuances, autrement mais non moins admirable.

—«Enfin, une troisième fois, la voici comme je la jouerais pour le public . . . à étonner, en charlatan!».

Et, allumant un cigare qu'il passait par instants d'entre les lèvres aux doigts, exécutant parmi ses dix doigts la partie marquée pour les pédales et se livrant à d'autres tours de force et de prestidigitation, il fut prodigieux, incroyable, fabuleux et remercié avec enthousiasme.

The translation of the first four paragraphs is largely the work of Catherine Bordeau, Associate Professor of French at Lyon College; the remainder is adapted from Rosen 1995, pp. 510–11. Original text from Eigeldinger 1973, pp. 176–77.

16. Rosen 1995, p. 511.

17. Walker 1988–97, vol. 1, p. 299.

18. Letter to A. W. Gottschalg of 25 January 1866. See Jung 1988, p. 202.

19. Ramann 1880–94, vol. 2, p. 157.

20. La Mara 1893, vol. 1, p. 67. Apparently, then, Liszt had lost the copy of the Six Great that he had used prior to the date of his letter.

21. Heinemann 1995, pp. 76–77; and MezŒ and Vikárius 1997, pp. xiii–xviii.

22. In the original, Liszt's inscription reads: *Die Pedal Zeile bleibt / durchgängig* [sic] *ganz / weg.*

23. "Sobald Sie Zeit dazu finden, machen Sie sich an die Bach'schen 6 Pedal-Fugen und schreiben Sie bitte recht deutlich und breit." See Mező and Vikárius 1997, p. xv; and Walker 1988–97, vol. 2, p. 157, n. 55.

24. "Gegenwärtig hat ihm sein Genius und seine musikalische Intelligenz noch eine andere Richtung vorgezeichnet: die Übertragung der grössten Joh. Seb. Bach'schen Orgelkompositionen aufs Klavier. Der Kenner und Verehrer Bachscher Werke wird in Erstaunen geraten, wie es möglich gewesen ist, erst überhaupt nur auf diesen Gedanken zu kommen und dann ihn in einer solchen Vollkommenheit auszuführen. Durch Übertragung der Partie des obligaten Pedals in die linke Hand hat dennoch keine der übrigen Stimmen an ihrer wesentlichen Originalität verloren—Bachs grosse Orgelfugen sind in ihrer Authentizität erhalten, vollständig auf das Pianoforte übertragen und auf demselben von einem einzigen Spieler auszuführen. Welcher Fortschritt des Klavierspiels seit Bachs Zeit, welche überraschende Anwendung der neuesten Technik!

Durch die vorliegende neueste Arbeit *Liszt's* ist wieder ein Abschnitt in der Geschichte des Klavierspiels angedeutet, und so wie die früheren Abschnitte durch die Namen *Bach, Scarlatti, Clementi und Pollini* bezeichnet sind, so trägt dieser den Namen *Franz Liszt.*"

25. See Reger's letter to Ferruccio Busoni of 11 May 1895, published in Norman and Shrifte 1927, pp. 335–36.

26. Letter to the composer (and possibly Liszt's illegitimate son) Franz Servais of 20 December 1869. See A. Williams 1998, p. 709.

27. Jerger 1975, p. 151.

28. La Mara 1895–1904, vol. 1, p. 242.

29. Letter of 14 March 1855. See La Mara 1898, p. 123.

30. From 1854 to 1882 Bülow is known to have performed Liszt's transcription of the E-minor prelude and fugue eight times; that of the B-minor, thirty-one times; and that of the A-minor, a whopping fifty-eight times. See Hinrichsen and Sackmann 2004, p. 41.

31. La Mara 1898, p. 295.

32. As figure 4–3 demonstrates, the G-minor fantasy was also published as a *Praeludium* in volume 15 of the Bachgesellschaft edition, which appeared in 1867.

33. Kaczmarczyk and Sulyok 1998, pp. xii–xiii.

34. Smith 1986, p. 69.

35. Gottschalg 1910, p. 27. Translation from Sutter 1977, p. 210.

36. "Glauben Sie wirklich, dass Bach beide Compositionen fortwährend mit vollem Werke gespielt hat? Nun und nimmermehr! Dazu war er ein viel zu grosser und feinfühliger Künstler! Haben Sie nicht gelesen, dass er ganz wundervoll registrirt haben soll?" See Gottschalg 1886, p. 338.

37. For a list of all the registration and manual changes in Töpfer's edition, see Weinberger 1995, p. 202. See also Sieling 1999, pp. 333–34. Gottschalg himself transcribed the Passacaglia for piano, four hands, and published it together with his four-hand arrangement of the Prelude and Fugue in A Minor, BWV 543. See Heinemann 1995, p. 235; and Schanz 2000, p. 512.

38. Gottschalg 1899, p. 505. Translation from Sutter 1977, p. 210.

39. Gottschalg correctly identifies this passage as contained in the fourth system of the edition, but he gives the wrong page number.

40. Chorzempa and Bähr 2001.

41. See the translation in David and Mendel 1998, pp. 438–39.

42. Gottschalg 1910, p. 144; and Walker 1995, pp. 169–73.

43. Gottschalg 1883, pp. 20–21.

44. Walker 1995, p. 172.

45. Gottschalg 1910, p. 151.

46. This program is reproduced in Jung 1988, p. 267.

47. Stradal 1929, p. 25.

48. Liszt praised Tausig's arrangement in a letter to Marie Lipsius ("La Mara") of 23 July 1871, two days after Tausig's death. See La Mara 1893, vol. 2, pp. 167–68. Tausig's mishandling of these mordents is pointed out in Stradal 1929, p. 26.

49. Publication date according to Schanz 2000, p. 545.

50. According to Göllerich 1908, p. 292, Liszt himself transcribed one of Bach's settings of "O Lamm Gottes," but surely this is a mistaken reference to Tausig's arrangement of the Great Eighteen chorale by the same name.

51. "Ich sendete Ihnen letzthin die Bachschen Choralvorspiele unter Kreuzband; N° 3 in Es-dur ist meine Passion, mögen Sie nicht auch dies erhabene traurige Stück?" Letter of 21 May 1871, published in La Mara 1895–1904, vol. 3, pp. 352–53. Liszt mentioned Tausig's transcriptions in a mournful letter to Princess Carolyne of 23 July 1871. See A. Williams 1998, pp. 730–31.

52. It is worth pointing out that Brahms owned copies not only of Tausig's chorale transcriptions but also of his toccata arrangement. See Helms 1971, p. 57.

53. Kellermann 1932, pp. 17–19.

54. Ibid., p. 44. Translation from A. Williams 1990, p. 485.

55. Ramann 1880–94, vol. 1, p. 166.

56. Jerger 1975, pp. 44–45 and 64.

57. Ibid., p. 50; and Walker 1995, p. 325. On Liszt's attitude toward Berger, see Walker 1995, pp. 231 and 247.

58. Walker 1995, pp. 133–34, 193; and Jerger 1975, p. 95.

59. Walker 1995, p. 236.

60. Jerger 1975, p. 46.

61. Walker 1995, p. 127. Lachmund's diary refers to C rather than A octaves in the left hand here, but this is due obviously to his misreading of the clef used by Tausig.

62. Stradal 1929, pp. 25–29. According to Gottschalg 1910, p. 143, yet another performance of Tausig's arrangement was given by Martha Remmert on 6 September 1882.

63. Stradal 1929, p. 101. According to Burger 1989, p. 290, Liszt had heard the same work in Erfurt two years earlier, on 10 May 1883.

64. Stradal's transcriptions are listed in Schanz 2000, pp. 508–9, 545, and 585. Another Liszt pupil from this period who went on to produce piano arrangements of Bach's organ works was Alexander von Siloti. See Schanz 2000, pp. 508 and 544.

65. According to Goetz 1953, the couple had lived in Hanover since 1873.

66. Tyler and Waters 1979, p. 276.

67. Walker 1995, pp. 259–62 and 401–2.

68. Ibid., p. 262.

69. Ibid., pp. 68–69.

70. Jerger 1975, p. 151; Sutter 1981, pp. 210–11; and Eigeldinger 1973, p. 179.

71. "Ich habe gar kein *f* und *p* angegeben, weil der grosse Bach nichts hinschrieb und man ja nicht etwas ihm hinzufügen dürfte; das wäre Versündigung." See Jerger 1975, p. 151.

Chapter 4

1. My discussion of Brahms's life is based on Bozarth and Frisch 2001 and Hofmann 1983.

2. Dietrich 1899, pp. 2–3. Translation from Musgrave 2000, p. 122.

3. Kalbeck 1904–14, vol. 2, pp. 26–27, n. 2.

4. On Brahms and canon, see Kross 1957.

5. During Schumann's years in Düsseldorf, he and Euler socialized together extensively. See Eismann and Nauhaus 1971–82, vol. 3, pp. 538–619.

6. See the description in McCorkle 1984, p. 741.

7. Brahms's personal copy of this edition still survives. See Helms 1971, p. 53; and K. Hofmann 1974, p. 146.

8. "Ich lege ein Orgelkonzert von Friedemann Bach bei des schönen Adagios wegen." See A. Moser 1908, vol. 1, p. 183. By "Adagio," Brahms must have meant the

"Largo e spiccato" movement, since there is no "Adagio" movement per se in the work, or any other slow movement at all.

9. See the table in Brodbeck 1994, p. 35.

10. Dietrich 1899, pp. 16–18.

11. Little 1994, p. 278.

12. WoO (works without opus number) designations according to McCorkle 1984.

13. Beechey 1983, p. 43; and Oortmerssen 1995, p. 358.

14. Brodbeck 1994, pp. 69–72.

15. Brahms's program for this concert is given in Hofmann 1983, p. 32.

16. Pascall 1983, p. 123.

17. Concerning the possibility that "O Traurigkeit" served as a memorial to Schumann, see Brodbeck 1994, p. 77; and MacDonald 1990, p. 93. On Brahms's use of the *Orgelbüchlein* as a model, see Frisch 1998, p. 121.

18. Little 1994, pp. 281–82.

19. "Die Stimmung erinnert mich immer an das herrliche Pastorale von Bach, welches wir zuweilen zusammen gespielt haben." See Litzmann 1927, vol. 1, p. 285.

20. E. Schumann 1925, pp. 173–74. On at least two occasions during 1893–95, Clara also performed the Pastorale for her piano students. See D.-R. Moser 1990, pp. 75 and 79. In a letter to Theodor Kirchner of 2 November 1862, Clara refers to the Pastorale as one of Bach's most significant works ("Ich meine, Sie müssten einige der bedeutendsten Sachen Bach's, also zum B.[eispiel] das Pastorale in F dur . . . immer in den Fingern haben."). See R. Hofmann 1996, p. 108.

21. Drinker 1952, p. 16.

22. Kalbeck 1904–14, vol. 2, pp. 26–27, n. 2.

23. Asow 1943, pp. 35–37. Wagner's reaction to this performance is unknown.

24. R. Hofmann 1999, p. 270.

25. Schauffler 1933, pp. 216–17. In 1884 Röntgen issued his own piano transcription of the F-major toccata, which he seems to have played regularly in concert. It is easy to imagine that he undertook this project in imitation of Brahms. On Röntgen's performances of his transcription, see Röntgen 1934, pp. 83 and 107.

26. Avins 1997, p. 260.

27. F. May 1905, vol. 2, p. 333.

28. "eigentümlich orgelmässig, klangvoll, mit grosser Ökonomie der Steigerungen, aber auch mit breit ausgelegtem Ton bei den Hauptstellen." See Ehrmann 1933, p. 136.

29. Quoted in Hübbe 1902, p. 50. Translation from Gotwals 1970, p. 42.

30. Gilbert 1994.

31. F. May 1905, vol. 1, p. 17. See also E. Schumann 1925, pp. 146–47.

32. In a letter to Joseph Joachim of 13 April 1863, Brahms characterized this melody as a "wonderful old Catholic song" and a "beautiful lullaby." It also serves as the basis for his song "Die ihr schwebet um diese Palmen" (*Geistliches Wiegenlied*), op. 91, no. 2. See Avins 1997, pp. 273–74; and McCorkle 1984, pp. 374–75.

33. See, for example, Plath 1974, p. 95, n. 5.

34. The edition in question is a reprint from the Peters edition of Bach's complete organ works. Brahms's personal copies of eleven such reprints are housed today at the Gesellschaft der Musikfreunde, Vienna. (For a complete list, see Helms

1971, pp. 52–53.) That of the "Legrenzi" fugue, BWV 574, preserves four brackets drawn by Brahms into the score to mark the first and third combined statements of the two subjects (mm. 70–73 and 76–79), an analysis that likewise illustrates the invertibility of the two themes. That of the Fantasy in C Minor, BWV 562/1, preserves three brackets in Brahms's hand that designate the first three statements of the new countertheme at measures 23–28.

35. F. May 1905, vol. 2, p. 40.

36. Fellinger 1997, p. 22.

37. Kalbeck 1904–14, vol. 4, p. 9, n. 1.

38. Ibid., vol. 4, p. 401.

39. Ibid., vol. 4, pp. 8–9.

40. Beckerath 1958, p. 84.

41. Leyen 1905, pp. 96–98; and K. Hofmann 1979, pp. 62–64.

42. Smyth 1919, vol. 1, p. 266.

43. Kalbeck 1907, vol. 1, p. 176. Brahms was referring here to volume 25, part 2, which had been published in 1878 and which contains the *Orgelbüchlein,* Schübler chorales, and the Great Eighteen chorales (see table 4–3). He cannot have meant volume 40, which contains over sixty miscellaneous organ chorales, since it did not appear until 1893. Nor can he have meant the chorale settings within Part 3 of the *Clavierübung,* since they had been published almost thirty years earlier in a volume devoted largely to harpsichord music. It is worth pointing out that the editor of the latter volume (volume 3) is C. F. Becker, who was a colleague of both Mendelssohn and Schumann.

44. Kalbeck 1907, vol. 1, pp. 54 and 144.

45. Hinrichsen 1999, p. 263. Further evidence of Frau Herzogenberg's interest in Bach's organ works is provided by a letter she wrote to Ethel Smyth (30 July 1880), in which she mentions her "ravenous devotion" to the composer's organ chorales. See Smyth 1919, vol. 2, p. 36.

46. Little 1994, pp. 290–91.

47. Boyd 1999, p. 396.

48. Scholz's arrangement had been published in 1874 under the title *Präludium für die Orgel von Joh. Seb. Bach. Für grosses Orchester bearbeitet von Bernh. Scholz* (Leipzig: J. Rieter-Biedermann). See Riethmüller 1990, p. 40. According to McCorkle 1984, p. 649, the performing parts used by Brahms for this performance have not survived.

49. Walker 1988–97, vol. 2, pp. 349.

50. Brahms left for Breslau on 26 December 1874 and returned to Vienna on 3 January 1875. See Hofmann 1983, p. 122.

51. Knapp 1989, pp. 6–8.

52. Frisch 2001–2, pp. 306–7; and Knapp 1989, p. 8. For a recent discussion of a possible fifth model, that of an aria from J.-B. Lully's opera *Phaëton,* see Ricks 2005.

53. Letter of 16–17 February 1869. See Kalbeck 1915, p. 218. In this same missive, Brahms refers rather cryptically to Bach's chorale partitas for organ as "a special case."

54. See Mast 1980, which, unless otherwise noted, is the exclusive source for the following discussion. The manuscript belongs today to the Gesellschaft der Musikfreunde, Vienna.

55. Gotwals 1970, pp. 49–50 and 52.

56. Brahms's personal copies of volumes 2 and 9 of the Peters edition, however, are still extant. See, respectively, K. Hofmann 1974, p. 169, item 858; and Helms 1971, p. 56, item 35.

57. According to C. Wolff 2002, p. 92, the octave doubling here is "nothing more than an emergency solution for creating a proper manual plenum on an organ lacking a 16′ stop."

58. These fifths do not appear in volume 3 of the Peters edition, as the alto reading there is a dotted quarter note on f″. See also Kilian 1978–79, p. 451.

59. On the composition date and contrapuntal shortcomings of this movement, see Stauffer 1980, pp. 96–97.

60. Spitta 1873–79, vol. 1, p. 416.

61. Brahms's personal copy of the Bachgesellschaft edition is housed today at the archive of the Gesellschaft der Musikfreunde, Vienna. My thanks to Otto Biba (the archive's director) for authenticating Brahms's script.

62. Hancock 1983, pp. 37–38 and 126. For a very recent reductive analysis of this work—but one inspired by Brahms's example—see Rampe 2003, pp. 349–55.

63. For a complete inventory, see Hancock 1983, pp. 18–39; and McCorkle 1984, pp. 715–24.

64. Kilian 1988, pp. 192–93.

65. The only statements missing from Brahms's analysis are those at measures 72–74 (tenor), 82–84 (tenor), and 91–93 (soprano).

66. For whatever reasons, Brahms allowed six of the motivic statements beginning with a whole note to stand without any alteration. See measures 61–63, 93–95, 154–56, 162–64, 171–73, and 175–77.

67. "Als ich im Sommer aus dem Norden zurückkehrte, fand ich Ihren schönen, von Ihnen selbst geschriebenen Orgelchoral 'O Traurigkeit, o Herzeleid' vor: 'Choralfantasie' würde ich ihn, nach der von mir gebildeten Terminologie, nennen. Ich finde ihn an Kunst und Tiefsinn, an Innigkeit der grossen Seb. Bachschen Vorbilder würdig. . . . Damit ist zugleich gesagt, dass dieses Orgelstück mir keineswegs als eine blosse Nachahmung erscheint, sondern als eine selbständige Nachbildung, wie das von Ihnen ja auch nur zu erwarten war." Letter of 29 December 1873. See Krebs 1920–22, p. 51.

68. See volume 1 of Spitta's study, pp. 601, 608–9; and volume 2, p. 694. In reality, Bach left behind between twenty and thirty organ works that match Spitta's description of a Choralfantasie. See E. May 1986, pp. 97–100.

69. See Brahms's letter to Spitta of January 1874, published in Krebs 1920–22, pp. 58–59.

70. Letter of 14 June 1873. See Krebs 1920–22, p. 49. On the publication dates of Spitta's Bach biography, see Sandberger 1997, pp. 76–77.

71. See Spitta's letter to Brahms of 20 December 1879, published in Krebs 1920–22, pp. 76–78.

72. For a brief description of this source, see Helms 1971, pp. 62–63.

73. Helms 1971, pp. 15–19.

74. For a general discussion, see Helms 1971, pp. 64–73.

75. Hancock 1983, pp. 9–101.

76. Kalbeck 1904–14, vol. 4, p. 515.

77. P. Williams 1980–84, vol. 2, pp. 323–26.

78. Brahms owned over twenty different hymnals, all of which are listed in Helms 1970, pp. 39–40.

79. The issue of pedal simplification figures prominently in the slow movements of the Trio Sonatas because of their relatively ornate themes. As if to call attention to this fact, Brahms bracketed examples of this technique in the slow movements of the first (mm. 6–9), fourth (mm. 40–41), and sixth (mm. 10–13 and 34–37) sonatas.

80. See the Dorian toccata, mm. 25 and 66; the Fugue in B Minor, BWV 544/2, m. 28; the Prelude in C Major, BWV 547/1, m. 13; the Prelude in E Minor, BWV 548/1, m. 33; and the Fantasy in C Minor, BWV 562/1, m. 38.

81. P. Williams 1980–84, vol. 1, pp. 169–70.

82. Hancock 1983, pp. 61, 85, 92, and 100–1.

83. See the musical example in Keller 1967, p. 189 (first paragraph). Brahms's awareness of this process would explain, too, why he notated the dual time signature of the work (C and 12/8) beside the one printed.

84. Brahms also marked instances of hemiola in the cantata volumes of the Bachgesellschaft edition. See Hancock 1983, p. 85.

85. According to P. Williams 1980–84, vol. 1, p. 54, these four bars may be the most "skillfully managed" in any of the six Trio Sonatas.

86. According to Humphreys 1985, the composer may be J. C. Kittel; according to Dirksen 2000, the composer may be Wilhelm Friedemann Bach.

87. See also Keller 1967, p. 102, n. 171.

88. Nor was this manuscript available to F. C. Griepenkerl and Ferdinand Roitzsch when they prepared volume 5 of the Peters edition (and which prints the same reading as the Bachgesellschaft edition). See Löhlein 1987, pp. 184, 188, and 193.

89. On this discrepancy, see also P. Williams 1980–84, vol. 1, p. 150, footnote.

90. Rust's comments are found on pages xxiii–xxiv of the preface to volume 15. See also Kilian 1978–79, p. 333.

91. The revised version appeared around 1900. See Kilian 1978–79, pp. 261–64 and 470.

92. See, for example, his letter to Clara Schumann of 20 August 1855, translated in Avins 1997, pp. 107–8.

93. On the performance of these ornaments, see also Emery 1953, p. 16. According to Little 2005, pp. 79–80, none of these mordents should be considered authentic.

94. Kilian 1978–79, pp. 30–33; and Stinson 1989, p. 15.

95. Hancock 1983, p. 94.

96. See, for example, Kalbeck 1904–14, vol. 4, p. 473.

97. Bond 1971, p. 899; Kern 1983, p. 130; Musgrave 1985, p. 245; and Oortmerssen 1995, p. 377.

98. Gotwals 1970, p. 48.

99. Kern 1983, p. 130; and Senn 1959, pp. 176–77.

100. Stinson 1993, pp. 463–64.

101. The latter work is sometimes cited as a model for the first number in Brahms's collection, "Mein Jesu, der du mich," owing to its imitative treatment of each phrase of the chorale and lengthy pedal point at the end. (The two works are also in the same key.) Both of these traits, however, are commonly found in baroque organ chorales. Furthermore, Brahms's setting is characterized by pre-imitation, a technique totally absent from Bach's work.

102. With regard to the partita movement, see Beechey 1983, p. 45; and Kern 1983, p. 131.

103. Bach also delays the pedals in this manner in the *Variatio* movement of "Als Jesus Christus in der Nacht," BWV 1108. But this work belongs to the so-called Neumeister Collection, which was discovered only about twenty years ago.

104. Excluding the Neumeister Collection, only a dozen of Bach's organ chorales contain this heading.

105. Stinson 1993, pp. 462–64.

106. Williams 1980–84, vol. 2, p. 252.

107. Hancock 1983, pp. 87–88; and Helms 1971, p. 67.

108. In the *Orgelbüchlein* setting of "Wir Christenleut," a work studied by Brahms because of its near use of parallel octaves, the last *three* chorale phrases are unnecessarily repeated. Brahms, though, would have been unaware of this feature—which is clearly indicated by Bach in the autograph manuscript—since not until 1984 did any edition (the Neue Bach-Ausgabe) include it. See Löhlein 1987, p. 114.

109. Schäfertöns 1999, pp. 220–21. It is now known that the compilation took place several years earlier. On this point, see Stinson 2001, pp. 29–33.

110. Stinson 2001, p. 105.

Works Cited

Albrecht, Christoph, ed. *Felix Mendelssohn Bartholdy: Neue Ausgabe sämtlicher Orgel-werke.* 2 volumes. Kassel: Bärenreiter, 1993–94.

Appel, Bernhard R. *Robert Schumanns "Album für die Jugend": Einführung und Kommentar.* Zurich: Atlantis Musikbuch-Verlag, 1998.

Asow, Erich H. Müller von. *Johannes Brahms und Mathilde Wesendonck: Ein Briefwechsel.* Vienna: I. Luckmann Verlag, 1943.

Atkins, W. M. "The Age of Reform: 1831–1934." In *A History of St. Paul's Cathedral,* edited by W. R. Matthews and W. M. Atkins, 250–99. London: Phoenix House, 1957.

Avins, Styra. *Johannes Brahms: Life and Letters.* New York: Oxford University Press, 1997.

Beckerath, Heinz von. "Erinnerungen an Johannes Brahms." *Die Heimat* 29 (1958): 81–93.

Beechey, Gwilym. "The Organ Music of Brahms." *The American Organist* 17, no. 5 (May 1983): 43–46.

Bischoff, Bodo. "Das Bach-Bild Robert Schumanns." In *Bach und die Nachwelt, Vol. 2: 2750–2850,* edited by Michael Heinemann and Hans-Joachim Hinrichsen, 421–99. Laaber: Laaber-Verlag, 1997.

Blume, Friedrich. *Two Centuries of Bach.* Translated by Stanley Godman. London: Oxford University Press, 1950.

Boetticher, Wolfgang. *Robert Schumann: Einführung in Persönlichkeit und Werk.* Berlin: Bernhard Hahnefeld Verlag, 1941.

———. *Briefe und Gedichte aus dem Album Robert und Clara Schumanns.* Leipzig: VEB Deutscher Verlag für Musik, 1979.

Bokum, Jan ten. *Johannes Gijsbertus Bastiaans.* Utrecht: A. Oosthoek's Uitgevers-maatschappij, 1971.

Bond, Ann. "Brahms Chorale Preludes, op. 122." *The Musical Times* 112 (1971): 898–900.

Bormann, Oskar. "Johann Nepomuk Schelble: Sein Leben, sein Wirken und seine Werke." Ph.D. dissertation, University of Frankfurt, 1926.

Bötel, Friedhold. *Mendelssohns Bachrezeption und ihre Konsequenzen dargestellt an den Präludien und Fugen für Orgel op. 37.* Beiträge zur Musikforschung 14. Munich: Emil Katzbichler, 1984.

Bovet, Marie Anne de, and Charles-Marie Widor. "Gounod." *The Fortnightly Review* (December 1893): 824–41.

Boyd, Malcolm, ed. *J. S. Bach.* Oxford Composer Companions. Oxford: Oxford University Press, 1999.

Bozarth, George S., and Walter Frisch. "Brahms, Johannes." In *The New Grove Dictionary of Music and Musicians,* edited by Stanley Sadie. Second edition. Vol. 4, 180–227. London: Macmillan, 2001.

Brodbeck, David. "The Brahms-Joachim Counterpoint Exchange; or, Robert, Clara, and 'the Best Harmony between Jos. and Joh.'" *Brahms Studies* 1 (1994): 30–80.

Burger, Ernst. *Franz Liszt: A Chronicle of His Life in Pictures and Documents.* Princeton: Princeton University Press, 1989.

Busch, Hermann J. "Sächsische Bach-Tradition im Rheinland: Eine Quelle zur Interpretationsgeschichte der Orgelmusik Johann Sebastian Bachs aus der Mitte des 19. Jahrhunderts." *Freiberger Studien zur Orgel* 7 (2002): 111–19.

Chorley, Henry F. *Modern German Music.* 2 volumes. London, 1854.

Chorzempa, Daniel, and Hans-Peter Bähr. "Töpfer, Johann Gottlob." In *The New Grove Dictionary of Music and Musicians,* edited by Stanley Sadie. Second edition. Vol. 25, 610. London: Macmillan, 2001.

Citron, Marcia J., ed. *The Letters of Fanny Hensel to Felix Mendelssohn.* Stuyvesant, NY: Pendragon Press, 1987.

Claus, Rolf Dietrich. *Zur Echtheit von Toccata und Fuge d-moll BWV 565.* Cologne-Rheinkassel: Dohr, 1995.

Coleridge, A. D. *Goethe's Letters to Zelter.* London: George Bell and Sons, 1887.

Cooper, Jeffrey. *The Rise of Instrumental Music and Concert Series in Paris, 1822–1872.* Studies in Musicology 65. Ann Arbor: UMI Research Press, 1983.

Cox, H. Bertram, and C. L. E. Cox. *Leaves from the Journals of Sir George Smart.* London: Longmans, Green, and Co., 1907.

Crum, Margaret, and Peter Ward Jones. *Catalogue of the Mendelssohn Papers in the Bodleian Library, Oxford.* 3 volumes. Musikbibliographische Arbeiten 7–9. Tutzing: Hans Schneider, 1980–89.

Dähnert, Ulrich. *Die Orgeln Gottfried Silbermanns in Mitteldeutschland.* Revised edition. Amsterdam: Frits Knuf, 1971.

Daverio, John. *Robert Schumann: Herald of a "New Poetic Age."* New York: Oxford University Press, 1997.

———. "Schumann, Robert." In *The New Grove Dictionary of Music and Musicians,* edited by Stanley Sadie. Second edition. Vol. 22, 760–816. London: Macmillan, 2001.

David, Hans T., and Arthur Mendel, eds. *The New Bach Reader: A Life of Johann Sebastian Bach in Letters and Documents.* Revised and enlarged by Christoph Wolff. New York: W. W. Norton, 1998.

Dietrich, Albert. *Erinnerungen an Johannes Brahms.* Second edition. Leipzig: Otto Wigand, 1899.

Dirksen, Pieter. "Het auteurschap van Praeludium en fuga in f (BWV 534)." *Het Orgel* 26, no. 5 (2000): 5–14.

Drinker, Sophie. *Brahms and His Women's Choruses.* Merion, PA: privately published, 1952.

Edwards, Frederick George. *Musical Haunts in London.* London: J. Curwen & Sons, 1895.

————. "Bach's Music in England." *The Musical Times* 37 (1896): 722–26.

————. "Thomas Attwood." *The Musical Times* 41 (1900): 788–94.

————. "Mendelssohn's Organ Sonatas." *The Musical Times* 42 (1901): 794–98.

————. Obituary notice for Elizabeth Mounsey. *The Musical Times* 46 (1905): 718–20.

Ehrmann, Alfred von. *Johannes Brahms: Weg, Werk und Welt.* Leipzig: Breitkopf & Härtel, 1933.

Eigeldinger, Jean-Jacques. "Liszt trascrittore e interprete di Bach." *L'Organo* 11 (1973): 171–81.

Eismann, Georg, ed. *Erinnerungen an Felix Mendelssohn Bartholdy: Nachgelassene Aufzeichnungen von Robert Schumann.* Zwickau: Predella-Verlag, 1948.

Eismann, Georg, and Gerd Nauhaus, eds. *Robert Schumann: Tagebücher.* 3 volumes. Leipzig: VEB Deutscher Verlag für Musik, 1971–82.

Elvers, Rudolf. "Verzeichnis der von Felix Mendelssohn Bartholdy herausgegebenen Werke Johann Sebastian Bachs." In *Gestalt und Glaube: Festschrift für Vizepräsident Professor D. Dr. Oskar Söhngen,* 145–49. Witten: Luther-Verlag; Berlin: Verlag Merseburger, 1960.

————, ed. *Felix Mendelssohn Bartholdy: Briefe an deutsche Verleger.* Berlin: Walter de Gruyter, 1968.

————, ed. *Felix Mendelssohn Bartholdy: Briefe.* Frankfurt: Fischer Taschenbuch Verlag, 1984. (English translation, *Felix Mendelssohn Bartholdy: A Life in Letters.* New York: Fromm, 1986.)

Elvers, Rudolf, and Peter Ward Jones. "Das Musikalienverzeichnis von Fanny und Felix Mendelssohn Bartholdy." *Mendelssohn Studien* 8 (1993): 85–103.

Emans, Reinmar. *Johann Sebastian Bach. Orgelchoräle zweifelhafter Echtheit: Thematischer Katalog.* Göttingen: Johann-Sebastian-Bach-Institut Göttingen, 1997.

Emery, Walter. *Bach's Ornaments.* London: Novello, 1953.

Fellinger, Imogen, ed. *Klänge um Brahms: Erinnerungen von Richard Fellinger.* Mürzzuschlag: Österreichische Johannes Brahms-Gesellschaft, 1997.

Frisch, Walter. "Bach, Brahms, and the Emergence of Musical Modernism." *Bach Perspectives* 3 (1998): 109–31.

————. "Reger's Bach and Historicist Modernism." *19th Century Music* 25, nos. 2–3 (Fall/Spring 2001–2): 296–312.

Fuchs, Ingrid. "Bach-Aufführungen im Spiegel der Berichterstattung der *Neuen Zeitschrift für Musik* unter der Redaktion Robert Schumanns von 1834 bis 1844." In *Festschrift Othmar Wessely,* edited by Manfred Angerer et al., 207–36. Tutzing: Hans Schneider, 1982.

Gauntlett, Henry John. "Mendelssohn as an Organist." *The Musical World* (September 15, 1837): 8–10.

————. Letter to George Grove about Mendelssohn's organ playing. *The Musical Times* 43 (1902): 96–97.

Gehring, Franz, et al. "Schneider." In *The New Grove Dictionary of Music and Musicians,* edited by Stanley Sadie. Second edition. Vol. 22, 553–54. London: Macmillan, 2001.

Gilbert, Kenneth, ed. *Johann Sebastian Bach: Pièce d'Orgue BWV 572.* Le Grand Clavier 13. Monaco: Éditions de L'Oiseau-Lyre, 1994.

Goetz, Walter. "Albrecht." In *Neue deutsche Biographie.* Vol. 1, 173. Berlin: Duncker & Humblot, 1953.

Göllerich, August. *Franz Liszt.* Berlin: Marquardt, 1908.

Gottschalg, Alexander Wilhelm. "Von Seb. Bach—Franz Liszt." *Urania* 40 (1883): 18–22.

————. "Die moderne Orgel in orchestraler Behandlung." *Neue Zeitschrift für Musik* 82, no. 31 (30 July 1886): 337–39.

————. "Dr. Franz Liszt als Orgelkomponist und als Orgelspieler." *Neue Zeitschrift für Musik* 95, no. 46 (15 November 1899): 503–5.

————. *Franz Liszt in Weimar und seine letzten Lebensjahre.* Berlin: Arthur Glaue, 1910.

Gotwals, Vernon. "Brahms and the Organ." *MUSIC / The AGO-RCCO Magazine* 4 (April 1970): 38–55.

Gounod, Charles François. *Memoirs of an Artist: An Autobiography.* Translated by Annette E. Crocker. Chicago and New York: Rand McNally & Co., 1895.

Griepenkerl, Friedrich Conrad, and Ferdinand Roitzsch, eds. *Johann Sebastian Bach's Kompositionen für die Orgel.* 8 volumes. Leipzig: C. F. Peters, 1844–52.

Grossmann-Vendrey, Susanna. *Felix Mendelssohn Bartholdy und die Musik der Vergangenheit.* Studien zur Musikgeschichte des 19. Jahrhunderts 17. Regensburg: Gustav Bosse, 1969a.

————. "Stilprobleme in Mendelssohns Orgelsonaten op. 65." In *Das Problem Mendelssohn,* edited by Carl Dahlhaus, 185–94. Studien zur Musikgeschichte des 19. Jahrhunderts 41. Regensburg: Gustav Bosse, 1969b.

Grove, George. "Mendelssohn." In *A Dictionary of Music and Musicians,* edited by George Grove. Vol. 2, 253–310. London: Macmillan, 1880.

Hamburger, Klára, ed. *Franz Liszt: Briefwechsel mit seiner Mutter.* Eisenstadt: Amt der Burgenländischen Landesregierung, 2000.

Hancock, Virginia. *Brahms's Choral Compositions and His Library of Early Music.* Studies in Musicology 76. Ann Arbor: UMI Research Press, 1983.

Heinemann, Michael. *Die Bach-Rezeption von Franz Liszt.* Musik und Musikanschauung im 19. Jahrhundert 1. Cologne: Studio, 1995.

Helms, Siegmund. "Johannes Brahms und das deutsche Kirchenlied." *Der Kirchenmusiker* 21, no. 2 (March–April 1970): 39–48.

————. "Johannes Brahms und Johann Sebastian Bach." *Bach-Jahrbuch* 57 (1971): 13–81.

Herrmann, Marcelle. "J. J. B. Laurens' Beziehungen zu deutschen Musikern." *Schweizerische Musikzeitung* 105 (1965): 257–66.

Herz, Gerhard. "Johann Sebastian Bach in the Age of Rationalism and Early Romanticism." In Herz, *Essays on J. S. Bach,* 1–124. Ann Arbor: UMI Research Press, 1985.

Hiemke, Sven. "Aspekte der französischen Bach-Rezeption." In *Bach und die Nachwelt, Vol. 2: 1850–1900,* edited by Michael Heinemann and Hans-Joachim Hinrichsen, 31–83. Laaber: Laaber-Verlag, 1999.

Hilse, Walter. Liner notes to his recording, *Great Organ Builders of America: A Retrospective,* vol. 3 (*Aeolian-Skinner Opus 985, 2939*). J A V Recordings 103 (1998).

Hinrichsen, Hans-Joachim. "Die Bach-Gesamtausgabe und die Kontroversen um die Aufführungspraxis der Vokalwerke." In *Bach und die Nachwelt, Vol. 2: 1850–1900,* edited by Michael Heinemann and Hans-Joachim Hinrichsen, 227–97. Laaber: Laaber-Verlag, 1999.

Hinrichsen, Hans-Joachim, and Dominik Sackmann. *Bach-Rezeption im Umkreis Franz Liszts: Joseph Joachim Raff und Hans von Bülow.* Stuttgart: Carus-Verlag, 2004.

Hofmann, Kurt. *Die Bibliothek von Johannes Brahms: Bücher- und Musikalienverzeichnis.* Hamburg: Karl Dieter Wagner, 1974.

———. *Johannes Brahms in den Erinnerungen von Richard Barth: Barths Wirken in Hamburg.* Hamburg: J. Schuberth, 1979.

Hofmann, Renate. *Clara Schumanns Briefe an Theodor Kirchner.* Tutzing: Hans Schneider, 1996.

———. "Die Briefsammlung August Walter." In *Johannes Brahms: Quellen—Text—Rezeption—Interpretation (Internationaler Brahms-Kongress, Hamburg 2997),* edited by Friedhelm Krummacher and Michael Struck, 267–77. Munich: G. Henle Verlag, 1999.

Hofmann, Renate, and Kurt Hofmann. *Johannes Brahms: Zeittafel zu Leben und Werk.* Publikationen des Instituts für österreichische Musikdokumentation 8. Tutzing: Hans Schneider, 1983.

Horsley, Charles Edward. "Reminiscences of Mendelssohn by His English Pupil." *Dwight's Journal of Music* 32 (1872): 345–47, 353–55, and 361–63.

Hübbe, Walter. *Brahms in Hamburg.* Hamburg: Lütcke & Wulff, 1902.

Humphreys, David. "Did J. S. Bach Compose the F minor Prelude and Fugue BWV 534?" In *Bach, Handel, Scarlatti: Tercentenary Essays,* edited by Peter Williams, 173–84. Cambridge, UK: Cambridge University Press, 1985.

Jansen, Friedrich Gustav. *Die Davidsbündler: Aus Schumanns Sturm- und Drangperiode.* Leipzig: Breitkopf & Härtel, 1883.

———. *Robert Schumanns Briefe: Neue Folge.* Second edition. Leipzig: Breitkopf & Härtel, 1904. (English translation of first edition, *The Life of Robert Schumann Told in His Letters.* London: Richard Bentley and Son, 1890.)

Jerger, Wilhelm. *Franz Liszts Klavierunterricht von 1884–1886 dargestellt an den Tagebuchaufzeichnungen von August Göllerich.* Studien zur Musikgeschichte des 19. Jahrhunderts 39. Regensburg: Gustav Bosse, 1975.

Joachim, Joseph, and Andreas Moser, eds. *Briefe von und an Joseph Joachim.* 3 volumes. Berlin: Julius Bard, 1911–13.

Jourdan, Paul. "Mendelssohn in England 1829–37." Ph.D. dissertation, University of Cambridge, 1998.

Jung, Hans Rudolf, ed. *Franz Liszt in seinen Briefen.* Berlin: Henschelverlag Kunst und Gesellschaft, 1988.

Kaczmarczyk, Adrienne, and Imre Sulyok, eds. *Franz Liszt: Transkriptionen IX*. Neue
    Ausgabe sämtlicher Werke, series 2, vol. 24. Budapest: Editio Musica, 1998.

Kalbeck, Max. *Johannes Brahms*. 4 volumes. Berlin: Deutsche Brahms-Gesellschaft,
    1904–14.

———, ed. *Johannes Brahms im Briefwechsel mit Heinrich und Elisabet von Herzo-
    genberg*. 2 volumes. Berlin: Deutsche Brahms-Gesellschaft, 1907.

———, ed. *Johannes Brahms: Briefe an Joseph Viktor Widmann, Ellen und Ferdinand
    Vetter, Adolf Schubring*. Berlin: Deutsche Brahms-Gesellschaft, 1915.

Keil, Siegmar. *Untersuchungen zur Fugentechnik in Robert Schumanns Instrumen-
    talschaffen*. Hamburger Beiträge zur Musikwissenschaft, 11. Hamburg: Karl Dieter
    Wagner, 1973.

Keller, Hermann. *The Organ Works of Bach: A Contribution to Their History, Form,
    Interpretation and Performance*. Translated by Helen Hewitt. New York: C. F. Pe-
    ters, 1967.

Kellermann, Berthold. *Erinnerungen: Ein Künstlerleben*. Leipzig: Eugen Rentsch, 1932.

Kern, Ernst. "Johannes Brahms und die Orgel." In *Zur Orgelmusik im 29. Jahrhun-
    dert*, edited by Walter Salmen, 127–31. Innsbrucker Beiträge zur Musikwissenschaft
    9. Innsbruck: Musikverlag Helbling, 1983.

Kilian, Dietrich. *Kritischer Bericht* to *Neue Bach-Ausgabe*, series 4, vols. 5 and 6 (*Prälu-
    dien, Toccaten, Fantasien und Fugen für Orgel*). Kassel: Bärenreiter; Leipzig: VEB
    Deutscher Verlag für Musik, 1978–79.

———. *Kritischer Bericht* to *Neue Bach-Ausgabe*, series 4, vol. 7. Sechs Sonaten und
    verschiedene Einzelwerke. Kassel: Bärenreiter; Leipzig: VEB Deutscher Verlag
    für Musik, 1988.

Klein, Hans-Günter. "Abraham Mendelssohn Bartholdy in England: Die Briefe
    aus London im Sommer 1833 nach Berlin." *Mendelssohn Studien* 12 (2001a):
    67–127.

———. "Eine (fast) unendliche Geschichte: Felix Mendelssohn Bartholdys Hochzeits-
    musik für seine Schwester." *Mendelssohn Studien* 12 (2001b): 179–85.

———. *Felix Mendelssohn Bartholdy: Autographe und Abschriften*. Staatsbibliothek
    zu Berlin - Preussischer Kulturbesitz, Katalog der Musikabteilung, Erste Reihe:
    Handschriften, Band 5. Munich: G. Henle Verlag, 2003.

Klingemann, Karl, ed. *Felix Mendelssohn-Bartholdys Briefwechsel mit Legationsrat
    Karl Klingemann*. Essen: G. D. Baedeker, 1909.

Klotz, Hans. *Kritischer Bericht* to *Neue Bach-Ausgabe*, series 4, vol. 2. Die Orgel-
    choräle aus der Leipziger Originalhandschrift. Kassel: Bärenreiter; Leipzig: VEB
    Deutscher Verlag für Musik, 1957.

Knapp, Raymond. "The Finale of Brahms's Fourth Symphony: The Tale of the Sub-
    ject." *19th Century Music* 13, no. 1 (Summer 1989): 3–17.

Knechtges, Irmgard. *Robert Schumann im Spiegel seiner späten Klavierwerke*. Kölner
    Beiträge zur Musikforschung 142. Regensburg: Gustav Bosse, 1985.

Kobayashi, Yoshitake. "Franz Hauser und seine Bach-Handschriftensammlung." Ph.D.
    dissertation, Georg-August-Universität, 1973.

Krause, Peter. *Originalausgaben und ältere Drucke der Werke Johann Sebastian Bachs
    in der Musikbibliothek der Stadt Leipzig*. Bibliographische Veröffentlichungen

der Musikbibliothek der Stadt Leipzig 5. Leipzig: Musikbibliothek der Stadt Leipzig, 1970.

———. "Carl Ferdinand Beckers Wirken für das Werk Johann Sebastian Bachs." *Beiträge zur Bachforschung* 1 (1982): 85–95.

Krebs, Carl, ed. *Johannes Brahms im Briefwechsel mit Philipp Spitta / Johannes Brahms im Briefwechsel mit Otto Dessoff.* Berlin: Deutsche Brahms-Gesellschaft, 1920–22.

Kross, Siegfried. "Brahms und der Kanon." In *Festschrift Joseph Schmidt-Görg zum 60. Geburtstag,* edited by Dagmar Weise, 175–87. Bonn: Beethovenhaus Bonn, 1957.

Krüger, Eduard. "Metronomische Fragen." *Neue Zeitschrift für Musik* 20, no. 31 (15 April 1844): 121–23.

La Mara (Marie Lipsius), ed. *Franz Liszt's Briefe.* 2 volumes. Leipzig: Breitkopf & Härtel, 1893.

———. *Briefe hervorragender Zeitgenossen an Franz Liszt.* 3 volumes. Leipzig: Breitkopf & Härtel, 1895–1904.

———. *Briefwechsel zwischen Franz Liszt und Hans von Bülow.* Leipzig: Breitkopf & Härtel, 1898.

Lampadius, Wilhelm Adolf. *A Life of Felix Mendelssohn Bartholdy.* Translated by W. L. Gage. Edinburgh and London: Ballantyne, Hanson and Co., 1876.

Lehmann, Karen, ed. *Felix Mendelssohn Bartholdy: Vom Himmel hoch.* Choralkantate über Luthers Weihnachtslied. Stuttgart: Carus-Verlag, 1983.

———. "Mendelssohn und die Bach-Ausgabe bei C. F. Peters: Missglückter Versuch einer Zusammenarbeit." *Bach-Jahrbuch* 83 (1997): 87–95.

Leipold, Eugen. "Die romantische Polyphonie in der Klaviermusik Robert Schumanns." Ph.D. dissertation, Friedrich-Alexander-Universität, 1954.

Leyen, Rudolf von der. *Johannes Brahms als Mensch und Freund.* Düsseldorf and Leipzig: Karl Robert Langewiesche, 1905.

Little, Wm. A., ed. *Felix Mendelssohn Bartholdy: Complete Organ Works.* 5 volumes. London: Novello, 1987–90.

———. "Brahms and the Organ—Redivivus: Some Thoughts and Conjectures." In *The Organist as Scholar: Essays in Memory of Russell Saunders,* edited by Kerala J. Snyder, pp. 273–97. Festschrift Series 12. Stuyvesant, NY: Pendragon Press, 1994.

———. "Felix Mendelssohn and J. S. Bach's *Prelude and Fugue in E Minor* (BWV 533)." *The American Organist* 39, no. 2 (February 2005): 73–83.

Litzmann, Berthold. *Clara Schumann: Ein Künstlerleben nach Tagebüchern und Briefen.* 3 volumes. Leipzig: Breitkopf & Härtel, 1902–8. (Abridged English translation, *Clara Schumann: An Artist's Life Based on Material found in Diaries and Letters.* 2 volumes. London: Macmillan, 1913.)

———, ed. *Clara Schumann—Johannes Brahms: Briefe aus den Jahren 2853–2896.* 2 volumes. Leipzig: Breitkopf & Härtel, 1927.

Löhlein, Heinz-Harald. *Kritischer Bericht* to *Neue Bach-Ausgabe,* series 4, vol. 1. Orgelbüchlein, Sechs Choräle von verschiedener Art (Schübler Choräle), Orgelpartiten. Kassel: Bärenreiter; Leipzig: VEB Deutscher Verlag für Musik, 1987.

Loos, Helmut. "Die Zwickauer Schumann-Feier von 1860." In *Schumanniana Nova: Festschrift Gerd Nauhaus zum 60. Geburtstag,* edited by Bernhard R. Appel, Ute Bär, and Matthias Wendt, 400–422. Sinzig: Studio, 2002.

Ludwig, Klaus Uwe, ed. *Niels Wilhelm Gade: Variationen über den Choral "Sey gegrüs-set Jesu gütig" von Johann Sebastian Bach für Orgel zu vier Händen.* Wiesbaden: Breitkopf & Härtel, 1996.

MacDonald, Malcolm. *Brahms.* New York: Schirmer Books, 1990.

Martin, Uwe. "Ein unbekanntes Schumann-Autograph aus dem Nachlass Eduard Krügers." *Die Musikforschung* 12 (1959): 405–15.

Mast, Paul. "Brahms's Study, Octaven u. Quinten u. A." *The Music Forum* 5 (1980): 1–196.

May, Ernest. "The Types, Uses, and Historical Position of Bach's Organ Chorales." In *J. S. Bach as Organist: His Instruments, Music, and Performance Practices,* edited by George Stauffer and Ernest May, 81–101. Bloomington: Indiana University Press, 1986.

May, Florence. *The Life of Brahms.* 2 volumes. London: Edward Arnold, 1905.

McCorkle, Margit L. *Johannes Brahms: Thematisch-bibliographisches Werkverzeich-nis.* Munich: G. Henle Verlag, 1984.

Mendelssohn Bartholdy, Paul, ed. *Reisebriefe von Felix Mendelssohn Bartholdy aus den Jahren 1830 bis 1832.* Leipzig: Hermann Mendelssohn, 1861. (English trans-lation, *Letters from Italy and Switzerland by Felix Mendelssohn Bartholdy.* Lon-don: Longmans, Green, Reader, and Dyer, 1863.)

Mendelssohn Bartholdy, Paul, and Carl Mendelssohn Bartholdy, eds. *Briefe aus den Jahren 1833 bis 1847 von Felix Mendelssohn Bartholdy.* Leipzig: Hermann Men-delssohn, 1863. (English translation, *Letters of Felix Mendelssohn Bartholdy, from 1833 to 1847.* London: Longmans, Green, Reader, and Dyer, 1863.)

Mező, Imre, and László Vikárius, eds. *Franz Liszt: Transkriptionen VII.* Neue Ausgabe sämtlicher Werke, series 2, vol. 22. Budapest: Editio Musica, 1997.

Moscheles, Felix, ed. *Briefe von Felix Mendelssohn-Bartholdy an Ignaz und Charlotte Moscheles.* Leipzig: Duncker & Humblot, 1888.

Moser, Andreas, ed. *Johannes Brahms im Briefwechsel mit Joseph Joachim.* 2 volumes. Berlin: Deutsche Brahms-Gesellschaft, 1908.

Moser, Dietz-Rüdiger, ed. *Clara Schumann: Mein liebes Julchen.* Briefe von Clara Schu-mann an ihre Enkeltochter Julie Schumann. Munich: Nymphenburger, 1990.

Musgrave, Michael. *The Music of Brahms.* London: Routledge & Kegan Paul, 1985.

———. *A Brahms Reader.* New Haven: Yale University Press, 2000.

Nauhaus, Gerd, ed. *The Marriage Diaries of Robert & Clara Schumann.* Translated by Peter Ostwald. Boston: Northeastern University Press, 1993.

Neumann, Werner. "Welche Handschriften J. S. Bachscher Werke besass die Berliner Singakademie?" In *Hans Albrecht in Memoriam,* edited by Wilfried Brennecke and Hans Haase, 136–42. Kassel: Bärenreiter, 1962.

Norman, Gertrude, and Miriam Lubell Shrifte, eds. *Letters of Composers: An Anthol-ogy.* New York: Alfred A. Knopf, 1927.

Novello, Vincent, ed. *Sebastian Bach: Prelude and Fugue in E Minor.* Select Organ Pieces 42. London: Novello, 1833.

Oortmerssen, Jacques von. "Johannes Brahms and 19th-Century Performance Prac-tice in a Historical Perspective." In *Proceedings of the Göteborg International*

Organ Academy 1994, edited by Hans Davidsson and Sverker Jullander, 353–82. Göteborg: University of Göteborg, 1995.

Pape, Matthias. *Mendelssohns Leipziger Orgelkonzert 1840: Ein Beitrag zur Bach-Pflege im 19. Jahrhundert.* Wiesbaden: Breitkopf & Härtel, 1988.

Parkins, Robert, and R. Larry Todd. "Mendelssohn's Fugue in F Minor: A Discarded Movement of the First Organ Sonata." *The Organ Yearbook* 14 (1983): 61–77.

Pascall, Robert. "Brahms' Orgelwerke." In *Johannes Brahms: Leben und Werk,* edited by Christiane Jacobsen, 123–24. Wiesbaden: Breitkopf & Härtel, 1983.

Pearce, Charles William. *Notes on Old London City Churches, their Organs, Organists, and Musical Associations.* London: Vincent, 1909.

———. *The Life and Works of Edward John Hopkins.* London: Vincent, 1910.

Plantinga, Leon B. *Schumann as Critic.* New Haven: Yale University Press, 1967.

Plath, Wolfgang. "Ein 'geistlicher' Sinfoniesatz Mozarts." *Die Musikforschung* 27 (1974): 93–95.

Pleasants, Henry, ed. *The Musical World of Robert Schumann: A Selection from His Own Writings.* London: Gollancz, 1965.

Polko, Elise. *Reminiscences of Felix Mendelssohn-Bartholdy: A Social and Artistic Biography.* Translated by Lady Wallace. New York: Leypoldt & Holt, 1869.

Ramann, Lina. *Franz Liszt als Künstler und Mensch.* 2 volumes. Leipzig: Breitkopf & Härtel, 1880–94.

Rampe, Siegbert. "Bachs *Piece d'Orgve* G-Dur BWV 572: Gedanken zu ihrer Konzeption." In *Bachs Musik für Tasteninstrumente: Bericht über das 4. Dortmunder Bach-Symposium 2002,* edited by Martin Geck, 333–69. Dortmunder Bach-Forschungen 6. Dortmund: Klangfarben Musikverlag, 2003.

Reich, Nancy B. *Clara Schumann: The Artist and the Woman.* Ithaca, NY: Cornell University Press, 1985.

Ricks, Robert. "A Possible Source for a Brahms Ground." *The American Brahms Society Newsletter* 23, no. 1 (Spring 2005): 1–5.

Riethmüller, Albrecht. "Zur Geschichte eines Musikwerks: Die Interpretation von Präludium und Fuge ('St. Anne') für Orgel Es-Dur (BWV 552) zwischen Bach und Schönberg." In *Berliner Orgel-Colloquium,* edited by Hans Heinrich Eggebrecht, 31–44. Veröffentlichungen der Walcker-Stiftung 12. Kleinblittersdorf: Musikwissenschaftliche Verlags-Gesellschaft, 1990.

Rockstro, William Smith. *Mendelssohn.* London: Sampson Low, Marston, Searle, and Rivington, 1884.

Röntgen, Abrahamina, ed. *Brieven van Julius Röntgen.* Amsterdam: H. J. Paris, 1934.

Rosen, Charles. *The Romantic Generation.* Cambridge, MA: Harvard University Press, 1995.

Rosenmüller, Annegret. *Carl Ferdinand Becker (1804–1877): Studien zu Leben und Werk.* Musikstadt Leipzig 4. Hamburg: von Bockel Verlag, 2000.

Rossner, Johannes. "Robert Schumanns Bezüge zur Orgel: Neue Erkenntnisse." *Freiberger Studien zur Orgel* 5 (1997): 37–48.

Rothe, Hans-Joachim, and Reinhard Szeskus, eds. *Felix Mendelssohn Bartholdy: Briefe aus Leipziger Archiven.* Leipzig: VEB Deutscher Verlag für Musik, 1972.

Sabatier, Francois. "Mendelssohn's Organ Works." *The American Organist* 16, no. 1 (January 1982): 46–56.

Sandberger, Wolfgang. *Das Bach-Bild Philipp Spittas: Ein Beitrag zur Geschichte der Bach-Rezeption im 29. Jahrhundert.* Beihefte zum Archiv für Musikwissenschaft 39. Stuttgart: Franz Steiner Verlag, 1997.

Schäfertöns, Reinhard. "Johannes Brahms und die Musik von Johann Sebastian Bach." In *Bach und die Nachwelt*, vol. 2: *2850–2900*, edited by Michael Heinemann and Hans-Joachim Hinrichsen, 201–24. Laaber: Laaber-Verlag, 1999.

Schanz, Artur. *Johann Sebastian Bach in der Klaviertranskription.* Eisenach: Karl Dieter Wagner, 2000.

Schauffler, Robert Haven. *The Unknown Brahms.* New York: Dodd, Mead, 1933.

Schmieder, Wolfgang. *Thematisch-systematisches Verzeichnis der musikalischen Werke von Johann Sebastian Bach.* Revised edition. Wiesbaden: Breitkopf & Härtel, 1990.

Schrammek, Winfried. "Zur Geschichte der grossen Orgel in der Thomaskirche zu Leipzig von 1601 bis 1885." *Beiträge zur Bachforschung* 2 (1983): 46–55.

Schulz, Günter, ed. *Felix Mendelssohn Bartholdy: Glückliche Jugend (Briefe des jungen Komponisten).* Bremen: Jacobi Verlag, 1971.

Schumann, Clara, ed. *Jugendbriefe von Robert Schumann.* Leipzig: Breitkopf & Härtel, 1885. (English translation, *Early Letters of Robert Schumann.* London: George Bell and Sons, 1888.)

Schumann, Eugenie. *Erinnerungen.* Stuttgart: Engelhorn, 1925.

Schumann, Ferdinand. "Erinnerungen an Clara Schumann." *Neue Zeitschrift für Musik* 84, no. 11 (15 March 1917): 85–88.

Schumann, Robert. *Gesammelte Schriften.* 4 volumes. Leipzig: Georg Wigand, 1854.

Schünemann, Georg. "Die Bachpflege der Berliner Singakademie." *Bach-Jahrbuch* 25 (1928): 138–71.

Seaton, Douglass. "With Words: Mendelssohn's Vocal Songs." In *The Mendelssohn Companion*, edited by Douglass Seaton, 661–700. Westport, CT: Greenwood Press, 2001.

Selden-Goth, G., ed. *Felix Mendelssohn: Letters.* New York: Vienna House, 1972.

Senn, Kurt Wolfgang. "Johannes Brahms: Elf Choralvorspiele für Orgel, op. 122." *Musik und Gottesdienst* 13 (1959): 172–83.

Sieling, Andreas. *August Wilhelm Bach (2796–2869): Kirchenmusik und Seminarmusiklehrer-Ausbildung in Preussen im zweiten Drittel des 29. Jahrhunderts.* Berliner Musik Studien 7. Cologne: Studio, 1995.

———. " 'Selbst den alten Vater Sebastian suchte man nicht mehr so langstielig abzuhaspeln:' Zur Rezeptionsgeschichte der Orgelwerke Bachs." In *Bach und die Nachwelt*, vol. 2: *2850–2900*, edited by Michael Heinemann and Hans-Joachim Hinrichsen, 299–339. Laaber: Laaber-Verlag, 1999.

Smith, Rollin. "Franz Liszt and the Organ." *The American Organist* 20, no. 7 (July 1986): 67–73.

Smyth, Ethel. *Impressions That Remained.* 2 volumes. London: Longmans, Green, and Co., 1919.

Spitta, Philipp. *Johann Sebastian Bach.* 2 volumes. Leipzig: Breitkopf & Härtel, 1873–79. (English translation, *Johann Sebastian Bach.* London: Novello, 1889.)

Sposato, Jeffrey S. " 'For You Have Been Rebellious against the Lord': The Jewish Image in Mendelssohn's *Moses* and Marx's *Mose*." In *Historical Musicology: Sources, Methods, Interpretations,* edited by Stephen A. Crist and Roberta Montemorra Marvin, 256–79. Rochester, NY: University of Rochester Press, 2004.

Stauffer, George B. *The Organ Preludes of Johann Sebastian Bach.* Studies in Musicology 27. Ann Arbor: UMI Research Press, 1980.

———. "Fugue Types in Bach's Free Organ Works." In *J. S. Bach as Organist: His Instruments, Music, and Performance Practices,* edited by George Stauffer and Ernest May, 133–56. Bloomington: Indiana University Press, 1986.

Stinson, Russell. *The Bach Manuscripts of Johann Peter Kellner and His Circle: A Case Study in Reception History.* Durham, NC: Duke University Press, 1989.

———. "Some Thoughts on Bach's Neumeister Chorales." *The Journal of Musicology* 11 (1993): 455–77.

———. *Bach: The Orgelbüchlein.* Monuments of Western Music. New York: Schirmer Books, 1996.

———. *J. S. Bach's Great Eighteen Organ Chorales.* New York: Oxford University Press, 2001.

Stradal, August. *Erinnerungen an Franz Liszt.* Bern: Verlag Paul Haupt, 1929.

Sumner, William L., ed. *Mendelssohn: Organ Sonata No. 2 in Cm.* New York: Edition Peters, 1962.

Sutermeister, Peter, ed. *Felix Mendelssohn Bartholdy: Eine Reise durch Deutschland, Italien und die Schweiz.* Zurich: Max Niehans, 1958.

Sutter, Milton. "Liszt and the Weimar Organist-Composers." In *Liszt Studien,* vol. 1: *Kongress-Bericht Eisenstadt 2975,* edited by Wolfgang Suppan, 203–13. Graz: Akademische Druck- und Verlagsanstalt, 1977.

———. "Liszt and the Performance of Bach's Organ Music." In *Liszt Studien,* vol. 2: *Referate des 2. europäischen Liszt-Symposions Eisenstadt 2978,* edited by Serge Gut, 207–19. Graz: Akademische Druck- und Verlagsanstalt, 1981.

Temperly, Nicholas. "Attwood, Thomas." In *The New Grove Dictionary of Music and Musicians,* edited by Stanley Sadie. Second edition. Vol. 2: 150–52. London: Macmillan, 2001.

Thistlethwaite, Nicholas. *The Making of the Victorian Organ.* Cambridge Musical Texts and Monographs. Cambridge, UK: Cambridge University Press, 1990.

Thomson, John. "Das Musikfest in Birmingham." *Neue Zeitschrift für Musik* 7, no. 30 (13 October 1837): 118–19.

Tittel, Karl. "Welche unter J. S. Bachs Namen geführten Orgelwerke sind Johann Tobias bzw. Johann Ludwig Krebs zuzuschreiben? Ein Versuch zur Lösung von Autorschaftsproblemen." *Bach-Jahrbuch* 52 (1966): 102–37.

Todd, R. Larry. *Mendelssohn's Musical Education: A Study and Edition of his Exercises in Composition.* Cambridge Studies in Music. Cambridge, UK: Cambridge University Press, 1983.

———. "New Light on Mendelssohn's *Freie Phantasie* (1840)." In *Literary and Musical Notes: A Festschrift for Wm. A. Little,* edited by Geoffrey C. Orth, 205–18. Frankfurt: Peter Lang, 1995.

————. "Mendelssohn, Felix." In *The New Grove Dictionary of Music and Musicians*, edited by Stanley Sadie. Second edition. Vol. 16, 389–424. London: Macmillan, 2001.

————. *Mendelssohn: A Life in Music*. New York: Oxford University Press, 2003.

Tyler, William R., and Edward N. Waters. *The Letters of Franz Liszt to Olga von Meyendorff*. Cambridge, MA: Harvard University Press, 1979.

Vesque von Püttlingen, Johann. *Eine Lebensskizze*. Vienna: Alfred Hölder, 1887.

Walker, Alan. *Franz Liszt*. 3 volumes. Ithaca, NY: Cornell University Press, 1988–97.

————. *Living with Liszt: From the Diary of Carl Lachmund, an American Pupil of Liszt, 2882–2884*. Franz Liszt Studies Series 4. Stuyvesant, NY: Pendragon Press, 1995.

Walton, Benjamin. "Urhan, Chrétien." In *The New Grove Dictionary of Music and Musicians*, edited by Stanley Sadie. Second edition. Vol. 26, 155. London: Macmillan, 2001.

Ward Jones, Peter. "The Library of Felix Mendelssohn Bartholdy." In *Festschrift Rudolf Elvers zum 60. Geburtstag*, edited by Ernst Herttrich and Hans Schneider, 289–328. Tutzing: Hans Schneider, 1985.

————. "Mendelssohn and his English Publishers." In *Mendelssohn Studies*, edited by R. Larry Todd, 240–55. Cambridge, UK: Cambridge University Press, 1992.

————, ed. *The Mendelssohns on Honeymoon: The 2837 Diary of Felix and Cécile Mendelssohn Bartholdy Together with Letters to Their Families*. Oxford: Clarendon Press, 1997.

Wehmer, Carl, ed. *Ein tief gegrünget Herz: Der Briefwechsel Felix-Mendelssohn-Bartholdys mit Johann Gustav Droysen*. Heidelberg: Lambert Schneider, 1959.

Weinberger, Gerhard, ed. *Johann Ludwig Krebs: Choralbearbeitungen*. Sämtliche Orgelwerke 3. Wiesbaden: Breitkopf & Härtel, 1986.

————. "Die klangliche Darstellung der grossen freien Werke." In *Zur Interpretation der Orgelmusik Johann Sebastian Bachs*, edited by Ewald Kooiman, Gerhard Weinberger, and Hermann J. Busch, 199–208. Kassel: Verlag Merseburger, 1995.

Weiss, Wisso. "Zum Papier einiger Bach-Handschriften in der Goethe Notensammlung." In *Bachiana et Alia Musicologica: Festschrift Alfred Dürr zum 65. Geburtstag am 3. März 2983*, edited by Wolfgang Rehm, 340–55. Kassel: Bärenreiter, 1983.

Weissweiler, Eva, ed. *Clara und Robert Schumann: Briefwechsel*. 3 volumes. Basel and Frankfurt am Main: Stroemfeld Verlag, 1984–2001.

————, ed. *Fanny und Felix Mendelssohn: "Die Musik will gar nicht rutschen ohne Dich" (Briefwechsel 2822 bis 2846)*. Berlin: Propyläen, 1997.

Werbeck, Walter. Liner notes to *Robert Schumann: Complete Organ Works* (performed by Rudolf Innig). MGD Recordings 317 0619-2 (1995).

Werner, Eric. *Mendelssohn: A New Image of the Composer and His Age*. Translated by Dika Newlin. London: The Free Press of Glencoe, 1963.

Williams, Adrian. *Portrait of Liszt*. Oxford: Clarendon Press, 1990.

————, ed. *Franz Liszt: Selected Letters*. Oxford: Clarendon Press, 1998.

Williams, Peter. "J. S. Bach and English Organ Music." *Music and Letters* 44 (1963): 140–51.

————. *The Organ Music of J. S. Bach*. Cambridge Studies in Music. 3 volumes. Cambridge, UK: Cambridge University Press, 1980–84.

———. "BWV 565: A Toccata in D Minor for Organ by J. S. Bach?" *Early Music* 9 (1981): 330–37.

Wirth, Julia. *Julius Stockhausen: Der Sänger des deutschen Liedes.* Frankfurter Lebensbilder 10. Frankfurt am Main: Englert und Schlosser, 1927.

Wolff, Christoph. "Bach's Organ Toccata in D Minor and the Issue of Its Authenticity." In *Perspectives on Organ Playing and Musical Interpretation: A Festschrift for Heinrich Fleischer at 90,* edited by Ames Anderson et al., 85–107. New Ulm, MN: Martin Luther College, 2002.

Wolff, Ernst, ed. *Felix Mendelssohn Bartholdy: Meister-Briefe.* Berlin: B. Behr, 1907.

Wolff, Konrad, ed. *Robert Schumann: On Music and Musicians.* New York: Pantheon Books, 1946.

Wollny, Peter. "Sara Levy and the Making of Musical Taste in Berlin." *The Musical Quarterly* 77 (1993): 651–88.

Wüster, Ulrich. *Felix Mendelssohn Bartholdys Choralkantaten: Gestalt und Idee.* Bonner Schriften zur Musikwissenschaft 1. Frankfurt: Peter Lang, 1996.

Zappala, Pietro. "Dalla Spree al Tevere: il diario del viaggio di Felix Mendelssohn Bartholdy verso l'Italia (1830–1831). Edizione e commento." In *Album Amicorum Albert Dunning,* edited by Giacomo Fornari, 713–88. Turnhout: Brepols, 2002.

Index